TEXT-BOOK

IN

INTELLECTUAL PHILOSOPHY,

FOR SCHOOLS AND COLLEGES;

CONTAINING AN OUTLINE OF THE SCIENCE, WITH AN ABSTRACT OF ITS HISTORY.

BY J. T. CHAMPLIN, D.D.,
PRESIDENT OF COLBY UNIVERSITY.

NEW EDITION, REMODELED.

POTTER, AINSWORTH, AND COMPANY,
NEW YORK.

CONTENTS.

INTRODUCTION.

CHAPTER I.

CONSCIOUSNESS.

SECTION I.

SECTION II.

CHAPTER II.

PERCEPTION.

SECTION I.

SECTION II.

SECTION III.

SECTION IV.

CHAPTER III.

MEMORY.

CHAPTER IV.

IMAGINATION.

CHAPTER V.

CONCEPTION.

SECTION II.

SECTION III.

SECTION IV.

SECTION V.

APPENDIX.

INTELLECTUAL PHILOSOPHY.

INTRODUCTION.

DEFINITIONS AND DIVISIONS.

1. *Definition of person.* — The human person embraces both the internal knowing principle, and the external material organism, the powers of knowing, feeling, willing, and acting, — the body as well as the soul, the mind as well as the matter which encloses it. When one says *my* body, *my* soul, *my* reason, *my* hand, and the like, he claims each of these as belonging to himself, and equally as constituting but a part of himself. To be present in person, is not merely to be present in thought, but to be present bodily.

---

1. An individual object is one which exists by itself, separate from other objects; or, at least, one which is capable of being separated from other objects in thought. A human person is a *conscious* individual; not only existing apart from other objects, a rounded whole by himself, but aware of his different parts, and recognizing them as his own. What is called *personal identity*, or the sameness of the individual at different times, includes the body only as a typal form, like the new grain of wheat which springs from that which is sown ("We are sown a natural body, we are raised a spiritual body"); but the internal knowing principle seems ever the same.

2. *Definition of mind.* — The mind, however (from the Latin *mens*, Greek *μένος*, *strength*), is recognized as the most important part of the human person, — as that which gives him his power, life, and motion. The body and its organs are made up of the same substances as the trees, rocks, and other material objects around us, only differently arranged and compounded. And as we never think of ascribing life and intelligence to these material objects, so we cannot believe that the phenomena of life and intelligence manifest in the human person belong to the body. Hence we must ascribe them to an altogether different principle; which is variously denominated the mind, the soul, or the spirit. As the manifestations of this principle are entirely different from the phenomena of matter, we call it immaterial.

3. *Definition of knowing, feeling, and willing.* — The distinctive phenomena of the mind are those of *knowing*, *feeling*, and *willing*. In its most general sense, knowledge is the being aware of any thing, the realization of what is going on within a certain sphere. It includes thus the consciousness of the various affections or changes which take place in the different organs or parts of the body, as well as the apprehension of external objects; the direct information which we receive through the senses, and recall by the memory, as well as the inductions and deductions which we make from the materials thus furnished us. In short, knowing is seeing, tasting, hearing, touching, remembering, un-

2. The term "soul" designates the mind more specifically as embracing the principle of life in the being; and the term "spirit" represents it as capable of being either embodied or disembodied. — "Phenomena" means appearances, or manifestations.

derstanding, reasoning, &c. As to feeling and willing, they are intimately connected with knowing, though different from it. The sensations in the organ connected with seeing, hearing, touching, &c., as well as the painful or pleasurable emotions which arise from the information derived from the exercise of these powers, or from memory, reasoning, and the like, are different forms of feeling; while willing is the determination and the final impulse given to act according to the suggestions of our thoughts and feelings. Thus, we may see a beautiful landscape, and may experience certain pleasurable feelings in consequence of the sight, and may determine or will to visit it again at some future time. *Mental* philosophy, therefore, embraces an account of the principles which pertain to all three of these classes of phenomena, while *intellectual* philosophy properly takes cognizance of those only which pertain to the intelligence, or knowledge.

4. *Definition of intellect.* — The term intellect, then, designates merely the intelligent or knowing principle of the mind, and even this more emphatically in its higher capacities and operations. By the intellect of man we understand more specifically his powers of comparing, judging, and reasoning; less definitely, his powers of perceiving, remembering, and imagining. Still, as intelligence is the primary, and by far the most important, function of the mind, the intellect is often used,

---

3. As the mind acts through the body, its *manifestations* are dependent upon the condition of the body, and cease when that becomes an unfit instrument for its use. The operations of the mind, too, affect the body, and not unfrequently strain and impair its condition, — somewhat, we may suppose, as the steam strains and impairs the engine in which it works. — Another term for mental philosophy is *psychology*, "the doctrine of the soul."

in a general way, to denote the mind as a whole, as an independent nature.

5. *Definition of understanding and reason.* — The terms understanding and reason, also, are used in a similar sense. Locke's "Treatise on the Human Understanding" is intended to embrace an account of all the operations of the mind, from sensation and perception upwards; though more properly the term represents the mind as comparing, comprehending, and elaborating ideas, rather than as simply receiving and retaining them. So, too, the reason is often put for the mind as a whole, though strictly the term designates only the very highest processes of the mind. The reason is the faculty of reasoning, and judging of the validity of proofs; and hence stands equally opposed to the receptivity of sense and the excitability of passion. Indeed, reason is the grand distinguishing faculty of man, who is called a rational animal, in distinction from all others.

6. *Definition of consciousness.* — There is another term which is used to designate the different operations of the mind as a whole, — *consciousness.* Or, rather, consciousness is the knowledge which we have of all our mental acts, and of every affection within our organism that reaches the mind. Every distinct act of the mind, whether it be of knowing, feeling, or willing, is a conscious act. Consciousness is internal knowledge. Denoting, according to its derivation ("knowing together"), associated knowledge, it is not commonly regarded as including fugitive thoughts, which flit by unnoticed, and hence unconnected with other thoughts. And, being internal knowledge, we cannot properly be

5. For a fuller account of the applications of the terms intellect, understanding, and reason, see Wight's Hamilton, pp. 79, and following.

said to be conscious of external objects, though we are conscious of the operations of the mind by which we gain a knowledge of these objects, as well as of all other operations of the mind. Indeed, it is of the very nature of mental action, as distinguished from mechanical or chemical action, that it is conscious. Consciousness, then, is the essential characteristic of mental action, and inseparable from it.

7. *The different faculties of knowledge.* — But the mind, though one, in obtaining knowledge acts through special forms, or by special *faculties:* such as perception by the senses, by which we obtain a knowledge of external objects; memory, by which we recall past experiences; imagination, by which we figure to ourselves objects like what we have perceived by the senses; conception, judgment, and reasoning, by which we generalize and combine our primary ideas, and enlarge our knowledge. These faculties are all regarded as capacities for doing something, and hence are often called powers, or energies.

8. *Definition of speculation.* — In addition to the above-named special faculties, we have the power of *speculation*, or of scrutinizing the materials of knowledge obtained by these faculties, and detecting their subtle relations, and the general ideas or notions which they imply, and which underlie them as their conditions or foundation. We find, upon reflection, that all the objects of our knowledge imply the existence of space and time, and necessarily arrange themselves in our

---

6. Consciousness is not to be regarded as a special faculty taking cognizance of the operations of the other faculties; but the realization rather of those operations themselves, or the sum of those operations as realized by us. The mind acts consciously, if at all: its action is necessarily conscious action.

mind under the relations of substance and attribute, cause and effect, means and end, and the like. The detection and establishment of these and the like fundamental principles assumed in all thinking constitute what is called speculative philosophy, or metaphysics.

9. *Office of feeling and willing.* — It only remains to point out more definitely the particular office of our capacities of *feeling* and *willing*. These, as the immediate antecedents and prompters to action, constitute the special basis of ethics, or moral philosophy. Intelligence, to be sure, is the guide, or should be the guide, to action; but feeling and will are the immediate impulse to it, without which it is impossible for it to exist. Right action is the right application and carrying out in practice of our best thoughts and feelings and volitions: it is thus the proper and fitting result of the exercise of all our conscious capacities and powers.

---

9. A capacity is a capability, first of *becoming* something, and then of *doing* something. Feeling, therefore, is but a passive capacity; but the will, even if it be necessarily determined by the strongest motive, as being capable of appreciating motives, should be regarded rather as a power. — Perhaps it will be thought that *instinct* should be named as an additional faculty of knowledge. But instinct belongs almost wholly to the lower animals; and, besides, is merely an internal impulse, resulting from the *organization* of the animal, and not properly a faculty of knowledge: indeed, it operates quite independently of knowledge, and is not at all improved by knowledge. The first acts of the young of all animals, and even of human infants, are instinctive. But while man governs, or is capable of governing, his later acts by intelligence, the acts of the lower animals remain chiefly instinctive, being but slightly controlled by the results of experience. Young quails and rabbits run through bushes, avoiding all obstacles, and young ducks swim, as well at first as in later life. And although the feats of instinct have often been exaggerated, yet the principle is sufficient for the wants of the animal. Man alone, by his wonderful powers of progress, seems destined for a future life.

10. *Divisions of the subject.* — From this account of the different operations of the mind, we see at once the natural divisions of the subject. Following the order and distinguishing the nature of the several processes and their results, we have, 1st, Simple or concrete knowledge, embracing consciousness, perception by the senses, memory, and imagination; 2d, Generalized or abstract knowledge, embracing conception, judgment, and reasoning; 3d, Speculative knowledge, or metaphysics; and 4th, Ethics, or knowledge carried out in practice through the impulse of the feelings and of the will. A complete treatise, therefore, on mental philosophy, would embrace these four divisions, or parts. In concrete knowledge, the mind deals with individual objects or things; in abstract knowledge it deals with combinations or classes of things; in speculative knowledge it searches after underlying principles and relations; while, in the applications of knowledge to practice, it deals with the principles of right and wrong in action. As to Logic, which treats of the right use of the concept and the judgment in reasoning, it naturally falls under the second of the above divisions.

11. *Philosophy and science.* — Philosophy and science, though dealing with the same general materials, are not entirely coincident. The philosophy of any thing is a rational account of it, or a general explanation of phenomena by referring them to certain causes or fundamental principles; while science is a detailed and systematic proof and establishment of the causes of such phenomena. Philosophy, being strictly the result of the pursuit of knowledge for its own sake, properly investigates only such matters as naturally arrest the attention, and hence is confined to the general underly-

ing principles of things. Science, on the contrary, aims at an exhaustive exhibition and verification of the truth on any subject. Hence the operations of the mind, as naturally arresting the attention of every one, and as fundamental to every thing else, are the proper and special subject of philosophy.

CHAPTER I.

CONSCIOUSNESS.

SECTION I.

NATURE OF CONSCIOUSNESS.

1. *Consciousness defined.* — Consciousness has been described as knowing that we know. It is also knowing that we feel and will and act. It is primarily a knowledge of any affection of our nervous system, or any impression made upon it through either of the five senses of seeing, hearing, touching, tasting, or smelling. We are thus conscious of all sensations and sense-perceptions ; and we are equally conscious of these sensations and perceptions when they recur to us in memory or imagination. So too, when we combine these perceptions and reason upon them, or form plans of action and exert our wills or our muscles to carry them out, we are equally conscious of what we are doing. Consciousness accompanies every intelligent act, whether external or internal : it is, indeed, those acts realized ; it is the mind acting in them.

2. *Impressions upon the senses and internal action of which we are not conscious.* — But may there not be external or internal action in the organs or limbs which does not reach the mind, and hence is unaccompanied

by consciousness? The senses undoubtedly may be so closed in sleep that the usual causes of sensation and perception do not reach the mind, or awaken any mental apprehension. The attention, too, may be so absorbed in some matter, even during our waking hours, that we are not conscious of ordinary impressions upon the senses. The senses, being at rest in sleep, are in a torpid condition, and do not receive and transmit impressions as they do when awake; and in the other case, the mind, being wholly absorbed in one thing, pays no attention to any other. So, too, the processes of circulation, appropriation, secretion, and the other internal functions of life, are generally unaccompanied by consciousness. These changes being necessary for the preservation of the system, are intrusted to the superintendence of the vital principle, leaving the mind free to perform its own work.

3. *Effect of habit in obscuring consciousness.* — There

---

2. We call a sound sleep a "deep sleep," as though the soul had withdrawn far from the surface. Sometimes, on our attention being relieved from its absorption, we recall an impression, as the striking of a clock, which we did not seem to notice at the time; or else we now first become conscious of it from the impression on the organ still remaining, the sound, as we say, still "ringing in the ear." So the eye retains the impression a longer or shorter time after the cause is removed, as is proved by the ring of light which is seen when a torch is whirled rapidly around. Vital action, i. e. the action necessary to preserve the system from decay and death, is always involuntary, but not necessarily unconscious. We are conscious of all our external involuntary motions, such as sneezing, winking, starting at a sudden noise, and the like; and of some of the internal involuntary changes, as of respirations, the beating of the heart, &c. Thus the vital principle is not wholly an unconscious principle: and it is also a plastic or formative principle; since, under its influence, animal bodies are formed by organs and limbs, after a fixed type. It is evidently no mere mechanical or chemical principle, but should be regarded as the lowest form or beginnings of mind.

is another class of actions apparently unaccompanied by consciousness, and which many regard as really so, — those that have been often repeated and are performed from habit; such as taking a familiar walk, repeating a familiar piece of composition, or playing a familiar tune. Each of these and the like processes consists of a series of external acts or motions, which at first are performed with the greatest attention and care, but which, by frequent repetition, have become so familiar that they require but little or no attention, and seem almost involuntary. And yet they do not appear to be wholly unconscious acts; for the performer of the most familiar piece on the piano will notice a misplaced note in the music before him, and the drowsy fiddler, whose arm appears to move automatically, will stop the moment the dancing ceases. Habit, as we say, is a second nature; and as we have seen that nature relieves the mind by devolving certain constant and laborious operations upon the vital principle, so habit seems to effect something of the same result. When processes have become familiar, they seem to be remitted very much to the unconscious reflex action of our nervous system.

4. *Consciousness is co-extensive with knowledge.* — Consciousness meaning "knowing together," or, as some interpret it, "knowing again" (knowing that we know), it may be inquired whether any of our thoughts are wholly unconnected with other thoughts, and thus escape consciousness. There would seem to be nothing improba-

---

3. Hamilton, following Leibnitz, refers such acts as are here described to the operation of *latent mental modifications*, through which the mind is supposed to act unconsciously in directing the external movements. Stewart, on the contrary, regards such acts as strictly intelligent acts, but so slightly attended to as scarcely to be realized.

ble in the supposition that there may be thoughts passing so rapidly, and so little attended to, as to bring with them no other thoughts, and hence to be wholly isolated and fugitive. But, whether there actually are such thoughts or not, we can never be certain, since, not being connected with any other thought, they can never be recalled. They are at most but momentary thoughts, serving a temporary purpose, and then passing into oblivion. To know any thing distinctly, we must *note* or attend to it with some care; and, when we do thus attend to any thing, other things are usually observed with it, or other thoughts come into the mind, and are associated with it. Hence all real knowledge must be conscious knowledge. Fugitive knowledge is but sub-knowledge, and is, therefore, but partially conscious: the consciousness however, at the moment, is just as clear and distinct as the knowledge is.

5. *Is the mind continually conscious?* — As we have seen that consciousness accompanies, or rather is involved in, all real mental action, the question arises, whether the mind is always active, and hence continuously conscious. If not, what evidence have we of the continuous existence of the mind? Consciousness being the special property under which the mind becomes known, if it lose this, it is said, it loses its identity, just as matter would lose its identity if it ceased to be extended. It is true that the mind *manifests* itself through consciousness; but these manifestations in turn are made through the body, and must depend, therefore, upon the condition of the body as a medium for spiritual manifestations. On the death of the body, these manifestations wholly cease within their accustomed sphere; and so they may during certain torpid states of the body, with-

out implying the non-existence of the soul. Indeed, it is not certain that there is not, or rather it is highly probable that there is, during all these torpid states of the body, an internal current of consciousness constantly in existence. We all know that one may train himself so as to keep a correct account of the passage of time in sleep, and awake at a definite hour; and, even in the deepest sleep, the subject, by ejaculations and other signs, often indicates the existence of consciousness. The same thing is shown by the phenomena of dreams. As certain vivid dreams arouse us sufficiently to become connected with our ordinary waking current of thought, and hence are remembered, we may well suppose that there is constantly going on in sleep a less vivid but continuous dream-life which is not remembered.

6. *Consciousness not precisely the same as knowledge.* — Though consciousness is involved in all knowledge, yet it is not precisely the same as knowledge. Knowledge resolves itself into perception, memory, imagina-

---

5. The dream-life seems to be directed wholly by the ideas present to the mind, without the control of the will. This is seen especially in that kind of dreaming called *somnambulism*, or walking and performing various external acts in sleep. The dreamer is wholly absorbed in a certain current of thoughts, and pays no attention to any thing else while the spell lasts. And for the same reason, if the bystander can get his attention, he can direct his acts to almost any thing which he suggests; and he will go through the performance, whatever it be. But, when the subject comes out of this state, he has no remembrance of what he has been doing; and yet, when he relapses into a similar state, the former ideas and acts may be resumed. The two different states of life, having nothing in common, do not suggest each other, but are each pursued independently of the other. *Mesmeric phenomena* are probably due to a similar state of the system induced by the manipulations or suggestions of the operator in highly-nervous persons. See, *Marshall's Physiology*, p. 317.

tion, conception, judgment, and reasoning. These are all regarded as processes leading to certain results which constitute knowledge. Now, we are conscious of every step taken in each of these processes, and also of the result as an internal fact, but not of the thing embraced in the result. As we are conscious of all that transpires within us in the process of perceiving a tree, and of our conviction that it exists, but not of the tree itself; so we are conscious of all the steps taken in the process of proving that the three angles of a triangle are equal to two right angles, and also of our conviction of the truth of the proposition, and yet are not properly conscious of the truth itself. This last is knowledge, or a conclusion to which we have come for reasons which seemed to us satisfactory.

7. *Consciousness is no authority for abstract truths or the reality of things.* — Hence we see that consciousness cannot be appealed to for the truth of abstract propositions or the reality of independent existences. It deals only with internal facts. It cannot be mistaken in regard to the phenomena which transpire within: but it does not profess to interpret these phenomena; this it leaves to our various faculties of knowledge. In the various illusions of vision, *as in mirage*, consciousness reports correctly what is presented in the organ; but we come to interpret them rightly only by the knowledge which we acquire through investigation and experience: and, as all apparent facts must be interpreted by our rational powers, so must all general truths be tested by these powers. Consciousness, then, is no authority for the reality of the external world, nor for the truth of general propositions. And, in like manner, it is no direct

authority for the existence of a separate spiritual nature in man. It is an *evidence* of the existence of such a nature in us, as all our powers are; but it reports nothing in regard to such a nature, except certain acts and states which seem to imply its existence, and from which we infer it.

8. *Confirmation of the above view.* — The view expressed in the last paragraph is quite different from that very generally held, and formerly entertained, by myself. But, on further reflection, I do not see how the doctrine of an immediate consciousness of external objects, or of general truths, or of our own spiritual nature, can be maintained. Can we be said to be conscious of a tree? to be conscious that the whole of any thing is greater than a part of it? or to be conscious of the nature of the soul, or of its existence distinct from the body? Even Hamilton, who held the first two of these doctrines, if not the third, usually avoids such expressions, as evidently incongruous and incorrect. "In the act of sensible perception," his language is, "I am conscious of *myself* as a *perceiving subject*, and of an *external reality*, in relation with my sense, as *the object perceived*." Yes, in the *act* of perception, or through perception, one becomes thus conscious: the process of perception brings him this knowledge of which he is conscious. Perception is a process and a conclusion as to what is implied in it; and we are conscious of the process and the conclusion, but not of the things implied. So we cannot properly be said to be conscious that the whole of a thing is greater than any of its parts; but our judgment or reason decides that it is so, and we are conscious of the decision. Consciousness reports the experience and the

conclusions of the mind; nothing more. In like manner, we infer the existence of a spiritual nature within us on account of certain phenomena of intelligence which seem to us plainly to imply it, not because we are directly conscious of that nature.

It is obvious that consciousness is not a special power of any kind, whether of knowing, feeling, or willing. We neither know nor feel nor will by consciousness; though we are conscious alike of all these operations. It is, then, merely a quality of mental action, the distinguishing characteristic of it. But, the mind being a conscious principle, it is often convenient to use the term "consciousness" for the mind as a whole; as where we speak of the concentration of consciousness, instead of the concentration of the powers of the mind itself.

SECTION II.

CONCENTRATION OF CONSCIOUSNESS (ATTENTION AND REFLECTION.)

1. *What attention is.* — *Attention* is a special concentration of consciousness upon some particular object, process, phenomenon, or passing event. When we give ourselves up to the influence of what is passing around us, without endeavoring to control our thoughts or feelings, there is no special exercise of attention. In such cases, there is barely the ordinary wakefulness of the mental powers, such as is secured to each object in turn, by the varying interest which they excite in the mind in its different moods. But the moment we make an effort to apply ourselves to any particular business or study, our consciousness is more or less concentrated on that, to the exclusion of other things;

and in the highest concentration of consciousness, every thing is excluded from the mind except the matter immediately under consideration.

2. *Attention carries the whole mind with it.* — As the acts of the mind are only conscious acts, and as, indeed, we know the mind only in its conscious acts, when the consciousness is specially concentrated upon any object, the whole mind is virtually concentrated upon it. Hence, when attention to any thing is complete, we are wholly absorbed in it, and are as incapable, while the concentration lasts, of any other intelligent process, be it perceiving, remembering, or reasoning, as though we had no mind. By attention, then, the whole mind is turned to some object, with the faculty, or faculties, required in the case, in the highest degree of wakefulness, and in readiness to exert themselves.

3. *How far the attention is under the control of the will.* — The special concentration of consciousness, called attention, is effected by the will, and hence the attention is said to be under the control of the will. This it undoubtedly is to a certain extent, but not absolutely. We can at any time, by an act of the will, concentrate our attention upon an object, but we cannot always, by an act of the will, keep it so concentrated, against the intrusion of wandering thoughts and the diverting influences of passing events. Hence the attention, after it has been concentrated on any object, is liable at any moment to be diverted. The will, doubtless, may resist these influences to a certain extent, but not to all extents, — they may become so powerful as to be irresistible. Here, then, are indicated the chief points to which we should direct our efforts in attempting to increase our control over the attention.

4. *To control the attention we should always act with a will.*—In the first place, then, we should cultivate resoluteness of purpose and persistence of will in controlling the attention. We should form a settled purpose of acquiring as complete control over our attention, and hence over our faculties generally, as possible. When we turn our attention to any thing, we should do so with the determination of holding it there to the end, if possible, against all distracting influences. We should make it a point to resist to the utmost all such influences. We should be resolute and in earnest in all that we do, working in all cases under a strong tension of the will. Such a course will greatly increase the power of the will over the attention amid distracting influences.

5. *We should cultivate orderly habits of thought, etc.* —Besides, these disturbing influences themselves may be very much diminished and controlled by proper internal habits and external arrangements. Wandering and intrusive thoughts come chiefly of desultory habits of thinking. Our minds are formed for regular and coherent thought. In the natural order, one thought leads to another by a regular succession. In memory, reasoning, and all the fundamental processes of thought, one step almost necessarily follows another in a given order, in a well-regulated mind. To exclude wandering thoughts, then, we have only to follow, and confirm in our practice, the order of nature as to the connection of our thoughts. We should persistently discipline ourselves to think in a connected order, and thus curb the erratic and capricious action of the imagination. So, too, we may protect ourselves very much against the disturbing influences of external objects by proper

external arrangements. When we engage in any thing requiring close attention, we should not leave ourselves at the mercy of any one of ten thousand influences, by undertaking it in the midst of the distractions of business, of society, or even of the family circle. All the more difficult and protracted mental efforts require retirement. Thus, and thus only, can the attention be preserved long enough to carry them through.

6. *We should so order our occupations that surrounding influences may promote attention to them.*—Another means of controlling our attention is, so to order our pursuits, as to always have something for our chief object of attention, of such a nature that the surrounding influences will tend to promote it prosecution, or at least not be adverse to it. As we should think, investigate principles, and examine books in the study so we should study human nature in society, works of art in travel, and objects of Nature out among her works. Thus the mind will always be kept wakeful, and exert itself to the best advantage.

7. *Reflection as distinguished from attention.*—Thus much of attention. And the same applies to *Reflection*, which is merely attention directed to mental phenomena. Or more strictly, reflection is attention directed to some truth, principle, mental state or act, for the purpose of *re*-examining it. As a mere passing phenomenon, a mental act, or state, is more commonly spoken of as an object of attention,—as when we say to one, "Attend now to what is passing in your mind." But when we think of the act again, and examine its character, it is properly called reflection.

8. *No extended remarks needed on reflection*—As all that has been said of attention, and the means of im-

proving it, applies equally to reflection, it need only be added here, that the power of reflection is particularly required in psychological studies. Psychology rests wholly on the observed facts of consciousness; and hence, the whole success of the student of this science depends upon his power of internal observation,—upon his ability to seize upon and examine the delicate machinery and fleeting thoughts of his own mind. It is a power not easily acquired; but, difficult of acquisition as it is, it may be gradually gained by persevering efforts. And a power so valuable will abundantly repay all the effort which it costs.

CHAPTER II.

SENSE-PERCEPTION.

SECTION I.

SENSATION AND PERCEPTION.

1. *Sensations and feelings.*—In the experience of life, we are conscious of various feelings, or sensations, in our organs. We have a highly delicate and sensitive nervous system, having its centre in the head, and branching out from the brain and through the spinal cord to all parts of the body. Whatever change or affection takes place in any part of this system is apprehended by the mind, and constitutes what is called a sensation, or feeling. When these affections take place in the nerves connected with either of the five senses, they are apprehended through the perceptions of that sense. These sense-affections alone are what are more commonly called sensations, as being the regular antecedents of perceptions. But besides these, there are numerous other affections of the nervous system usually denominated *feelings*,—such as those connected with the processes of circulation and digestion, the healthy or unhealthy action of the lungs, the stomach, and the heart, called *organic* feelings; and the various *muscular* feelings, arising from any change, exertion, injury, or disease, of the muscles. Indeed, the nervous system so thoroughly pervades the body in all its parts, that scarce-

ly any chance can take place in any part of the body without our being conscious of it.

2. *The stimulus and the character of the different sensations.*—The stimulus which excites the sensations in the organs of the senses proper is partly mechanical, and partly chemical. In touch, hearing and sight, the action upon the organ seems to be mechanical; and in taste and smell it is probably chemical. But, whatever the stimulus, if it be too powerful it interferes with perception. The sensation should be strong enough to arouse the mind: if too strong, it distracts and confuses it. Hence it has become a maxim, "That the energy of perception in any of the senses is inversely as the intensity of the sensation." The sensation in the different senses may be briefly described thus: In hearing, it is the consciousness of an agitation or ringing in the ear; in taste and smell it is the consciousness of a stinging quickening, soothing, or the like impression, on the tongue or in the nostrils; in sight, it is the consciousness of a pictured outline projected upon the retina of the eye; and in touch, it is the consciousness of a smooth, rough, yielding, or resisting object in contact with some part of the surface of the body.

---

1. Feeling is the more internal sensation connected with the sense of touch, arising from some internal action, or from pressure, disease, and the like. Touch, unlike the other senses, is a general sense. The nerves of touch, or feeling prevade the whole body,—even the special organs of the other senses.

2. We are not, it is true, directly conscious of the retina, or of its position in the organ, any more than we are of the position or action of the other nerves at any point between the surface and the centre in the brain; nor, indeed, of the brain itself, in ordinary perception. Consciousness directly reveals nothing of the nature of the nervous system beyond certain affections, which, in the senses proper, always appear to be at the surface. Dissection alone discloses the internal

3. *Sensations are referred to the localities where the affections actually are.*—All our sensations and feelings appear to us to be each in that part of our organism or body where the affection really is. Thus any disturbance in the brain—as from over-exertion, disease, or too great a supply of blood to that organ—is realized by a pain, or some other unpleasant feeling, in the head; and a disease in the stomach is attended with uneasiness in that organ; while a cut or bruise in any part of the body is felt where it is made. And the same is true of the sensations in the nerves connected with the several senses: they are all realized at the surface where the impressions are made; as a smell in the nostrils, a taste on the tongue, a sound in the ear, and a touch on some part of the skin. In vision, however, while there may be some feeling realized in the eye, color, the special sensation of this sense, seems projected outside of the organ to the object which is seen; but this, as we shall presently see, is the result of experience.

---

structure of the system; and it was not till the time of Descartes that the retina was discovered by John Baptist Porta.—See Porter's Human Intellect, p. 227. But it is well known that persons born blind, and afterwards restored to sight, at first regard the colored object, which is seen, not at a distance, but on or in the eye; showing that our original cosciousness in this, as in the other senses, locates the affection at the surface. And that the image is within the eye is proved by taking out the eye of an ox, and holding it before an object: when its image will be seen on the retina in the back part of the organ.

3. The science of pathology would be impossible if sensations did not appear to be where the affection or disturbance really is. Without this, there could be no diagnosis nor application of remedies in diseases. Possibly the reference of sensations and feelings to their real place may be the result of experience. When external, our other senses help us locate them; and, when internal, the feeling in many cases may extend to the nearest surface, or its place be determined by local pressure.

4. *But sensations must be apprehended by the mind at the centre of the organism.*—And yet it is certain that all these sensations must be apprehended by the mind at the centre of the organism in the brain. This is plainly indicated by the very structure of the nervous system. In each of the senses the nerves and their branches run in pairs from the surface to the brain directly, or else indirectly to it through the spinal cord. And it is found that one of these pairs in each case, called the *afferent*, bears to the brain the stimulus which excites the sense at the surface; and the other, called the *efferent*, contracts at the bidding of the will, in order to produce any motion which may be required in the case. This is proved by the fact, established by Sir Charles Bell, that if the root of the afferent nerve (i. e., the posterior root of each pair) near its interior termination—where its fibres are separate, and not interlaced with those of the efferent, as they are in its branches—be cut across, all sensation in the parts to which its ramifications extend ceases; while the power of motion ceases in those parts when the other root is severed. And again: if the posterior root, while still connected with the brain, be pinched or irritated in any way near its interior termination, a sensation of pain it produced; while the other root, under the same conditions and treatment, contracts. Thus the susceptibility of sensation and motion in the nerves, which may be traced up from the surface to the centre, is found to cease the moment they are severed from that centre. The conclusion is inevitable, that the real source of that susceptibility or power is some way connected with the brain; and many other things suggest the same conclusion.

5. *While the mind occupies the centre of the organism,*

it commands the whole.—The mind, then, must occupy the centre of the organism in the brain. Here, evidently, is the original susceptibility and power. It is here that what in the ear is a mere agitation becomes a sound; that what upon the tongue or in the nostrils is merely the chemical action of some foreign substance taken into the mouth, or drawn into the nose by the inspiration of the breath, becomes an agreeable or disagreeable taste or odor; that impressions upon the skin of the hand and other parts of the body become the signs of form and extension; and that different quantities and qualities of light distributed upon the retina of the eye transformed into the pictured landscape which we behold. These are not the works of matter. Matter may produce mechanical changes: only mind can make such transformations as these.

But the mind, though it occupies the centre of the organism, evidently traverses or commands the whole. Through the nervous system, it holds, as we may say, telegraphic communication with all its parts, receiving and returning dispatches to every organ and limb. The whole system is animated by the mind, and becomes its special sphere, of which it seems to be directly conscious in all its parts. The body thus becomes the ***microcosm*** of the human spirit, as the universe is the *macrocosm* of the Divine Spirit.

6. *Through sensations external to each other the mind*

---

5. The reference of the sensations excited by irritating the extremities of the nerves of an amputated arm to the fingers of the hand may be supposed to be the result of habit, such sensations having been frequently realized there before by the mind. They are recognized as sensations of the same character as those formerly realized in the hand, and hence are located there.

apprehends the body as extended.—The mind, then, realizes the various sensations in all parts of the body. And, what it is important to observe, these sensations all appear out of each other. They do not reveal themselves as all in the same place, but as occupying different locations; and they seem so, undoubtedly, because they are so. At any rate, through the mutual externality of our sensations to each other, we apprehend our bodies, in which these various sensations are realized, as *extended objects.* The body being visible to our eyes, and tangible to our hands, admitting of the motion of the eyes and of the hands over its surface, possessed itself of locomotive powers, and pervaded in all its parts by life and conscious action, can but be apprehended by us as an extended object. The mind connects the *here* and the *there* of which we are conscious through our experience of sensations, and putting together the different organs, parts, and limbs which it has traversed, makes out a rounded whole, which it objectifies and apprehends as an object distinct from itself. The mind thus first perceives its own enclosing organism as extended and external to itself. Sensations have been transformed into a perception.

6. Perception, it will be seen, is an active process of the mind; while sensation is but a passive process. Perception gathers up, connects, and interprets sensations, supplying what is implied in them, and thus making up the notion of an object. The term perception is used to signify both the act of doing this, and the power of doing it; and also the idea attained by the process, or the mental representation which we form of the object perceived; though this last is more properly called a *percept.* And, further, the term perception is frequently used to denote any mental apprehension; as when we say, "I perceive the point," "I perceive the truth," and the like. **But, since the time of Reid, the term perception has come to mean almost wholly sense-perception.**—In the language of metaphysics, the per-

7. *It then learns to distinguish other objects from the body.*—The mind now knows its own body as extended and external to itself. How early in life the soul learns this is uncertain: but it must quite early learn to distinguish the body, not only from itself, but from other things; for, until it knows this, other objects must appear merely as affections of the body itself. Their presence or contact with any of the senses would at first seem to be but sensations in the organs of sense. Not yet being able to judge of distance by sight, external objects would appear to this sense only as pictured on or in the eye; while to touch they would appear as but more or less deep sensations in different parts of the body; and to smell and taste and hearing they would seem only as more or less pungent or thrilling feelings in the nose, on the tongue, or in the ear. Thus, in infant life, the world is all within. But experience rapidly enlarges this world. The child, laying one hand upon the other, and then upon its mother's breast, is conscious, indeed, of feeling in both cases; but in the first he is conscious also of *being felt*. So he soon finds that the free motion of his hands is resisted and arrested; and by moving in different directions, and grasping objects which lie in his way, he early comes to distinguish himself from other things, and to project the picture-world in which he has thus far lived outside of himself to an outward world actually existing in space.

---

ceiving mind is called the *subject*, while that which it perceives is called the *object*. To "objectify" the body, therefore, is to view it apart from our spiritual nature as a distinct object.

7. It is not pretended, of course, that this is the precise process by which we learn to distinguish ourselves from external objects. The experience by which this is learned will differ in different cases; but in all cases it must be accomplished through experience, and, very naturally, would be accomplished through some such experience as that described above.

8. *We next distinguish various qualities in external objects.*—Having thus learned to distinguish other objects from ourselves, we by degrees learn various things about these objects. By attempting to move against or through them, or by coming into collision with them, we learn that they resist in different degrees our power of motion, and call them hard or soft, according to the degree of their resistance; and, since in such contact or collision they affect more or less extended portions of the body, we infer that they also are extended. And, in grasping or moving the hand over them, we discover that they have form; or we place some of them in the mouth, or snuff in particles thrown off from others, or receive in the ear agitations caused in the air by vibrations in others, and thus learn that they have the power of producing in us the sensations of taste, of smell, or of sound. In this way we learn more or less of the qualities of the different objects around us, and from our notion or idea or mental representation of each. such a notion, embracing the qualities of an individual object, is called a *percept.*

9. *Primary and secondary qualities of objects.*—The qualities of objects thus apprehended have usually been divided into two classes,—primary and secondary qualities. The primary qualities are extension, and the subordinate qualities implied in it, as divisibility, size, density or rarity, impenetrability, and figure. The secondary qualities are the assumed causes of certain sensations or affections in our organism known as resistance or pressure, color, sound, flavor, savor, heat, electrical and galvanic effects. While these are apprehended as mere sensations in our organism, they are supposed to be caused by corresponding qualities in objects, which,

therefore, usually bear the same names as the sensations; though the term caloric is sometimes used for the cause of the sensation of heat, and hardness is regarded as the cause of resistance, or pressure. The primary qualities, however, are not apprehended as mere sensations in us, but as having a real objective existence in bodies, and as essential to their very nature. They are apprehensions of the mind, reached, it is true, through sensations, but of an entirely different and a far higher character. Indeed, the apprehension of extension in objects is the chief intellectual element in perception.

10. *Objects are not directly apprehended by consciousness.*—From the preceding account of the process of perception, it will readily be inferred that the doctrine of an immediate intuition or apprehension of external objects through consciousness is abandoned. As we are directly conscious of the sensations or affections of our own organism, we may perhaps be said to be conscious of this as an object. But the existence of any thing beyond and outside of this is an inference, made, indeed, on the most satisfactory grounds, but yet an inference, not a direct apprehension of consciousness. Hamilton's statement on this point is briefly this: "In this case" (i. e., of the free motion of a limb being evidently arrested by some external object) "I cannot be conscious of

---

9. I can see no good reason for regarding resistance and the subordinate qualities involved in it as partaking of the nature of both the primary and secondary qualities, and hence constituting the so-called intermediate class of qualities, called by Hamilton secundo-primary qualities. Pressure, or the consciousness of resistance to our locomotion, is but a subjective feeling, realized in the organism. It is merely the sign of something external, not the perception of it; a ground of inferring the presence of the external object, a little more conclusive, perhaps, than other sensations, but not at all different in nature.

myself as the resisted relative without at the same time being conscious, being immediately percipient, of a not-self as the resisting correlative." Yes, "immediately percipient," perhaps; or rather I would say, indirectly percipient of it through an inference, but not conscious of it. Consciousness is not the same as knowledge. One may be conscious that he is resisted, and that the resistance does not come from within himself; but he can only know by *inference* (not by consciousness) that he is resisted from without.—See chap. i. sect. i. 6 and 7.

11. *Perception, then, is far from a simple process.*—Perception, then, is by no means a simple direct act. It is not simply receiving through the senses what is presented to them. In its largest sense, it is the result of an experience commenced in our earliest days, and continued to the end of life. Our perceptions are continually increasing, not only in number, but in completeness. Repeated acts of observation and closer attention are ever dispelling illusions, and purifying and perfecting our perceptions. But, not to speak of the continual enlargement of our knowledge through perception, every intelligent act of perception presupposes and requires several mental acts and experiences. Through a variety of experiences which have already been described, we must first have acquired a knowledge of our animated organism as an extended object, and learned how to use it in acquiring a knowledge of other things. And the perception of every external object, besides an appropriate use of the organ of sense, requires, first, some degree of attention; second, the judgment that it is an object external to us; and, third, the discriminating of it from other objects by its

qualities, place, &c. By repeated acts of observation, we may learn more and more about an object: having exhausted all its directly perceptible qualities, we may proceed to divide it into parts mechanically, and decompose it chemically, but can never arrive at an absolute knowledge of its nature as distinguished from its qualities, elements, and parts. Matter in its essence, not less than spirit, is incognizable to us.

12. *It is only in a limited sense intuitive.*—It is only in a very limited sense, at most that perception is intuitive. The term intuitive comes from the Latin word *intueor*, "I see," "behold:" it means, therefore, the direct vision of something, primarily through the sense of sight, and secondarily by the mind itself. In sense-perception, then, what addresses itself directly to the eye is perceived intuitively; as colors, forms, and the outward aspects of Nature. But even these are intuitively perceived only as phenomena or appearances; the real form, size, and distances of objects are determined by the judgment. So, too, tastes, smells, sounds, contact, and pressure, being *directly* perceived as phenomena or appearances, may be considered as intuitively perceived. But all phenomena must be interpreted and judged of by the reason. The reason alone determines what they imply; and what is implied or involved in these appearances is what constitutes the real perception as a form of knowledge.

11. The parts of an object obtained by mechanical or chemical separation are called its *integrant parts;* while its qualities (such as form, color, odor, &c.) are called its *metaphysical parts.* The process by which we mentally view an object as composed of parts is called *analysis;* while that by which these parts are re-united and viewed as a whole is call *synthesis.* In our study of objects, we are constantly performing these two counter processes upon them.

SECTION II

THEORIES OF PERCEPTION.

1. *View of perception by the earliest Greek philosophers.*—In the speculations of the early Greek philosophers (Thales, Anaximander, Anaximenes, and Heraclitus), man was not very sharply distinguished from nature nor the soul from the body. They were conscious, of course, of possessing an intelligence greater than that of other objects and animals around them. But this they regarded as the result of a more refined material nature within, not as the manifestations of a soul different in its nature from the body. They generally assumed some material element, as *water*, *air*, or *fire*, as the general constitutive principal of all things,—as that of which all things consisted, only in different states and under different forms. With them the soul was but a refined form of this material element, and its sensations and perceptions but the response which it made to the agitations or action upon it of the coarser forms of the element without. This, in a rude way, corresponds to the modern theory of the materialists, that sensation and perception are wholly the result of our organism, acted upon by external objects.

2. *View of perception by later Greek philosophers and the schoolmen.*—The Greek philosophers of a later period (Anaxagoras, Socrates, Plato, Aristotle) introduced and gradually developed the doctrine of an intelligent principle in man more or less distinct from his material organism. Such a doctrine would necessarily work some change in the received view of perception. Perception being no longer regarded as the mere result of the ac-

tion of the organism acted upon by external objects, but an apprehension of external things by an intelligent principle within, some provision must be made for bringing the external object into relation with this internal principle. Accordingly there was gradually developed, more particularly by Aristotle, the distinction of the *form* and the *matter* of an object, the former of which alone was perceived; the soul receiving it as the wax does the impression of the signet, taking no knowledge of the material of the signet itself. It was felt that the spirit within could not directly apprehend the gross external object, but only its form or image (τὸ εἶδος as it was called). This doctrine was further developed by the schoolmen of the middle ages (who substituted the term *species* for form) and continued in vogue till the time of Descartes.

3. *Descartes' theory of perception.*—Descartes, the father of modern philosophy (born at La Haye, in Touraine, 1596), distinguished the soul from the body more sharply than any of his predecessors, regarding it as entirely different in its nature and mode of existence. He regarded the brain, or more definitely the *peneal gland* of the brain, as its special presence-chamber, or sensorium. In his view, sensation is purely a spiritual affection, or thought; and perception consists in the apprehension by the mind of external objects through motions in the brain caused by the contact or influence of these objects upon the organ of sense, and conveyed

---

2. Pythagoras and the Eleatic philosophers (Xenophanes, Parmenides, and Zeno) rather attempted to construct a world out of their own thoughts than to learn what the world actually was. Absorbed in the combination and evolution of their concepts, they entirely overlooked perception. As every particular thing exists and is therefore embraced under the general concept Being, they concluded that all things were one (τὸ ἓν και παν).

inward by the *animal spirits.* These motions were not regarded as representing the external object, but, by the divine assistance, were made the occasion of awakening in the mind a representation of it, which alone was perceived,—not the external object itself, either in its nature or qualities. Thus we have substituted for the representative form or species of the earlier philosophers motions conveyed to the brain by a mysterious agent called animal spirits. External objects being thus perceived, not in themselves, and only indirectly through their representative forms or species, arbitrarily occasioned by motions or signs in the brain, the question immediately arose as to the trustworthiness of these perceptions, which has ever since been the great point of dispute among philosophers. If sensations are mere thoughts of the mind, and not mental apprehensions of organic affections, the validity of sense-perceptions may well be doubted.

Descartes relied upon his capacity of thought as proof of his spiritual existence. *Cogito ergo sum* ("I think, therefore, I exist") was his formula. And this is the best proof possible of our possession of a spiritual nature. The phenomena of thought are entirely different from the phenomena of matter as witnessed everywhere else: hence we cannot believe them to be due to the body in our own person.

4. *Pantheistic theory of perception.*—From the Cartesian philosophy sprang the most elaborate development of the pantheistic view of nature which has yet been made. Spinoza, an earnest student of Descartes, despairing of being able to bring mind and matter into relation with each other on Cartesian principles, boldly transferred *thought* and *extension*—by which Descartes

characterized mind and matter respectively—to a single substance, itself imperceptible, but manifesting itself phenominally in different cases under the two attributes just named: in man it took the form of thought; in inanimate objects, the form of extension. Perception, which is one phase of thought, was the apprension of extension, and, like extension, was a mere transitory development from the one underlying imperceptible substance; and hence, and far as they were any thing, they were one and the same. Hence this has sometimes been called the *theory of absolute identity*. The underlying or absolute substance was called God by Spinoza: by others it has been called Nature. It is quite immaterial which it is called, as it is in itself without relations, and unconscious indeed, except in the transitory conscious objects called men, and the like. In such a system man is but an appearance, and thought but an illusion awakened by the endless evolution from the absolute substance of apparently-extended objects. Though not without its advocates, even at the present day, I cannot but regard the system as the fruit of a great but perverted ingenuity.

5. *Ideal theory of perception.*—Another ingenious, but, as I must regard it, perverted theory of perception, is what has been called the *ideal theory*. As we are confessedly conscious of only what is present to the mind, and as the external object cannot be present to it, but merely an idea or mental representation of the object, Berkeley and others have held that our apparent perceptions of external objects are merely a consciousness of ideas, thoughts, or feelings, in our own minds. How these ideas come to exist in the mind, if not produced there by real objects, has been variously accounted for

by different advocates of the theory. Berkeley regarded them as presented to the mind by the direct agency of God. Fichte regarded the external object as merely a self-limiting form of thought, as necessarily assumed in order that thought might be realized at all. Schelling regarded the mind and its object as really the same, and as consciously so in its highest moods of thought, they being consciously different and contrasted only in practical life. And Hegal regarded thought itself as the all-in-all, and as representing in itself all things; since in its development it had passed through all possible forms,—forms of thought, in his view, being the same as forms of being. Hegel, therefore, was not only an idealist, but a nihilist, holding that nothing exists except thoughts. David Hume, of Scotland, had previously professed such a doctrine, though on different grounds. He denied the existence of every thing except states of consciousness; regarding our idea of material substance as wholly generated by our various sensations of the so-called material qualities, and our idea of self by many rapidly-succeeding states of consciousness. And similar views to these of Hume, of the subject and object of thought, are now held by J. S. Mill and others. According to this theory, cooking and eating a dinner are merely mental processes, and growing pumpkins and melons only gradually expanding ideas. Let him believe it who can.

6. *Materialistic theory of perception.*—Materialism is the precise opposite of idealism. As idealism develops the object out of the subject, making it but a result of the activity of the soul; materialism, on the contrary, develops the subject out of the object, making but a result of the action of the organism of the body. Ac-

cording to this view, perception and every other form of thought and feeling are produced by the action of external objects upon our nervous organism, and its reactions upon them, without the intervention of any intelligent principle, or any principle whatever other than the organism itself. It regards the nervous system as so constructed as to produce these results in response to the action of other things upon it. Thus, while an agitation in the water of a river is merely an agitation there, an agitation in the water of the labyrinth of the ear, conveyed to the brain along the auditory nerve, becomes a sound, and this solely by virtue of the organism itself. And while the light of the sun merely warms and quickens other objects, falling upon the eye and conveyed to the brain, it is transformed into a picture-world within. But who hears the sound, or sees the vision? The organism, of course; as there is nothing else to hear it. The organism, then, both produces and realizes these phenomena. Who can believe or even conceive this? Much less can any one believe that the organism remembers, imagines, judges, and reasons.

Difficult as it is to conceive how a spiritual nature can be connected with a material organism, and act through it, and be acted upon by it, yet it is far less inconceivable than that the material organism itself is percipient. And yet many of the scientific men of the present day seem to be tending strongly to materialism. They have studied the structure of the organs, and find the mechanism so perfect, that they imagine it competent to the production of thought: and still there is not one of them who does not recoil from expressing in words what he is trying to believe; viz., that the brain or nervous system thinks.

7. *Theory of immediate perception.*—To the preceding views of perception should be added that which, since the time of Reid, has commonly been held by the Scotch school of philosophers,—the doctrine of an immediate perception of external objects. And by immediate perception is meant a direct perception of the object itself in certain of its qualities, without the intervention of any intermediate representative, whether material or immaterial. From the preceding account of the different theories of perception, it will be seen that it has generally been felt that the external object could not itself be perceived, but only some form, image, or shadow of it which approached more nearly to the mind in nature. This representation was called the *species* by the schoolmen; but, since the time of Descartes, has generally be called the *idea*. It has assumed three different forms: 1st, That of an image or real representative of the external object, regarded by some as material and by others as immaterial, presented through the senses to the mind for its apprehension; 2d, An image or change somehow produced in the mind itself through the action of the organism: and, 3d, An image or representation of the object formed in and by the mind in the very act of perception.

The first two of these views are neither of them susceptible of an intelligible explanation, and are now

---

7. It may be thought, that, in ever so brief an account of the theories of perception, some notice should be taken of the views of so distinguished a philosopher as Kant. But Kant was a metaphysician rather than a psychologist, and taught nothing important on the subject of perception, except that the notions of space and time enter as a necessary or *a priori* element into every act of perception. For a fuller account of the different representative theories of perception, see Wight's Hamilton, pp. 180–237.

almost universally abandoned; and the third view also, which is here regarded as the true view, is rejected by Hamilton, who strenuously advocates in its stead the theory of an immediate perception of external objects through consciousness. But I am confident that this view cannot be maintained. Knowledge is merely realized in consciousness, not acquired by it. The objections to the theory have already been stated (see sect. i. 10). We undoubtedly obtain a knowledge of external objects in perception, and form a notion or idea of them in the process, as already described (see sect. i.), but do not perceive them through this notion as a representative, nor apprehend them directly through consciousness.

SECTION III.

PERCEPTION BY THE DIFFERENT SENSES.

TOUCH (FEELING, PAIN, MUSCULAR SENSE).

1. *Definitions of touch, feeling, etc.*—The sensation caused by bringing an external object gently into contact with the skin is called *touch;* the more internal and subjective sensation caused by the pressure of the object touched, or other causes, is called *feeling;* while that occasioned by the violent contact of an external object, or by any injury of the tissues of the body, or by internal or external disease, is called *pain.* The Muscular Sense, sometimes called the *active sense*, embraces the sensations felt in the muscles when exerted in overcoming resistance. Besides these general sensations, there are other peculiar and occasional feelings, caused by local or special stimuli, such as those felt in sneezing, shuddering, or from the effects of fear, heat, cold, etc.

2. *The seat of these various sensations.*—All these different sensations have their seat in the *nerves of touch or feeling*, which proceeding from the brain and spinal chord, are distributed to all parts of the body, and branching out into innumerable minute filaments as they approach the surface, protrude themselves through the skin to the cuticle, in the form of *papillæ*, or little prominences, with varying degrees of proximity to each other in different parts of the body, but at minutely small distances in all parts. All the proper feeling experienced in any part of the system, even in the use of the other senses, is yielded by this class of nerves. The nerves of each sense yield but a single class of sensations, whatever be the stimulus applied; as we learn, in the case of sight, by pressing upon the eye, when we are conscious of the sensation of color, as if the organ were under the stimulus of light. So our nerves of touch yield nothing but feeling, and yield all the feeling of which we are conscious.

3. *The experience of which we are susceptible through this sense.*—If all the various sensations which have there seat in the nerves of feeling be grouped together under the sense of touch, as they more commonly are, we are susceptible of a more varied experience through this sense, than through any other. Its sensations furnish more obtrusively than those of the other senses, the conditions for perceiving extension in our own organism and inferring it in external objects, while through the feeling of resistance we reach our first knowledge of external objects. It is through the nerves pertaining to this sense, also, that we experience the sensations of heat and cold, of the healthy and diseased action of all the organs, of disorganization, of injury done to

any part of the body, and various other sensations so essential to our comfort or preservation. (N. I. 3, p 252).

4. *The hand the most important organ of this sense,* —The hand is the most important organ of this sense. as well on account of its delicate sensibility to external objects, as on account of the freedom of its motions and its adaptedness to grasping and thus ascertaining the form of objects. The blind man, by passing his fingers over the lines of a book printed in raised letters, reads almost as readily and rapidly as one does by sight. But while the form of small objects which can be grasped, or are easily compassed by the motion of the hand, is very readily determined by touch, it is very difficult, if not impossible, to ascertain the form of large objects by this sense alone. The form of such bodies is more readily learned by sight, through its acquired powers.

II. TASTE.

1. *The organ of this sense.*—The tongue is the organ of taste, the skin of which, at innumerable points, is pierced to the mucous membrane by minute filaments of the *gustatory nerve*, producing the little prominences, or *papillæ*, which are plainly discernible all of its surface, but especially on the tip, edges, and near the root. Although this organ, like all other organs and parts of the body, is supplied with nerves of feeling, it is the gustatory nerve alone which is susceptible of the distinctive sensation of taste. As it is necessary that the substance should be diffused over the organ and be brought into close connection with the terminations of the nervous filaments, in order that it be tasted, only such substances as are soluble in the

saliva affect the sense; and hence, while the mouth is furnished with teeth for crushing substances, the tongue is surrounded by the salivary glands which secrete this fluid. Hence it is, that if from any cause the saliva is scantily furnished, or the tongue becomes coated so as to cover the *papillæ* to any considerable depth, the taste, for the time being, is greatly injured or destroyed.

2. *A taste is a mere sensation.*—Taste is a mere sensation, and conveys to us directly no knowledge of its cause. As, however, we soon learn that the sensation arises only when certain substances are placed in the mouth, we infer that these are the cause of it. But what the particular property in objects is which causes the sensation, at least in its nature, is still unknown. As a mere subjective sensation yielding no perception of an external extended object, a taste involves but few physical elements,—barely those embraced in the physical changes produced in the mouth by the substance tasted. But even these are often sufficient to afford the ground for a description of it, and are always present to the mind in recalling the sensation. In recalling tastes, we often smack the lips, or spit, as though rejecting something offensive from the mouth, in evident allusion to the impression which they originally made upon this organ.

3. *Taste as a test of wholesomeness.*—Whatever is taken into the mouth and has an agreeable taste, we have a disposition to swallow, while we involuntarily reject whatever has a disagreeable taste, However, the taste of substances is but a poor test of their wholesomeness. Some of the most deadly poisons, as, for instance, arsenic, are sweet and agreeable to the taste, while most of the useful medicines are very offen-

sive to the taste. And even of articles of food, it is not always those which are the most agreeable to the taste that are the most healthful. It is only by experience that we learn what is hurtful to be eaten, and having learned this, the other senses enable us, without resorting to taste, to recognize, on their recurrence, articles which have been found to be of this character, as well as those which have been found to be of an opposite character.

III. SMELL.

1. *The organ of this sense.* — The nose is the organ of smell, in the back part of which are situated the *turbinated bones*, which consist of thin convoluted plates, like a piece of crimped paper, exposing a large surface in a small space. Over these bones is spread the *olfactory nerve*, in which resides the susceptibility to odors; and this, again, is covered by the mucous membrane which lines the nose and mouth, and secretes the mucus necessary to keep the surface soft and in a condition favorable to perception. An organ thus situated and constructed, can be reached by external objects only through minute particles thrown off from them, and borne through the air to the interior of the nose. Hence only those substances are odoriferous which are capable of throwing off such particles.

2. *Smell is a mere sensation.* — Smell, like taste, is a mere sensation, conveying no direct knowledge of its cause. The cause is discovered only by experience. By observing that the presence of certain objects is accompanied by the sensations of smell, we infer that these sensations are somehow caused by these objects. On further examination, we learn that particles of the

substance smelled, called *effluvia*, are actually present in the air, and must be drawn into the nostrils with every inspiration of the breath. We conclude, therefore, that these substances cause the sensations by throwing off particles into the surrounding air, which by due process are brought into contact with the organ. As to the physical character of the sensation, and its capability of being recalled in memory, much the same may be said as in the case of taste. We often recall an agreeable or disagreeable odor so vividly, as to seem now to be smelling it, and snuff or snort with the nose as an indication of our conception of its character.

3. *Importance of the sense.* — Smell is an important sense, not only as assisting in determining what is wholesome to be taken into the system (and for this reason, as remarked by Socrates of old, placed near the mouth), but also, on account of its informing us of the existence of objects at a distance, out of the reach or range of the other senses, or inappreciable by them. It thus greatly enlarges the boundary of our knowledge of external things.

IV. SIGHT OR VISION.

1. *The organ of this sense.* — The eye is the organ of sight. The rays of light proceeding from an object, on reaching the eye, first pass through the *cornea* and *aqueous humor*, and are admitted into the chamber of the eye through a small opening in the *iris*, called the *pupil.* From this point the rays pass on through the *crystalline lens* and the *vitreous humor* to the *retina*, which is a fine network expansion of the *optic nerve*, embedded in the black pigment of the *choroid coating*, in the back part of the eye. The rays of light from the

different parts of an object proceeding in straight lines cross each other on their entrance at the pupil, and slightly refracted, or bent inwards, in their progress through the eye, form a diminished and *inverted picture* of the object on the retina.

2. *Conditions of vision.* — The susceptibility of sight resides in the retina, and all that is required for producing perfect vision in a sound eye, is, that a given amount of light should proceed from an object and be formed into a distinct image upon the retina. To secure this, the eye has certain powers of adjustment, such as contracting and expanding the pupil, in order to let in less or more light, and perhaps, of changing the form or the position of the crystalline lens, so as to secure the distinctness of the image. These powers of adjustment, however, are quite limited. A great excess or deficiency of light, or an unusual convexity or flatness of the eye, cannot be remedied by any power of adjustment which it possesses, though the latter defect may be in certain cases by external appliances, as by concave or convex glasses.

3. *What vision is.* — Our consciousness of an affection of the optic nerve is vision, just as our consciousness of an affection of the gustatory nerve is taste. The light falling upon the retina from an object produces in it a certain change or modification, varying in the different parts of the nervous expanse, according to the quality and quantity of the rays, and this affection reveals itself as a pictured outline. That the organ is thus affected we know from observation, and that it is this organic affection of which we are directly conscious, and not the external colored objects, is evident from various considerations, and especially from the

fact, that light proceeds from a body to the eye, and is seen, and can be seen, only when it reaches the eye; i.e., it is nothing to us till it becomes an organic affection. Hence, sight or vision, in the first instance, and without the elements derived from experience, is simply the consciousness of an affection of the visual organ.

4. *Color, as apprehended by us, is a mere sensation.* — Consequently, color, as far as it is directly apprehended by us, is a mere sensation. It is merely the recognition in our organism of an extended nervous expanse as colored. As to the nature and character of a sensation so elusive and so much under dispute among philosophers, I gladly avail myself of the following clear, and, to me at least, satisfactory, statement of Sir W. Hamilton * on the subject. (Notes, p. 252.)

5. *Remarks of Hamilton.* — "I hold that color, in itself, as apprehended, or immediately known to us, is a mere affection of the nervous organism; and therefore, like the other secondary qualities, an object, not of perception, but of sensation proper. The only distinguishing peculiarity in this case, lies in the three following circumstances: —

"(1.) That the organic affection of color, though not altogether indifferent, still, being accompanied by comparatively little pleasure, comparatively little pain, the apprehension of this affection, *qua* affection, i.e., its sensation proper, is consequently always at a minimum.

"(2.) That the passion of color first rising into consciousness, not from the amount of the intensive quantity of the affection, but from the amount of the extensive quantity of the organism affected, is necessarily apprehended under the condition of extension.

* Wight's Hamilton, p. 431.

"(3) That the isolation, tenuity, and delicacy of the ultimate filaments of the optic nerve afford us minutely and precisely distinguished sensations, realized in consciousness only as we are conscious of them as out of each other in space.

"These circumstances show, that while in vision, perception proper is at its maximum and sensation proper at its minimum, the sensation of color cannot be realized apart from the perception of extension: but they do not warrant the assertion, that color is not, like the other secondary qualities, apprehended by us as a mere sensorial affection."

6. *Fallacies of vision.* — According to the above view of vision, the various *fallacies of sight*, as they have been called, vanish at once; such as the crooked appearance of a straight stick when thrust into the water, the apparent suspension of objects in the air in *mirage*, the small apparent size of the sun and moon, and other large bodies, which are far removed from us. As vision is merely the apprehension of the actual affection of the organ, there is no deception in these cases. The visual image is precisely what it appears to be. The actual form, size, position, etc., of the object represented by the sensation is reached only by the co-operation of the other senses and powers.

7. *Vision leads to a knowledge of external objects.* — But vision, though in itself a mere sensation, is not practically confined to the subjective affection. As in the case of other sensations, we soon learn to infer its cause. As we are conscious of the affection only when the eyes are open, we at once infer that the cause is without. On further experience, we learn that the affection varies as we turn in different directions, and

that the same affection recurs when we occupy the same position and our eyes are in the same direction The unavoidable inference, therefore, is, that each affection has a particular cause, lying in a particular direction from us. Coming to this conclusion, we soon verify our conjecture by moving in different directions, and, by means of our other senses, identifying as their cause certain objects appreciable by the other senses. Having thus established as the cause of visual affections, certain external objects in a given relation to us, we come to take a visual affection as the sign of the existence of a corresponding object in a particular direction and relation to us, — nay, transfer the appearance directly to the object in space. The rest is learned by after-experience, particularly by the *motion* and *scrutiny* of the eyes.

8. *We learn the relative position of the different parts of an object to us by the motion of the eyes.* — We not only learn by experience that the objects of vision are external to us, and the general directions in which they lie from us, but by the motion of the eyes over an object we learn the exact *relative position* of its different parts towards us. The picture of an object on the retina, as we learn from science, is inverted relatively to the object without. But this we can never become conscious of, or deduce from our own experience, only as the actual position of the different parts of the external object to the eye are learned by the use of the sense itself. And in learning this, and just as fast and as far as we learn this, we learn, also, as we shall soon see, that, following out the ascertained lines of vision, every point in the object corresponds to its projected image on the retina; so that there never can be any

conscious discrepancy between the position of the different parts of an object and its perceived affection or image. The law of *visible direction*, which shows the position of an object and its image on the retina to differ relatively, shows them to agree actually. (N. 8, p. 252.)

9. *The law of visible direction.* — How, now, do we learn this law of visible direction? Although we receive the general image of all parts of an object within the field of vision when we open the eyes before it, still, it is distinctly and satisfactorily seen only as every part in succession is scrutinized by the eyes, with the axes more or less concentrated upon it. And all objects presented to our view are thus scrutinized by the eyes, which are constantly traversing in concert every object before them. By this scrutinizing movement of the eyes, up and down, to the right and left, over an object, the relative position of every part of it to the eye is learned, and we soon come to understand that each point of an object is seen in the direction of a perpendicular to that point of the retina upon which the rays from it fall, which is called the *law of visible direction.* Thus the image, at one end of the complement of rays, corresponds throughout to the object at the other, and any perceived discrepancy is impossible.

10. *How we learn the form of objects by sight.* — It is by the active and scrutinizing use of the eyes, also, that we learn to judge of the *form* of external objects by sight. As the light from all parts of an object reaches the eye in straight lines, we cannot, of course, directly see the *form* of any thing, except in two dimensions; i.e., as a mere surface outline, just as it is pictured upon the retina. All that we can see is different varieties and shades of color covering a certain expanse.

A solid body is discovered to be such by the sight: — in part, from the different degrees of brightness in the light from the more distant and averted portions and those nearer and more directly before us; and in part, by the varying effort and angle under which the axes of the eyes are concentrated upon the different parts of it, or of the objects which surround it and determine its form. When the object is a solid of such shape and size that no rays of light from it reach the eyes except from the surface towards them, we make out its form from the appearance of surrounding objects.

11. *How we learn to see things single.* —The question here is not, why we do not in looking at an object see two images of it which are *precisely alike*, since we never can, at the same time, see two images of an object precisely alike. But the real question is, why we are not conscious of two images of an object, since two *different* views of it are actually imaged upon the two eyes? This question may be answered in a general way, by saying that it is for the same reason that we hear but one sound with two ears, or feel but one object with two hands; viz., that knowing the object to be one by other means, as well as by the general sameness of the two impressions on the double organ, we have learned to disregard the difference, and are not at all conscious of it unless the attention is specially called to it. Two ears, two eyes, and two hands are given us for the precise purpose of observing opposite sides of things — for enlarging our experience on the right and on the left— but our Creator has abundantly provided by the principle of habit that no confusion shall arise from this beneficent arrangement. And this, perhaps, is an ade-

quate answer; but it may be rendered more convincing by a more precise statement.

12. *A more precise answer.* — From the relative position of the two eyes towards an object, one must always take in a different aspect of it from the other, when they are opened before it. This becomes consciously so to a cross-eyed person, who attempts to use both eyes in looking at an object; also, to any one who receives upon his eyes the image of an object lying beyond some point on which he is steadily fixing his gaze, — the more remote object, in such a case, always appears double. And all objects would appear so to us were not the two images, in ordinary vision, actually brought together and blended into one. Not only do the two images seen in looking at any object necessarily lap on to each other, but as vision is clear and distinct only at those points where the axes of the eyes are more or less concentrated, we are constantly traversing objects from point to point by both eyes in concert, which reduces all to unity. Yet, that we are familiar with the aspect of an object as seen by each eye, and actually combine these two aspects in vision, is evident from the illusion produced by the Stereoscope. By this contrivance, two photographic pictures of a person or thing, such as would be seen were it looked at first with one eye and then with the other, are enclosed in a case, and viewed through two eye-glasses brought near to the eyes. The result is, that the two pictures are combined into one, and we seem to be looking at a single object standing out in relief, as in nature.

13. *How we learn to judge of distance by sight.* — It is by experience, also, that we learn to judge of the *distance* of objects by sight. It is obvious that we do not

directly *see distance;* and this has been proved experimentally in the case of persons born blind and afterwards restored to sight. Such persons are found, at first, incapable of forming any idea of distance by sight.* But we learn by experience to *infer* distance from sight with great certainty. We soon learn that distance greatly affects the brightness of the color and the distinctness of the outline of objects. We are also conscious of a varying muscular effort in adjusting the eyes to see objects distinctly at different distances. From these circumstances, and the intervention of other objects of known size and character, in the field of vision between the eye and the object looked at, we learn to judge quite accurately by sight of the distance of objects from us. And having thus formed a notion of their distance, we infer also their *size.* Thus, by experience, vision, like our other senses, becomes the source of knowledge, of which, at first, it is entirely incapable.

14. *But our judgments from vision suppose uniform conditions.* — It is true, that vision in itself being merely the recognition of the actual affection of the retina, and the knowledge which we acquire by it of the position, form, size, and distance of objects being only inferential, our judgment in regard to these qualities of objects can be relied upon only under normal conditions in the atmosphere, which is the medium through which light reaches the eye. If in passing through this medium the light from any object is bent out of its course, as it often is by a change of density in different strata, the object is not seen in its proper place or po-

* See the account of the young man couched by Cheselden, Hamilton's Reid, p. 136.

sition, as is the case in *looming* or *mirage*. So a hazy atmosphere, giving an indistinctness of outline to an object near by, while it does not, of course, diminish its apparent size, makes us judge it to be larger than it really is; since we imagine it, from the indistinctness of its outline, to be farther off than it is, — we allow too much for distance. Bishop Berkeley attributes to this source of illusion the increased apparent size of the sun and moon when seen in the horizon, compared with their apparent size in mid-heaven. But this would seem to be due, rather, as explained by Descartes, to the intervention of objects of *known size* within the field of vision, when they are seen in the horizon, with which these heavenly bodies are brought into comparison, and judged to be larger in consequence, because known to be vastly farther off, — the comparison forces us to magnify the apparent size of the distant luminaries.

15. *But any illusions of sight are easily corrected.* — But these and the like illusions of sight are comparatively few and unimportant, and are either wholly corrected or rendered harmless by experience. They are all explained by a knowledge of the laws of nature, and easy means of correction supplied. Sight thus opens to us a wide and diversified field for perception, and by the cheerful light and varied hues with which it clothes nature, imparts the crowning charm to life.

V. HEARING

1. *The organ of this sense.* — The ear is the organ of hearing. At the point where it joins the head, the ear becomes contracted to a small tube, across the bottom of which is stretched the membrane that forms

the head of the *tympanum* or drum, which is a cavity containing a succession of bones so arranged as to propagate vibrations most effectively. Below the tympanum is the *labyrinth*, which is filled with a watery fluid, in which the fibres of the *auditory nerve*, the seat of the sensation of sound, are spread out. The external ear collects the vibrations proceeding from sonorous bodies through the air, which are conveyed to the drum through the tube, and from that propagated with greatly increased intensity to the fluid of the labyrinth, and thus to the auditory nerve which floats in this fluid; the vibratory affection of which is recognized by the mind as sound.

2. *Sound is a mere sensation.*— Sound, too, as perceived by us, is a mere sensation. Its immediate cause we learn to be, the vibratory motion of the surrounding air; and its remote cause, the vibratory motion of the particles of some body, which causes the agitation in the air. As the whole movement originates with this remote cause, this is considered the real cause. In determining the direction of a sound and tracing it to its source, we are greatly assisted by having two ears, and the capacity of turning the head in different directions. It is on the fact that we judge of the direction whence a sound comes from the manner in which it strikes the ear, and of its distance by its strength and distinctness, that the art of ventriloquism is founded. The ventriloquist, with some peculiarity, perhaps, in the organs of speech, has acquired such power over his voice, that he is able, aided by an artful direction of the attention of the hearers, to speak in such tones as may seem to proceed from any point he pleases.

3. *Importance of this sense.*— The sense of hearing

is important to us, not only by informing us of the clash of objects, the roar of waters, the agitations of the elements, the cries of animals, the artificial sounds, whether produced for pleasure or utility, but especially as the means of catching the tones of the human voice, and receiving the thoughts of others conveyed to the ear in winged words. Nay, even the exercise of our own powers of speech depends upon our possession of the sense of hearing. The voice can be articulated only as its tones are heard by the speaker himself.

SECTION IV.

IMPORTANCE OF THE SENSES.

1. *Comparative importance of the senses.* — Of the comparative importance of the different senses it seems difficult to judge. They are all so important, so necessary, that it is hard determining which is the most so. As of the members of the body in general one cannot say to the other, "I have no need of thee," so of the senses in particular, it is hard to say which we could spare best. Yet, it is obvious that the loss of feeling must be the most fatal, though the loss of sight seems the most deplorable. But it is found, as matter of fact, that the loss of hearing, accompanied, as it always is, by the loss of the power of speech, is a greater obstacle to improvement than the loss of sight, and I doubt if it be not a greater deduction from one's happiness.

2. *Their individual and combined importance.* — But, of the individual and combined importance of the senses, there can be no doubt. It is by them that na-

ture is unlocked and disclosed, being transformed from what would be to us a universal blank to the cheerful scene in which we ever move. By Taste her various sapid qualities are elicited — her treasured stores of sweet and pleasant flavors, with their opposites, the bitter, the sour, the acrid, and the nauseous. Smell snuffs up her odors, and Hearing drinks in her harmonies; while under the power of Touch and Sight she discloses her huge masses, her vast distances, her endless variety of forms, all invested with a robe of light, so bright, so cheerful, so variegated, so tinted and beautified, as to defy all imitation, or even description.

3. *The senses collect the primitive materials used by the mind.* — The senses, then, collect the primitive materials, and indeed, the whole mass of materials from without, used by the other powers of the mind. Besides perception, we have the powers of memory, imagination, conception, judgment, and reasoning. Of these powers, memory simply retains what has been acquired by perception; while conception, judgment, and reasoning combine perceived and remembered ideas, and make inductions and deductions from them. The means for exerting our higher powers, therefore, and the legitimacy of their results, all depend upon the extent and character of the primitive materials collected by the senses. It is obvious, therefore, in general, that the man who neglects to use his senses assiduously and carefully, can have but little knowledge, and that of a very vague and indistinct character. Without the proper use of the senses, there must always be an indefiniteness, an inaccuracy, an insufficiency in our views, which can be remedied by no other powers.

4. *The sciences are founded upon perceived facts.* — Most sciences are founded upon facts, and of these, all

but mental science, upon facts observed by the senses. And in many, if not in most, of these sciences, the observed facts are the chief thing. In all the branches of Natural History, there is nothing but classification, beyond the collection of facts. And while the collection and proper inspection of these require a vast amount of time, labor, and care, the principle of classification is usually quite obvious, and is generally of itself suggested to the mind during the collection of the materials, if only the senses be properly used in scrutinizing them as they pass under their observation. And even in Natural Philosophy, not excepting Astronomy, the facts are not only the foundation, but a large part of the science.

5. *Even language is based upon the perceptions of the senses.* — And not only so, even language is built very largely upon the knowledge acquired by the senses. The first meaning of most words is physical. A large part of the words of a language, of course, refer solely to things physical — to natural objects, changes, or phenomena. Of the rest, very many, not excepting those referring to mental states, acts, relations, etc., have a physical element as their basis. Hence much of the force and meaning of language must depend upon our having observed the physical objects, facts, changes, phenomena, to which the words refer, or from which they take their coloring.

6. *These elements of knowledge are accessible to all.* — Now it is benevolently arranged by our Creator, that these facts, thus lying at the foundation of all knowledge and improvement, are generally close at hand, addressing themselves to our senses, and soliciting our attention on all sides. We have but to open

our eyes and unseal our senses, to perceive the great mass of them. As a whole, they are so accessible, and even obtrusive, that an ever-wakeful attention will enable even the common man, in connection with his ordinary pursuits and experience, to collect a vast store of them.

7. *Importance of cultivating the senses by observation.* — We see, then, how great importance attaches to our early forming the habit of close and accurate observation of all the objects and changes around us. This is the way to cultivate our senses and make them in the highest degree useful to us. The man who forms this habit early and continues it through life, keeping up, wherever he goes, and however employed, a lively wakefulness of attention to what exists and is occurring around him; examining everywhere nature and art, earths, minerals, insects, animals, man, chemical and mechanical processes and arrangements, the aspects of the earth, the sea, and the sky, will acquire a vast store of most interesting and useful knowledge, and have in his possession the materials for making a great philosopher. One thus furnished, only wants an intellect capable of evoking order from the mass, and connecting his materials by the natural threads of classification and law, to become a Cuvier, a Humboldt, a Miller, or an Agassiz.

8. *Importance of training the senses in youth.* — In conclusion, I cannot refrain from suggesting, as a most obvious inference from what has been said, that more attention should be given to the training of the senses to habits of observation in youth. Parents should endeavor to form the habit in their children, and teachers in those committed to their charge. Observation by

the senses should be a very important branch of instruction in all schools, from the lowest to the highest. Natural objects of all kinds should be examined and analyzed before the pupils, while they are required accurately to note all their peculiarities. And if our schools would adjourn to the fields, *en masse*, for an hour or two each day, and carry on the study of nature there, it would be greatly to the advantage of the pupils, both physically and intellectually.

CHAPTER III.

MEMORY.

SECTION I.

CONDITIONS OF MEMORY (ASSOCIATION).

1. *Memory and recollection.* — Memory is the common undiscriminating term employed to designate the recovery or reproduction of our past experience, whether it be our thoughts, feelings, volitions, or actions. But, in distinction from recollection or reminiscence, it means that ready reproduction of the past as though it were an ever-present possession. According to its derivation, memory means *the being mindful of, the having something in mind.* Whatever we perfectly remember seems a part of the ready furniture of the mind, — something which we can rely upon for use whenever we need it; so that we have but to turn our attention inward to perceive the objects of memory, just as we have but to open the eye to see outward objects. Recollection, or reminiscence, on the contrary, recognizes the reproduction of our past experience as a process, — as the *collecting again*, or *becoming mindful again*, of something known before. In recollection we are conscious of a search for the object, and realize that it is reached only by several steps. The

difference, however, between memory and recollection, is only apparent. They are both processes; only, in the former case, the steps are more readily, and hence less consciously, taken. Familiar objects, being more largely associated with our experience, are readily remembered; since, whichever way we look, or turn our thoughts, we meet with something which reminds us of them. Thus the steps are so readily and rapidly taken, that we are scarcely conscious of taking them at all.

2. *Statement of the conditions of memory.* — The conditions of memory, or what have usually been called the laws of association, were well known and clearly stated by Aristotle, and have been distinctly recognized by all competent writers on the human mind ever since. These conditions are, THAT WHATEVER IS REMEMBERED MUST BE RECALLED OR REACHED, EITHER THROUGH SOMETHING IN OUR PRESENT THOUGHTS OR EXPERIENCE SIMILAR TO IT IN SOME RESPECT, OR THROUGH SOMETHING RELATED TO IT BY CONTIGUITY OF TIME OR PLACE, OR THROUGH SOMETHING RELATED TO IT BY CONTRARIETY OR CONTRAST. Some things are reached through one of these relations, and some through another; but nothing can be remembered on any other conditions. Some minds recall more things by one of these laws, and some more by another; but no mind can recall any thing except by one or another of them.

3. *Of the condition of similarity.* — The first condition of memory, then, is similarity, or likeness. The likeness may be either direct or fanciful; but some likeness is essential. Instances of things recalled by a direct likeness are such as the reviving in the mind of some taste, smell, feeling, or emotion, by the recurrence in our experience of a similar taste, smell, &c.; or the

recalling of some familiar face by the present sight of a face with some resembling feature. As is well known, a single resembling feature in a face often awakens the recollection of an absent friend; and a single resembling strain in a tune, the recollection of a once familiar air. So of fanciful likenesses: the decay of plants or the falling of the leaves tends to remind one of death, pensive music inspires solemn thoughts, and vast solitudes suggest ideas of God and of eternity. We often avail ourselves of this principle of similarity in order to secure the ready recollection of a name, for instance, which it is important that we should have at our command; as when we recall the name Walker by looking at the feet.

4. *Of the condition of ideas having been in the mind together.* — The second condition of memory is, that, in regard to time and place, only those things recall each other which happen or exist together, and, as such, have been perceived together. And, when things have been thus perceived together, it is found that the recurrence of one of them afterwards in our thoughts or experience tends to reproduce the other, or others. Thus the successive words on the page which we are studying are perceived in immediate connection with each other and with the page itself, and we find that they tend to recall each other in the order in which they were perceived. For the same reason, the name tends to recall the thing, and the thing its name. So a native air in a foreign land will remind one of home, where he has so often heard it before. Feelings or emotions, also, are recalled

---

3. In what is called *recognition*, or the reviving of a former perception of any object by its recurrence in our experience, the thing recalls itself, instead of something connected with it.

or revived on the same principle. Thus, on the sabbath, and in the house of God, the mind readily takes on the tone which it has so often experienced there before; while, for the same reason, it is exhilarated with lightness or gayety in the ball-chamber or the festive hall.

5. *The so-called condition of contrast is not a condition.* — The condition of contrariety, or contrast, does not seem to be a distinct principle of memory. As far as it is a principle of memory at all, it appears to be but a particular application of the last principle. Much of our knowledge comes into the mind in the form of contrasts; and, coming in thus, is naturally recalled in the same order, according to the preceding law. In our experience, we meet in close proximity with each other the good and the bad, the rich and the poor, the high and the low, the bitter and the sweet, day and night, hill and dale, woodland and prairie, land and water, the hovel and the palace, and all the ten thousand varieties and contrasts of life. Now, if these contrasts tend to suggest each other by memory proper, it must be through the tie formed between them by thus coming into the mind near together. But it seems to me, rather, that in most of such cases the contrasted pairs are but relative ideas, each essential in defining the other. They thus imply each other in thought, rather than are suggested by each other in memory. The terms good and bad, rich and poor, high and low, bitter and sweet, day and night, part and whole, true and false, parent and child, debtor and creditor, simple and complex, equal and unequal, and the like, mutually imply and define each other; so that, when one occurs to the mind, the other comes with it as its limiting opposite, or contrast. As Hamilton says, "The knowledge of relatives is

one:" when we attempt fully to realize the one, it is found to imply the other.

6. *Things are remembered only by the recurrence of the same or the similar.* — Our past experience and absent thoughts then, if recalled at all, must be recalled by the recurrence in our present experience of something which is either similar in some respect to that which is recalled, or something which on some former occasion has actually occurred in connection with that which is recalled. Thus the recurrence of the same and of similar thoughts or experience alone gives us any clew to what is past or now absent from the mind. And this is enough, as life repeats itself every day either in the same or similar forms; and the oftener it repeats itself thus in any one's experience, the surer and more ready is his memory. This, indeed, is one of the chief circumstances which determine the lines of association, or the methods of recovering their past experience, in different men.

7. *Of the effect of the repetition of the same on the memory.* — Repetition, then, of the same or similar experience, exerts an important influence on the memory. The narrower one's course of life, the more frequently it repeats itself in the same forms, and the more complete is the mastery of the past experience. Men remember best what has been oftenest in their minds; and hence, in recovering any thing past or absent, run along the line which their occupation or daily life has led them so frequently to trace. Accordingly, it has always been observed that our associations are very much determined by our business or profession. As one cannot remember at all what has never been in his thoughts, so he remembers best what has oftenest

been there. Every time a thought, feeling, or action, is repeated, it is done in connection with some other thought, thing, feeling, or action, and thus forms a new association or tie at every repetition. Such associations are necessarily formed in the oft-repeated routine of our daily business, or among the oft-recurring thoughts in our habitual modes of thinking: and hence every thing within such a sphere becomes, as we say, perfectly familiar to us, and is easily called up when wanted; since the whole round of thoughts, actions, &c., are thoroughly associated and bound up together.

8. *Of the effect of the repetition of the similar.* — In like manner, repetition and familiarity determine the lines of association through which we reach things absent on the principle of likeness. Thus an old Lutheran divine (quoted by Hamilton) naturally regarding the pope of Rome as a monster, and, familiar with the interpretation which makes the Apocalyptic Babylon only a mystical representation of Papal Rome, reaches the recollection of Babylon through a chain of association starting with the thought of the hydra, the monster killed by Hercules. Thus: "The thought of the *hydra* reminds me of the *pope;* the memory of him, of *Rome;* and the memory of Rome, of *Babylon.*" An astronomer, on the contrary, from his habits of thought might reach the memory of Babylon from an observation of the stars; since the Chaldeans, who lived at Babylon, were among the earliest cultivators of this science.

9. *Of the effect of interest on the memory.* — Another circumstance which greatly affects the memory is the degree of interest felt in the things to be remembered. When an unusual degree of feeling or interest accom-

panies any experience or the reception of an idea, it is much more firmly associated with the attendant circumstances, and hence is more likely to be recalled afterwards by the repetition of any of these circumstances. Hence it is that the events of a battle or a campaign always remain fresh, as we say, in the mind of a soldier, and that the young, to whom every thing is new, and hence interesting, remember facts better than those who are older. Interest, also, gives new potency to the principle of similarity in calling up absent thoughts or things, as is so happily represented by Shakspeare in his "Merchant of Venice:" —

> "My wind, cooling my broth,
> Would blow me to an ague when I thought
> What harm a wind too great might do at sea.
> I should not see the sandy hour-glass run
> But I should think of shallows and of flats;
> And see my wealthy Andrew docked in sand,
> Veiling her high-top lower than her ribs
> To kiss her burial. Should I go to church
> And see the holy edifice of stone,
> And not bethink me straight of dangerous rocks,
> Which, touching but my gentle vessel's side,
> Would scatter all her spices on the stream;
> Enrobe the roaring waters with my silks;
> And, in a word, but even now worth this,
> And now worth nothing?"

10. *Of the effect of attention.* — Attention to any thing when it is experienced or received into the mind tends largely to strengthen the memory. The chief source of the influence on the memory of the natural interest felt in any thing, already spoken of, is that it excites the attention. But, beyond this, we often, by a special effort of the will, concentrate the attention on

something which we wish to remember. We do this in committing a lesson, or when we charge the memory with any thing, or attempt to pre-arrange any matter for recollection. In all such cases we fix the mind intently, for a longer or shorter period of time, upon that which is to be remembered in connection with certain other familiar things which are likely to occur to us, and thus remind us of the thing desired. If one is going to a certain village, and wishes to obtain some article at a certain store, he thinks intently of the article and the store together, that, when he passes by the store, the sight of it may remind him of the article to be obtained there; and the more intently and repeatedly he thinks of them together, the more sure will be the remembrance. All artificial memory, so called, is effected in this way. The string that is tied upon the finger of the child must be made to mean something to the child, by calling his attention distinctly and repeatedly to that which it is intended to suggest, before it can be of any avail. Such artificial arrangements are useful in many simple cases which every one practises; but any extended system of mnemonics for recalling dates or historical facts by forced and artificial associations is worse than useless, it being more difficult to retain the mnemonic symbols employed than the things themselves.

---

10. As a speaker who had various points to present in his discourse might first visit the building in which he is to speak, and associate the different points with different objects in the audience-room; so some of the earlier systems of mnemonics recommended the association of different things to be remembered with the different parts of an artificial picture or drawing, or with different numbers or letters in a word. Gray's *Memoria Technica*, one of the most elaborate systems of mnemonics, recommends, in order to remember dates, the association of the

11. *Of remarkable memories.* — Some persons are endowed with wonderful powers of memory. Some clergymen are able, by reading over their sermons a few times before service, to repeat them *verbatim* from beginning to end. Seneca states that he could repeat two thousand words in their order upon hearing them once recited. He also says that Cyneas, the ambassador of King Pyrrhus to the Romans, in a single day so well learned the names of the people whom he saw, that the next day he saluted all the senators and all the people assembled, each by his proper name. Pliny says that Cyrus knew every soldier in his army by name, and L. Scipio all the people of Rome. Such wonderful powers of memory are very striking, and for this reason often prove a fatal gift by preventing all persistent and profound study. In such cases, too, the powers of memory are very apt to be greatly in excess of the other powers of the mind. It is only in the very best minds that all the powers attain any thing of this extraordinary efficiency. But, however great the feats of memory, they are all accomplished through the operation of the two laws already so often referred to. Such minds recall what they remember by the usual associations; only, by a keener perception and greater concentration of the attention, they make them much more rapidly and securely: though it is usually found in such cases that the whole series of remembered objects

---

different letters in the alphabet with certain numbers, and then so to change the historical names connected with the dates as to suggest them. Thus: If the letter *a* be placed over 1, and the letter *i* over 3, and *t* under it, so as to be associated with each other by being seen and studied together, and then Alexander be changed to Alexandr*ita*, it will suggest 331, — the date of the founding of his empire.

vanishes as soon as the effort ceases. By an extraordinary effort they are held securely for the occasion, and, as soon as this is past, vanish at once.

12. *The principle of similarity the most fruitful principle of memory.* — Of the two principles for recalling our past experience or thoughts, the recurrence of the same and the recurrence of the similar, the latter is obviously of the widest application. There are many similarities among events and things to one sameness ; so that, to a mind with any aptitude for analogies at least, the like must recur with much greater frequency than the same. Both the same and the similar thought or object which is to recall another may recur by a fresh perception, or be itself recalled by the recurrence of the same or the similar in our previous thoughts; thus producing the perpetual round of thoughts which we realize in our daily experience. Each principle, therefore, has a very wide application ; but the principle of similarity must be much the most fruitful. Indeed, it is by this principle that most of our remote thoughts are recovered, and frequently without any voluntary effort of our own. The oft-quoted case of reminiscence from Hobbes is of this kind. "In a discourse," says he, "on our late civil war" (i.e., in the time of Charles the First), "what could seem more impertinent than to ask, as one did, what was the value of the *Roman penny?* Yet the coherence to me was manifest enough: for the thought of the *war* introduced the thought of *delivering up the king to his enemies;* the thought of that brought in the thought of *the delivering up of Christ;* and that, again, the thought of the *thirty pence*, the price of that treason."

13. *It is, however, doubtful if it be an indedendent prin-*

ciple of memory. — But although the recurrence of the similar is more fruitful in reviving other thoughts than the recurrence of the same, still it is doubtful if it be an independent principle of memory, or any thing more than a form of the recurrence of the same. The similarity which recalls some other object, thought, or feeling, is usually a likeness in a certain particular; and may we not suppose that the similarity first recalls that particular in the other object, and then that particular recalls the rest of the object, on the principle of its having been before perceived in connection with the rest, as it must necessarily have been? As, in perception, things substantially alike make the same impression upon us, and are regarded as substantially the same, why may it not be so in memory, and hence the similar be taken for the same? When I see a feature in a face, or any thing in the carriage of a man, like the same in a friend, it immediately reminds me of that friend. In such a case, there can be no doubt, I think, that I recall first the resembling particular in the friend, and then his whole person.

14. *Memory always starts from something present to the mind.* — The process of memory, or recollection, being such as it has been described above, it is obvious that it must always start with something now present to the mind, — either a present perception, or a present thought suggested by something antecedent to it. The call to recite will start one in the process of rehearsing a series of words which he has been studying as a task; and so the desire to recover something lost will incite one to run over in memory the whole course of a journey on which he supposes he lost the article. If we are inquired of whether we remember any particular event

which has faded from the memory, or if for any reason we wish to revive our recollection of such an event, we always begin by searching in the mind, as we say, for something to start with. The process is well stated by Longinus, in a passage quoted by Hamilton: "For as dogs," says he, "having once found the footsteps of their game, follow from trace to trace, deeming it already all but caught; so he who would recover his past thoughts from oblivion must scrutinize the parts which remain to him of those thoughts, and the circumstances with which they chance to be connected, to the end that he may light on something which shall serve him as a starting-point from whence to follow out his recollection of the others."

SECTION II.

THEORIES OF MEMORY.

1. *Memory is not a recognition of impressions on the brain.* — Such being the conditions of memory, — viz., that nothing can be recalled, or re-introduced into the mind, except by the recurrence of something formerly perceived or thought of in conjunction with it, or of something similar to it in some respect, — how may the process be best accounted for? What theory will best explain the facts? In the first place, it is obvious that the popular representations of the condition and connection

---

14. It is evident that we cannot recall any thing by a direct effort of the will. We may put ourselves upon a search for something by an act of the will; but we can reach the object desired only by falling upon something in our search which shall suggest what we are in quest of.

of our thoughts among themselves are no explanation of the facts of memory, but are rather misleading than otherwise. Our perceptions are often spoken of as inscribed or engraved upon the mind, or as leaving impressions upon the brain. But neither of these representations is even intelligible in itself, and does not at all account for the recurrence of our thoughts in memory. If the mind is of a spiritual nature, how can ideas be inscribed upon it? and how can the myriads of perceptions and feelings of which we are conscious leave impressions on the brain which can be distinguished from each other? The experience of a single day would produce inextricable confusion there. But, supposing it so, it does not explain at all why these impressions are recognized by the mind only on the recurrence of some associated or similar thought. If they are there, why should they not be continually recognized?

2. *Ideas are not bound together by any real tie.* — So, too, our ideas are often spoken of as having an attraction for each other, as bound together by some tie, as stored away in the mind, as committed to the memory, and the like; or the mind or the memory is spoken of as retentive, tenacious, &c. The effects, indeed, are very much as though these representations were true, and we can hardly avoid such language when speaking of the phenomena of memory; but they do not explain any thing. The question still remains, *why* our ideas are bound together by such fixed ties as we find them to be, and what is really *meant* by the tenacity, retentiveness, &c., of the mind. What is meant, for instance, by committing any thing to the memory, or charging the memory with any thing, as we say? Do we really consign it to the memory, as one of the compartments

of the mind for safe keeping, till called for? Certainly not. We rather associate it or think of it with special attention in connection with something which we suppose likely to attract our notice, or fall in our way about the time we wish to recall the object to be remembered, and thus remind us of it. Suppose, for instance, I have written a letter, which I wish to drop into the post-office at a certain hour. I either place it where I expect to be at that time, so that it may attract my notice; or I think of it in connection with some object, place, or duty, which is to occupy my attention at that hour, and will thus remind me of it. The effort which we make in any case of memory evidently is not directly to retain our thoughts in the mind, but rather so to connect them with other thoughts or things, by fixing the mind upon them in conjunction with each other, that the recurrence of one will recall the others. The fact, then, is, that our thoughts are bound together by being in the mind together; and we are to inquire why this should be so.

3. *Memory not explained by the law of redintegration.* — Is memory explained by what has been called the law of *redintegration*, or the tendency of the mind to restore all the particulars which have been before united in a single mental state on the recurrence of one? This, at most, can be regarded as only a comprehensive statement of the general laws of association, and indeed a statement less simple and less exact than the ordinary statement of those laws. But the statement of a law or a fact is surely no explanation of it: it merely describes what the mind does, or has a tendency to do, not *why* it does it. To say that the mind, on the recurrence of a single particular, has a tendency to restore all the other particulars which have been united with it

in a single mental state, is to say nothing more than that it has a tendency in such a case to restore all that on a particular occasion had been in the mind together; thus wholly leaving out the law of similarity. Though supported by great names, and favored by Hamilton, I can but regard this famous law as a defective statement of the facts, and as very far from explaining them.

4. *Nor by President Porter's principle.* — Is the coherence of our thoughts which have been in the mind together explained by the principle propounded for its explanation by President Porter? ("Human Intellect," p. 282): viz., "that the mind tends to act again more readily in a manner or form which is similar to any in which it has acted before, in any defined exertion of its energy." . . . "This tendency explains the principle that underlies the laws of association." Increased facility, it is true, whether in thought or action, does result from habit; but habit is not formed by a single repetition: and how does it happen that a coherence among our ideas is established by a single association? and why do only those thoughts follow each other which have before been in the mind together? All our experience, of course, must occur at some place and time, and some associations may be formed at each; but, as place and time are continually changing, more of our experience must be separated in these respects than conjoined. And yet those experiences which occur at different places or times do not tend to recall each other, however often they may thus occur. If I witness a murder in one place, and a wedding in another, the thought of one has no tendency to introduce the other; but, if I witness them both together, the thought of one will be pretty sure to revive the thought of the other.

It is only when perceptions at different times and places are like each other in some respect that they tend to recall each other, as where the thought of a wedding witnessed at one place might recall the thought of a festival at another, they having certain points of similarity. It seems, then, that while the energy of the mind is more frequently exerted in perceiving things in different places and times, yet only those things which are perceived together tend to recall each other. It is clear, therefore, that the above principle is not sufficient to account for the coherence of our thoughts in memory.

5. *May be explained by the repetition of the organic action which took place at the original perception.* — In short, I know of no principle which at all accounts for the reviving of our thoughts in memory, unless it be that of an actual repetition in each case of the same action in our organism which occurred at the original perception of the object remembered, and of that by which it is remembered. If, in accordance with a suggestion already made (see sect. i. 13), we may consider the similar as equivalent to the same, then the universal condition of memory will be, that nothing can be recalled which has not previously been in the mind with another thought or thing now present to the mind. Now, if we trace back our thoughts to their origin, we shall find that they represent things; and these things, when first perceived, we must suppose, produced a certain effect, or caused a certain action in the organism; which action, by the theory now under consideration, is supposed to be renewed or repeated in every case of memory. It is universally admitted that there is a certain action in the organism connected with every perception; and we may well suppose that this action is different when two or more

things are perceived in conjunction with each other, from what it is when they are perceived separately. Now, we have only to suppose this action to be renewed on the recurrence of one of the conjoined objects to account for all the facts of memory. In this case memory is but a second perception, reviving in the mind the previous perception. But there is still a difficulty in seeing why the whole of the complex organic movement should be renewed on the presence or thought of only one of the several objects which were originally perceived together, and still more why in so many cases the movement is not renewed at all on the perception or thought of one of the conjoined objects; since it is well known that we never recall more than a small fraction of those things which have been perceived together.

6. *This by far the most conceivable theory, and the difficulties not insuperable.* — This theory, then, though by far the most conceivable, is not without its difficulties; and, besides, is often objected to on other grounds. It is regarded by many as tending to materialism. But the mind is confessedly dependent upon the action of the organism in perception; and why may it not be in recollection? That the organism is the medium of the mind in perception by no means proves that there is no mind; and why should it be thought to prove or imply this, if it be found that the organism is its medium in recollection? A percipient power beyond and above the organism is plainly implied in both cases, and especially in recollection; since what is recollected is recognized as something which has been perceived before. There must, therefore, be a permanent percipient principle, existing not only *now*, but *then*. In like manner, the objection sometimes made to this theory of memory, that

it cramps and confines the movements of the mind in association, restricting it to those necessary rounds which our experience awakens in our organism, does not seem very weighty. The theory does not change the facts of memory, but merely attempts to account for these facts. Whatever freedom the mind really has in its associations remains untouched; and, in point of fact, it must have as much freedom and spontaneous action here as it has in perception. As we can disregard or turn away from hurtful objects which are presented to us in perception, so we may from the like thoughts presented or suggested by memory; and as the mind, of itself, forms its idea of an object on the action of the organ in perception, so it must re-form or re-present this idea on the recurrence of the same action in memory. The action of the organism can no more constitute the idea in the one case than in the other. And as to rigidness in our associations, the more fixed and certain they are the better, provided they are wholesome; and, in order that they may be such, it is only necessary that our lives should be upright and pure.

---

6. Even J. S. Mill, who seems to be a sort of materialistic nihilist, in his "Examination of Sir William Hamilton's Philosophy" (vol. ii. p. 261), makes the following concession: "If, therefore, we speak of the mind as a series of feelings, we are obliged to complete the statement by calling it a series of feelings which is aware of itself as past and future; and we are reduced to the alternative of believing that the mind, or ego, is something different from any series of feelings, or possibilities of them; or of accepting the paradox, that something which *ex hypothesi* is but a series of feelings, can be aware of itself as a series."—In our present state of existence, it is probable that the mind is not wholly independent of the organism in any of the processes of thought; and, in the future life, we are told in Scripture that we shall be furnished with a more refined or spiritual body, which may serve the same purpose there that our gross body does here.

At the same time, it should be stated, that this theory best accounts for the abnormal operations of memory and imagination in an excited state of the nervous system, arising from capricious movements in the organism, which seem to be mistaken by the mind for real sensations caused by external objects.

SECTION III.

WHAT WE REMEMBER.

1. *The object remembered is suggested by something else present to the mind.* — To remember any thing is to be reminded of it, or more exactly, *to be put in mind of it again.* It is the reviving again of a previous knowledge of something. It is not to have a direct present knowledge of any thing in itself, but to have a previous knowledge recalled. The mind, in memory, is not directly occupied with the thing remembered, but searches for something to suggest it. The external object remembered is never present within the sphere of sense, and is often very far removed from us, both in time and space. The mind, then, must really be occupied with its own thoughts. The thought of the object is suggested by some other thought present to the mind. Or if the remembrance be occasioned by the recurrence of the object itself, still, it is the object in our past experience which is remembered, — the present perception of the object reminds us, at the same time, of a former perception of it, and recalls it as it was then perceived.

2. *Memory pictures out the thing remembered.* — Memory is an imaging out or thinking of something of which we have been previously conscious. If one re-

flects upon his state of mind in memory, especially in recollecting an object of sight, as, for instance, a family circle with which he has been familiar, he will find himself picturing out the whole scene and contemplating it in all its minutiæ. As, however, the object or scene, as far as it is distinctly recalled and dwelt upon, is always pictured out with its surroundings, or in its actual connections of time and place, as originally perceived, it does not appear to be in the mind, but in the position of the thing itself; nay, almost the very thing itself. By a law of our nature, universally recognized, the representation is received as irresistible evidence of our former perception of the object, and by the force of habit, we come to think only of that object. Thus, in the regular operation of those laws of our nature which the Creator has impressed upon it, our knowledge of the past, as far as it goes, becomes as simple, as vivid, and as reliable as that of the present. With this explanation of what memory is, both really and practically, we are prepared to consider, more particularly, what objects are capable of being recalled in memory.

3. *We may thus remember objects perceived by sight.* — It is quite obvious, then, at the outset, that we may distinctly remember objects which have been perceived by sight. Objects of sight being perceived under the illumination of light, and being apprehended as pictured forms, are easily imaged or represented to the mind in memory. A tree, a house, a human form, or any other visible object, stands out in memory, almost as distinctly as in perception. The object remembered is not only as clearly conceived by the mind, but may be as clearly described to another, as if directly perceived

The mental image being the exact counterpart of the external object or scene, may, of course, be described in the same terms.

4. *Also objects perceived by touch.* — It is universally conceded, too, that we may distinctly remember objects of touch. In the perceptions of this sense, also, the object is revealed as having a definite form and outline, and hence, like the object itself, may be distinctly described to another. The blind man who reads by raised letters, remembers the form of the letters as distinctly as does the man who reads by his sight. But, as most objects of touch are also objects of sight, and, by those who have the use of both senses, are almost always actually perceived by the latter, they are, of course, more commonly recalled as objects of sight than as objects of touch.

5. *So, too, we may remember sounds.* — It is generally allowed, also, that we can remember sounds. The person who, having heard a variation of sounds, as in a tune, repeats or imitates these sounds by his voice or on an instrument, must remember the original harmony. And yet we can form no such distinct image of sound, as we can of an object of touch or sight, and hence a sound cannot be adequately described to another, except by repeating it, or by a series of conventional signs, as musical notes, which have come, by usage, to have a given significance, like language. Still, sound being a particular phenomenon to the mind, possessing a specific character or marks, must be susceptible of reproduction in memory. Indeed, as a particular local affection of the organ of hearing, as a succession of impulses on the ear, it is not without physical elements, which are capable of being likened to objects of sight and

touch; as, for instance, to a succession of waves, a rising or falling, a moving or shaking, of an object in space. At all events, we know that sounds are remembered, and that a musician can not only repeat a complicated variation of sounds which he has heard, but run over them in thought, without any accompanying sound.

6. *Nor can it be denied that we remember odors and flavors.* — And if it be admitted that we remember sounds, I do not see how it can be denied that we remember odors and flavors. These, too, as specific affections of the organs of smell and taste, are not without physical elements enough to give them local associations, and constitute the basis of a veritable representative image. At all events, they are specific phenomena to the mind, susceptible of such mental associations as to be capable of being recalled. And there is abundant evidence that we do recall them even by their physical associations, as in the smacking of the lips, the snuffing up of the air, etc., which are often witnessed in persons when referring to certain tastes or smells. All recognize them, too, on their recurrence, which is virtually an act of memory.* The recurrence of the thing itself is substituted in place of the usual related thought. But the immediate recognition of it as what has been before perceived, shows the mind not to have lost its former knowledge of it.

7. *Feelings, etc., may also be remembered.* — We may remember, also, all the various local affections, sensations, feelings, and pains, of which we are conscious, as well as the various unlocalized emotions and states of

---

* "If I be not mistaken, we must recur to repetition as an ultimate principle of reproduction (i.e., in memory)." — *Hamilton.*

the mind; such as, on the one hand, the feelings occasioned by heat, cold, stimulants, narcotics, pressure, disorganization, disease, etc., and on the other, the emotions of fear, joy, compassion, and the convictions of truth, duty, etc. Many of these, as affections of certain organs or parts of the body, or being attended with certain physical perturbations, are remembered under local relations, and all of them are recognized at once, on their recurrence.

8. *Even a process of reasoning, as a series of steps, may be remembered.* — In a certain sense, too, we remember processes of reasoning. Reasoning itself, however, is not, either as a new or as a repeated process, mere memory. Reasoning proceeds by the assent of the understanding to the truth of a series of propositions, and in order to make it reasoning, there must be the same assent of the mind at every step, on its repetition. We may remember that we have before given our assent to the truth of a proposition, or a series of them, but unless we now give it, also, it is no reasoning to us. But the whole process, as consisting of a series of propositions assented to, or of steps taken by the mind, may be made as much an object of memory, as any thing whatever.

9. *This illustrated.* — Thus it is that the public speaker fixes in his mind beforehand the chief points or propositions which he wishes to establish in his speech, and recalls them in order, as he advances, and establishes them, too, by subordinate propositions, also pre-arranged. Here, doubtless, the memory is aided by language, and the propositions may be, in part, suggested by their logical dependence. In like manner, also, the mathematician, by going over a demon-

stration, fixes the successive steps of the process in his mind, so that he can recall them at any time. In this he is greatly assisted by diagrams or other symbols. The geometric construction, or other combination of symbols, is made to represent the process, and recall it whenever it is itself recalled.

10. *In short, we may remember any state of consciousness.* — In short, it is evident that we may remember any simple or complex state of consciousness, and any mental experience whatever. There are none of them that are not so associated with something else, either external or internal, as to be recalled by the associated object or thought, and they all appear as old acquaintances on a fresh recurrence. Indeed, unless one is the most empty of nominalists, he must believe that every thing which has a name is recalled by the recurrence of that name, which serves as its representative, and often as a sort of description.

11. *But it is admitted that things visible and tangible are the most readily remembered.* — But while all this is true, it is admitted that things visible and tangible are the most easily and vividly remembered. Not only can they be distinctly imaged by the mind, but they are capable of much more varied associations. The gradations and analogies among forms, places, and colors, are so numerous and obtrusive, that objects possessing extension, position, and color, are readily associated with a greater variety of things than any others, and consequently are more easily recalled. Hence, as much of our knowledge as possible should be introduced through the senses of sight and touch, or at least be represented by objects which address themselves to these senses. And here, again, we see the importance

of diagrams, models, and symbols of all kinds, in imparting knowledge. The mind not only apprehends knowledge more distinctly when thus presented, but retains it better.

12. — *What is meant by locating one in Memory.* — On seeing a former acquaintance, we often experience a difficulty in recalling the place where we formed and enjoyed his acquaintance. The effort to do this is called *locating* him, and, when successful, makes the recognition much more perfect.

SECTION IV.

ASSOCIATIVE AND LOGICAL THOUGHT.

1. *Reminiscence and reasoning distinguished.* —Reminiscence, as we have seen, is a movement or progress in thought from one particular to another, sometimes voluntary, and sometimes involuntary. In like manner, also, logical thinking is a discursive movement through a connected series of ideas. But logical thinking is chiefly, if not exclusively, voluntary. Besides, logical thought, or reasoning, proceeds by ideas as contained by and containing each other, respectively; whereas reminiscence proceeds by ideas only *contingently connected*, or associated, according to certain laws of mental suggestion, not as contained one under the other, or necessarily implying each other. Association, then, proceeds by contingent relations, reasoning by natural or necessary relations. The latter is a much higher kind of thought, as being regularly voluntary, and determined only by a perceived dependence among ideas.

2. *The logical order of thoughts.* — Among the ideas

pertaining to any subject, there is a certain order to which the intellect assents as fit, appropriate, or true, as opposed to the casual order in which they occur in the promiscuous experience of life, and in which they are remembered. This is their natural order, or when the inquiry is after truth, their logical order. Whenever our thoughts on any subject are so arranged, that the intellect admits the *sequence* of one from the other, as where they stand related as means and end, premises and conclusion, cause and effect, part and whole, etc., they are arranged in their logical order. Ideas so arranged are not so much a subject of memory as of thought. When viewed in these relations, the process of passing from one to the other is logical, not associative. The mind which feels the force of the reasoning traces the process logically the first time it goes over it, and equally so, though with increased rapidity and ease, at all subsequent times.

3. *Reasoning is a subject of memory in its outward relations.* — Still, as remarked in a previous section, when the steps of a reasoning are once drawn out, they may, in their merely outward relations, be made matter of memory, and thus a semblance of knowledge be obtained, instead of the reality. For, besides that reminiscence is vastly less reliable for recalling the steps of the process, than logical thought, the mind is only burdened by a succession of associated points, instead of being enriched by a series of dependent thoughts leading to some important conclusion. Hence so much importance attaches to our arranging our thoughts on all subjects as much as possible in their logical order, that they may become matter of inspiring thought, rather than a mere dead weight of details upon the memory.

4. *All science is arranged in the logical order.* — And it is surprising how large a part of the materials of thought may be thus arranged. All science naturally arranges itself thus. The treatment of any subject becomes a science, only as its materials are arranged in their *knowable* order, which is their natural or logical order. The materials of every science must be arranged under the relations of means and end, premises and conclusions, media and proof, part and whole, cause and effect, or of some other necessary or mutually implied relations.

5. *History may be so arranged to a considerable extent.* — And even history has been said to be but "philosophy teaching by examples." At first its materials seem to be only a confused mass of facts, and such they probably always remain to most minds. But when profoundly studied by a mind of a philosophical turn, they soon begin to marshal themselves as causes and effects, principles and illustrations, means and ends, and the like. History, when understood in its internal nature, is not merely a succession of events connected by the thread of time, but a dependent succession, connected by the thread of thought.

6. *So may even geography and much of the common experience of life.* — So, too, of geography and the daily experience of life, much is capable of being connected by a thread of dependent, and not merely associated thought. We have no occasion to remember that large cities are upon the coasts, rivers, and the great channels of communication; we know that in the nature of things they necessarily must be. For their particular locations on these coasts, etc., and their individual names, we rely upon memory, as we must for all indi-

vidual, isolated facts. But in all the great subjects of study and attention, there is an internal connection of parts, an underlying theory, which really explicates the whole nature of the subject, and which is traced by thought proper, rather than by memory.

7. *Incoherence of thought an evidence of a diseased mind.* — As the result of the laws of association and logical thought, the ideas of the mind, in a healthy state, always have a certain order and coherence about them. Any considerable degree of incoherence in the thoughts is always taken as evidence of a diseased state of mind. Insanity is but a wild incoherence of thought, and the ravings of the maniac only a setting at naught of the ordinary laws of associative and logical thinking.

SECTION V.

IMPORTANCE OF MEMORY.

1. *All our faculties are necessary for the completeness of knowledge.* — Absolutely, memory is as indispensable to the general purposes of thought and of life as any other faculty. No faculty can be dispensed with; they are all necessary for the acquisition, the retention, and the arrangement of knowledge. The facts received by the senses are preserved by the memory, and arranged and reasoned upon by the other faculties. The loss of either of the faculties would be fatal to the completeness of knowledge. Indeed, it is not quite clear that any one of the faculties can act without the co-operation of some of the others. At all events, it is certain that in our mature experience, not

only does one sense greatly assist another, but one faculty, also, another. Still, the different faculties have different, and, in the main, distinct offices to perform, which must relatively, at least, differ in importance.

2. *But relatively memory is inferior to perception.* — Relatively, then, memory is inferior in importance to perception. It is not, like perception, a receptive faculty. It does not, like that, furnish the primitive materials of thought, nor indeed, any original materials. It is simply the faculty of retaining or recalling what has been furnished by the senses and our internal experience. We might have a passing knowledge of facts without memory, * but without perception, we could have no knowledge at all. Memory is wholly dependent upon perception, but not perception upon memory.

3. *Also to reason.* — In the scale of the human faculties, memory ranks below the reason, also. It cannot be said, indeed, that reason is wholly independent of memory in its operations, although the logical relations of things, as we have seen, are traced by the reason alone. The assistance rendered by the memory here, is in bringing the related objects before the reason and holding them before it till their mutual dependence is perceived and felt. All comparison and judging of relations between ideas necessarily involve memory. But reason is the distinguishing endowment of man, and must, therefore, be higher than either perception or

* Hamilton makes memory a condition of perception. But if so, how could there ever be a first perception, since there can be no memory antecedent to experience? Doubtless memory greatly assists perception, in our mature experience, but perception cannot be wholly dependent upon its co-operation.

memory, which are possessed by the lower orders of animals. Its movements are more independent, being determined by its own spontaneous energy, rather than from without.

4. *Experience shows this.*—The attempt so often made, by a certain order of minds, to make memory do the work of reason, shows its vast inferiority to that godlike power. Memory attempts to retain knowledge as a succession of facts barely associated together by contingent relations, while reason arranges them according to their relations of mutual dependence, and thus connects them by a line of thought, which can be traced at any time. And although a vast amount of knowledge may be retained by the memory, when thus taxed with a double duty, yet it is comparatively uninstructive, and rests like an incubus upon the mind, preventing all free and fruitful action.

5. *But memory is not an unimportant power, as appears from its connection with the imagination.*—But memory, in its proper office, is far from being a useless or unimportant faculty. As a reproductive power, it seems to be generically the same as imagination. The only difference between the two powers is, that memory recalls perceived objects as wholes, precisely as they occurred to sense; while imagination reproduces them disconnected from their surroundings, or in fragments, or variously mixed and compounded, so that they are no longer simple representations of what has been perceived, though always made up of the elements of what has been perceived. Memory, then, is of the same general nature as imagination, but is evidently an inferior energy. It is wholly confined to things *as perceived*, while imagination creates new forms

from perceived elements. Hence, though a good memory may exist without a fine imagination, a fine imagination must always be accompanied by a good memory. When the representative faculty rises high enough to constitute a lofty imagination, it must necessarily embrace the lower energy of memory; though it may rise high enough to constitute a good memory, without reaching the elevation necessary to a fine imagination. And this we find to be the case in fact. A man with a vivid imagination always has a good memory, though we often see persons with a good memory who have but an indifferent imagination. Memory, therefore, though often existing without genius, and far from being a uniform sign of genius, necessarily accompanies it, as far as genius consists in extraordinary powers of imagination.

6. *Its importance is best seen in practical life.*—But it is in practical life that the importance of memory appears the most conspicuously. The details of everyday life must mainly be committed to the memory. They cannot, to any great extent, be arranged in the order of mutual dependence, and thus be recalled by logical thought; they can generally be reached only through association and habit. This is especially the case in the heterogeneous and multifarious duties of private and business life. And even the professional man and the scholar must rely largely on the memory in the prosecution of their duties. After all that can be done in arranging their knowledge in its logical order, there must necessarily remain a vast amount of detached and loose material, hovering within the sphere of their action, and essential to their success, which can be connected only by association, and recalled only by memory.

7. *Memory is all-important in its place.* — Memory, therefore, though not relatively one of the very highest endowments of the mind, is yet, in its place, a highly useful power, and deserving, like all the other faculties, of the most assiduous cultivation. What has disparaged memory most, is the attempt, so often made, to substitute it for reason, and make it do its work. Such an attempt is always unsuccessful, and exposes memory to reproach. Besides, as it is entirely unnatural and out of place, such an attempt seems to imply a *want* of reason in the one who makes it, and hence begets a contempt for an order of mind in which memory is largely developed. Memory, like the other faculties, is most honored and improved when confined to its proper sphere, and within that, tasked to the utmost on all occasions requiring its use.

CHAPTER IV.

IMAGINATION.

SECTION I.

NATURE OF IMAGINATION.

1. *Imagination distinguished from other powers.*—"Imagination* or Phantasy," says Sir W. Hamilton, "in its most extensive meaning, is the faculty *representative* of the phenomena both of the external and internal world." Imagination is thus distinguished generically from perception and self-consciousness, which are faculties *presentative* or *intuitive*,—the one of the phenomena of the external, and the other of those of the internal world. On the contrary, imagination and memory are distinguished from each other only specifically. They are generically alike, in both being representative faculties,—specifically different, inasmuch as memory represents an object with its surroundings as it actually came into the mind; while imagination represents an object out of its original connections, or in some way distorted, or combined with other images.

2. *Imagination and memory.*—In consequence of

* "The Latin *imaginatio*, with its modifications in the vulgar languages, was employed both in ancient and modern times to express what the Greeks denominated *Φαντασία*. Phantasy, of which Phancy, or Fancy, is a corruption, and now employed in a more limited sense, was a common name for Imagination with the old English Writers."—*Hamilton.*

this difference between memory and imagination, the representative thought in the former is taken as the undoubted counterpart of what *actually has been*, while in the latter it is taken only as a representation of what *possibly may be*. Hence, the one involves an absolute belief in the (former) existence of the object *as represented*, while the other does not. The images, in imagination, are recognized as mere images. When I remember any object, as a house, a tree, a tune, I think of it with its surroundings, just as it came into the mind; but when I simply imagine such an object, I disconnect it from its surroundings, and give it any position, or conjoin it with any other object, as I choose. Thus, I can imagine a tree inverted in the air, an anthem chanted by angels, or a human face attached to the neck of a horse.

3. *Imagination only combines perceived elements.*— Imagination, however, is limited for its materials to what has been actually perceived, either by external or internal perception. It creates no new elements of its own. It can combine the elements received through perception in innumerable forms and proportions — can variously attenuate, spiritualize, idealize them, — but can never wholly transcend them. Centaurs and Sphinxes, as well as the infinite succession of images presented by poets and other imaginative writers, are all composed of materials furnished by perception and self-consciousness, — only variously arranged, compounded, diminished, distorted, sublimated, or idealized. The giant of the imagination is only a man enlarged, and the Venus of Praxiteles, or the Fairy Queen of Spenser, only the ideal of all that is fair in woman.

4. *The images of the imagination are concrete.* — Hence, too, the images of the imagination must always be concrete in form. Things are perceived only in their concrete form, and the representations of the imagination being wholly composed of the elements of perceived objects, — not of an abstract of their qualities, — must also be concrete. The most extravagant and grotesque images of the Oriental imagination, embodied in their monsters or gods, are but the exaggerated forms of various heterogeneous parts, limbs, organs, etc., combined into certain fantastic wholes. The thinking of abstract or generalized ideas is conception, * not imagination.

5. *Images are either drawn from the inspection of objects, or are suggested.* — Sometimes we form these images from a direct inspection or recollection of the different objects from which they are compounded. Thus the sculptor forms his ideal image of the perfect human form which he wishes to represent, from a combination of the most perfect limbs, organs, lines, and features, which he has observed in different persons. So the painter forms his fancy landscape by combining in his picture the most attractive features in the different scenes which he has witnessed. But in other cases,

* This is in accordance with the better usage of philosophers; though Mr. Stewart makes conception merely that form of imagination which consists in reproducing, without change, what has been previously perceived. Conception, as the act of thinking, realizing, or construing something to the mind, is of the same general character as imagination, and hence is often used in referring to the thought of individual, concrete things, especially of such as really present no adequate image, as sounds, flavors, and odors; or where the image is reached through a process of comparison and combination, as in case of the ideal embodied in a work of art, or the hypothesis by which the different parts of the solar system, or other related phenomena, are connected in the mind.

images come to us ready formed, being *suggested* by something present to the mind. The unreal images of the imagination, like the real images of memory, and the thoughts and feelings of our rational and emotional nature, are suggested, or recur, according to fixed laws and relations, such as those already described in the chapter on memory.

6. *The images contained in figures of speech are suggested.* — It is in this latter way that the images contained in figures of speech are awakened. In thinking or writing upon any subject we fall upon ideas which, by resemblance, contrast, or the relations of cause and effect, part and whole, etc., suggest other ideas or images, which are either directly introduced as *illustrations* of the thought under consideration, or, by the use of some term which is applicable to the related rather than to the main thought, are *suggested* to the mind of the reader or hearer. Thus, in speaking of the period of youth, I may be reminded, by resemblance, of the spring, and say directly, in the form of an illustrative comparison, " youth, like the spring, is fresh and blooming," or, on the same principle of resemblance, I may be reminded by it of the opening of day, and say of it, by a metaphor, " youth is the *morning* of life." And thus of the other figures of speech, used more or less by all writers, but especially by those of the imaginative sort, and treated of in books on Rhetoric.

7. *These images come either voluntarily or involuntarily.* — And here, too, as in reminiscence, the suggested images either come unbidden, or only after a predetermined search. They always come involuntarily in sleep, and for the most part, also, in our waking hours. But not unfrequently, in thinking or writing upon any

subject, having brought the discussion to a certain point, or having reached a certain idea which seems specially to require illustration or adornment, we halt, and cast about for some image fitted to illuminate or beautify it. This must be done to some extent by all writers, and especially by those of no more than ordinary liveliness of imagination, in any elaborate or finished style. Thus Demosthenes, wishing to animate the Athenians in their contest against Philip, and inspire them with confidence in the favor of the gods towards the city, notwithstanding some recent reverses, closes a series of observations on the subject by the following apt and striking illustration, which condenses the whole spirit and force of what he had previously said into a single burning point: "I think it is with the favors of the gods as with the gifts of fortune; if we retain and improve them, we retain also our gratitude for them; but if we misimprove and lose them, we at the same time lose our gratitude — our state of mind in each case being very much determined by the last event."

8. *Fancy as distinguished from imagination.* — The lighter, more airy, more capricious movements of the imagination are called *fancy*. An image is said to be fanciful, when it is not suggested by an obvious, natural, substantial similarity, which is approved on reflection as sound and important, but by some casual, factitious, unobvious, slight, shadowy, or recondite similarity, which occurs only to minds of a peculiar cast, or to the ordinary mind, only in its gayer, more sportive and fantastic moods. The fancy forms such characters as Ariel and Queen Mab, the imagination such as Calaban, the Satan of Milton, or the Mephistopheles of

Goethe. The Paradise Lost is more the work of the imagination, the L'Allegro and Il'Penseroso, of the fancy; the plays of Skakspeare and the discourses of Jeremy Taylor are woven of materials supplied about equally by each.

9. *Fancy, conceits, wit, etc.* — Fancies are the playful, subtile, evanescent, witching, and often, affected and extravagant, images of the imagination. At the same time, Conceits are only affected fancies, and Wit, which aims at producing pleasurable surprise, by placing words or images in unexpected or unusual relations to each other, works chiefly by this faculty. So, the Ludicrous and the Grotesque, which depend upon odd or fantastic conjunctions among ideas, are but the wanton freaks of fancy.

SECTION II.

USES OF THE IMAGINATION.

1. *Imagination one of the chief constituents of genius.*— In order to the possession of any thing which deserves the name of intelligence, knowledge must, at least, be obtained, preserved, and arranged. Sense, memory, and understanding, therefore, are absolutely indispensable to any proper intelligence. Imagination, however (as distinguished from memory), does not seem to be thus absolutely essential to intelligence; and hence, more minds, perhaps, are deficient in this power, than in any other. This, however, does not prove imagination to be an inferior gift, but rather the reverse. We might live and know without it; but our life becomes nobler, and our knowledge grander with it. The intelligence which

has simply the least number of powers necessary for knowing, is the lowest form of intelligence, and every additional power, as being a rarer, is also a higher, gift. Thus it is with the imagination, — it is among the higher and diviner gifts of the mind. It is one of the chief constituents of genius.

2. *Is of great service in conversation.* — But to proceed to particulars; the imagination is of great service in *conversation.* As one could not converse at all without memory, so he cannot converse well, i.e., with any elegance or force, without imagination. Any topic of conversation is comparatively barren of interest, and soon exhausted, if considered simply by itself, or only in its commonest relations. But when amplified, by following it out in its logical connections, by clustering about it associated thoughts, and illustrating and adorning it by appropriate comparisons, figures, and images, drawn from the wide range of analogies throughout nature, the dryest subject becomes attractive. As conversation is best when somewhat discursive, proceeding from one related thought to another in an easy and graceful manner, and drawing in materials from a wide range of objects, no faculty is more serviceable to the converser than the imagination or fancy. Its light and airy movements buoy up the mind and bear it along with nimbleness through pleasing and deversified fields of thought.

3. *Is of great service to the orator.* — Imagination is of great service to the *orator;* not so much, however, in giving a light discursiveness to his thoughts, as in giving them vividness and life. The Orator must think thoroughly and systematically, but the line of his thoughts must be illuminated and vivified through its

whole extent by the imagination. The source of this life and power, doubtless, is passion, but passion arouses the imagination and opens its storehouse of images. The figures of the orator are chiefly what rhetoricians call *figures of passion*, i.e., figures of the imagination called forth by passion. They are of the vivid, the strong, and the illustrative sort, rather than of the calm and beautiful.

4. *Illustrated from Demosthenes.* — The object of the orator is, to carry his hearers with him, — to make them converts to his ideas and purposes. Hence, he must secure their attention, must make his ideas palpable and vivid and convince them that he is thoroughly in earnest. Beyond the simple power of logical thought, his most important auxiliary for doing this is the imagination. Thus, to quote again from that most cogent and earnest of orators, and master of the illustrative comparison; Demosthenes, having exhausted all his power of direct appeal and argument in attempting to arouse the Athenians from their tardy and fitful policy in opposing Philip, closes an indignant strain of remark upon that point by the famous comparison of the unskilful boxer: "O Athenians! your contest with Philip is like that of unpractised boxers against their antagonists; who, struck in one place, cover it with their hand, — struck in another, place their hand there; and thus, always occupied with the blows they receive, know not how to strike and defend themselves."

5. *The imagination is a great aid to the poet.* — The imagination is a great aid to the *poet*. It is by this power, more than by all others, that the genuine poem is made. A true poem is but a tissue of various and softly blending images drawn from "all that

is fair and bright" through the universe. Selecting some of the loftier, more affecting, or more interesting themes, the poet, as he advances, traces in imagination the long lines of analogies, both material and spiritual, connected with each succeeding thought, and instinctively appropriating such images as are best calculated to beautify and ennoble his theme, sets them as gems in the general ground of his subject. Those striking and pleasing ornaments, which sparkle thus on the pages of Homer, of Shakspeare, of Milton, and other great poets, are all the work of the imagination.

6. *Also to other classes of writers.* — And thus, to some extent, of *all writers.* There are few species of writing which are not improved by an occasional figure of the imagination. The philosophical style, perhaps, should wholly eschew tropes, but there is no kind of style which does not admit of, and which may not be greatly improved by, the illustrative comparison. In the treatment of almost any subject, there are points in the progress of the thought where an illustrative comparison, founded upon some striking analogy, may be made to illuminate the whole matter. These a good writer always feels the need of at such points, and if they do not occur to him at once, searches for them in his imagination.

7. *Is indispensable to the artist.* — Imagination is indispensable to the *artist.* Painters and sculptors, even more than poets, have to do with images. Where they copy direct from nature, they must first form in the mind a connected image of the object or scene. But in the higher efforts of art, the object or scene is always more or less ideal; i.e., it is a model formed in the im-

agination, composed, indeed, of elements which have been perceived, but so selected, arranged, and retouched by the fancy, as to be more perfect than ever actually occurs in any one object or scene in nature. Without this there can be no high art. An imagination capable of forming appropriate ideals is an indispensable requisite for an artist. (N. 7, p. 253.)

8. *Is a great assistance to the student of nature.*— The imagination, also, is a great assistance to the *student of nature.* All objects, and systems of objects, in nature, have a certain conformity and relation of parts, and all agents, a certain definite mode of operation, which we must be able to form a correct image of, before we can understand either the objects or their relations, or the operation of agents. The manner in which we image out to ourselves these objects, their relations, and modes of action, constitutes our theory, hypothesis, or conception,* in the case. When our conception is proved to be in accordance with all the facts in the case, it is no longer hypothesis, but knowledge. Thus, the Ptolemaic conception of the solar system was gradually changed and purified, till in the mind of Newton it was brought into conformity with nature, and is now familiarly illustrated by a concrete sensible illustration, in the orrery. In reaching such a result, the imagination performs an important part. The physical philosopher succeeds in interpreting nature, just in proportion to his capacity of forming correct conceptions of the relations and modes of action between objects and agents, from hints, analogies, etc.

---

* Called conception, because reached through a process of comparison and combination, though there is really nothing but a concrete image formed in the case. See Sec. 1. note 2d.; also n. 8. p. 253.

9. *Also to the student of geometry, geography, and history.* — In a similar way, the imagination greatly assists the *student of geometry, of geography,* and *of history.* Geometric figures, whether applying to the heavenly bodies, to the earth, or to empty space, consist of a certain combination of lines, surfaces, and angles, constituting a definite outline or form, which must be distinctly imaged as a whole in the mind before they can be constructed, or understood in their application, or even well retained, supposing them already constructed to our hand. Consequently, the success of the student of geometry must depend largely upon the facility with which his imagination pictures the outline and relation of parts in a figure. So in geography and history, one's ideas must always be extremely vague and inadequate, and his progress but small, unless he readily catches the image of coasts, rivers, mountains, cities, costumes, fortifications, plans of campaigns, lines of march, orders of battle, and the general figure and relations of men and things on the earth, from such hints and descriptions as can be conveyed by language.

10. *Imagination of less service to the abstract thinker.*— The mere *thinker* or *speculator* in abstract truth, and things wholly immaterial, is less assisted by the imagination than any other class of men. As the imagination deals only with the concrete, we should expect it would be of the least service in abstract reasoning. But even abstract subjects require, in their development, concrete means of proof, and thus need the aid of the imagination. Hence, while it is of no little service to the abstract thinker and reasoner, the imagination, as is implied in what has already been said, is of the greatest importance to the inductive discoverer, as well as to the analogical and

general reasoner. In such kinds of reasoning there is a demand for something besides logical inference. There is room for the play of the imagination, and it plays with the best effect in suggesting media of proof and means of illustration. The discursive power of the mind lies wholly in the imagination (including the memory) and the reason; and all invention, discovery, and advancement of the boundaries of thought, as well as the enriching and beautifying of our ideas, depend upon these powers.

SECTION III.

TRAINING OF THE IMAGINATION.

1. *The imagination needs chastening as well as strengthening.*—The great influence of the imagination, both for good and for evil, on our intellectual habits and pursuits, makes its proper training an object of the utmost importance. On the one hand, it needs strengthening and developing, on the other, curbing and chastening. If it be well to have a ready and vigorous imagination, it must still be subject to reason and taste. And while it is strengthened, like the other faculties, by use, it is chastened by being used only in subordination to the dictates of reason and taste. Now, there are three ways in which the imagination may be used, and thus strengthened and improved, when used aright. It may be employed in forming and contemplating the images presented by the objects of nature, or those suggested by the writings or works of men, or in combining and embodying these in works of our own. Each is a useful exercise of the faculty, though differing somewhat in their effects.

2. *It may derive images direct from nature.* — Whatever we perceive, and, more especially, whatever we perceive by the eye, by the ear, or by the touch, leaves its image in the mind, or rather is capable of being imaged by the mind afterwards. Wherever we go, therefore, among the works of God, we are filling the imagination with images. The hills, the vales, the mountains, the forests, the rivers, the ocean, the sky, abound in objects whose images may be used in illustrating and adorning our ideas, or be embodied in works of art for the instruction and admiration of others.

3. *But these are valuable only when the result of careful observation.* — But it is not sufficient simply to ramble among the works of nature. One may do this and get but little that is valuable. Only those images are of much value which are true to nature, and hence characteristic. The variety of nature is endless and inexhaustible, so that it has been said, that no two leaves, even from the same tree or shrub, are exact facsimiles of each other in the lines which variegate the surface. Hence, a writer whose imagination is filled with images which are exact copies of natural objects, will never fail in variety and freshness. But to obtain these, nature must be closely scrutinized, and every object be perceived exactly as it is. This, of course, can be done only by the most careful and accurate observation. Hence, again, we see the vast importance of having an ever-wakeful attention, wherever we are, and however engaged. He who is much abroad among the works of nature, and observes objects with a careful and wakeful attention, is filling his mind with an

inexhaustible store of the most pleasing and useful images.

4. *The imagination may be improved, also, by the study of books and art.* — The imagination is improved, also, by reading books, and contemplating works of art. The writings of men, — especially those of the imaginative sort, as fiction and poetry, — and the various creations of art, embody the best conceptions or combinations of images of which the human imagination is capable, and hence are most useful studies for the improvement of this faculty. These, however, and particularly as presented in books, are to the reader but suggested images. They are, at best, but images at second-hand, — images of images, — and hence, necessarily more or less imperfect, inadequate, and indistinct. This they would be, supposing them to have been original and exact in the mind of the writer who employs them; but a large part of them have come down, as commonplaces, through a long series of writers, one borrowing them from the other, till they have lost all freshness and point. They are no longer the distinct, characteristic images of nature, but only their dim and wasted ghosts. No book, therefore, nor work of art even, can be compared with nature as a study for improving the imagination, and too many of these productions tend rather to pervert than to improve the power.

5. *And most of all in combining images for works of our own.* — Again, we improve our imagination by embodying its images in works of our own, or, more properly, by employing it in forming images for the purpose of embodying them in some production of our own. In the previous cases, the imagination is com-

paratively passive, but here it is decidedly active. The artist who is at work in forming and embodying his ideal, and the poet, or other writer, who sends forth his imagination, at every step, in quest of some appropriate image to illustrate or adorn his ideas, is exercising his imagination in the most effectual way. The other methods furnish the imagination with the materials for its images, this practises it in producing and combining them, as the case requires. And, as is the case in the exercise of the other faculties, every creative effort of the imagination strengthens it for another effort of the same kind, till at length we acquire a facility in calling images to our aid, as we need them, which astonishes ourselves.

6. *But the imagination should be subject to a sound taste.* — But the imagination does not need strengthening alone, it needs chastening. It will be to little purpose that we are able to call up images, if they are not appropriate. Improper images employed by a writer are worse than no images at all. A strong imagination, without a just *taste*, is a dangerous power. Hence, the imagination should never be cultivated to the neglect of the taste, but only in connection with and in subordination to it. It is the special province of taste to control the imagination in the use of imagery. Without this the imagination becomes grotesque and fantastic.

7. *Also to an enlightened reason.* — Nor should the imagination be allowed to override, or in any way to interfere with, *reason.* Bishop Butler, who was a sturdy thinker, calls the imagination a "forward, delusive faculty, ever obtruding beyond its sphere." And this, undoubtedly, is its tendency. If the reason be not

cultivated and made to assert its authority, the imagination usurps its place, and substitutes its wild and empty images for truth. It does this with the savage, and with all, just in proportion as the cultivation of their rational powers is neglected, so that they are incapable of distinguishing truth from fancy.

8. *Otherwise it interferes with thinking.*— As already remarked, any great vigor of imagination is probably of little service to the mere deductive reasoner or investigator of abstract truth. It would, of course, be an aid to him in setting forth the results of his investigations in a popular way to others, but as a mere investigator of truth in its logical and abstract relations, it is rather a hinderance than a help to him. To such a one, it is truly a "delusive faculty." It not only thrusts forward its vain images for truth, but by its wild and capricious habits of association, often diverts the attention, and draws off the mind from the direct line of thought.

9. *And becomes wild and fantastic.*— While, therefore, it is necessary to strengthen and cultivate the imagination, it is necessary at the same time to cultivate the other powers, and especially the taste and the reason, to which it owes subordination. If these be not cultivated in conjunction with it, the imagination being unrestrained, runs riot, and does violence to all propriety and truth.

CHAPTER V.

CONCEPTION.

SECTION I.

NATURE OF CONCEPTION.

1. *Definition of conception.* — Conception means *taking together*, in allusion to the common marks or attributes of different objects, which are taken together or thought as one nature, in the act. Conception denotes both the power of thus grasping the common nature of different related objects, the act of doing it, and the result or product of the act; though the latter is sometimes, and more properly, called a *concept.* Conception, therefore, corresponds to the Simple Apprehension of the Logicians; and the concept, as embracing certain attributes and hence characterized by certain marks, means the same as Notion, or General Notion, which is kindred to the Latin *notæ* (marks).

2. *Nature of the cognition in conception.* — Conceiving, then, is cognizing objects, not by their individual features and peculiarities, as is done in perception, but by certain common features, to the neglect of individual peculiarities. It is thus rather thinking of objects, than perceiving them. The concept, being indifferently applicable to any one of a class of related objects, represents no particular object existing in time and space, but only some possible object. But its marks or attributes must not be contradictory of each other, so that

we cannot think them together, and hence cannot suppose them capable of co-existing in any object whatever. Standing thus as the representative of no one particular object, the concept is capable of being *fixed*, so as to be reproducible in thought, only in some representative sign, as a *word*, or other symbol. Concepts, then, have no specific embodiment except in general terms, or common names. In the operations of thought, they are regularly suggested or recalled by these, and indifferently applied, as the case may require, to any individual of the class designated by the term.

3. *A concept cannot be represented in a concrete image.* — But although the concept is thus fixed, or individualized, in a common term, and is capable of being applied in thought to any one of the class of objects whose common attributes it includes, still, as not embracing the special nature and peculiarities of any particular sensible object, — i.e., as not being a simple *intuition* of some one object, — it is incapable of being itself presented in a *concrete image*. As, however, the concept embraces only compatible attributes, it is always capable of individualization in a possible object of intuition, and is often so individualized in its application to the different objects of the class which it represents. In such application, when consciously and formally made, the imagination presents the individual to which it is made; as where the general concept of *man* is applied to this or that particular man. This, however, is imagination, not conception.

4. *How we may have a concept of a general triangle.* — Hence we see how we may have such a concept as that of a general triangle, which is neither equilateral, isosceles, nor scalene, and yet is virtually each and all

of these. It is obvious, at once, that there can be no such general notion of triangle as shall, *at the same time*, embrace all the possible varieties of triangle. A triangle which shall be at once oblique and rectangle, equilateral and scalene, is clearly inconceivable, since it is required that it have contradictory attributes, which cannot be thought together. It was on this ground that such a general notion was rejected by Hobbes, Berkeley, Hume, etc. But no such concept is contended for by any intelligent advocate of general notions. Indeed, such a concept, were it possible, would not be a general notion, as it would embrace the special features of triangles of all forms. All that is required is, that there should be such a general notion of a triangle as is capable of being applied in thought to every form of the triangle *at different times*, as occasion requires us to reason about this or that sort of triangle. Such a concept of a triangle is simply that of a figure having three sides and three angles, without any regard to the special character of those sides and angles.

5. *It is not generally necessary to individualize our concepts in using them.* — But in using our concepts in thought, it is not generally necessary to individualize them. In the majority of cases we make no attempt to realize the concept either in an actual or possible object of intuition. We, in fact, substitute general terms for general notions, and use them in our judgments and reasoning, very much as we do algebraic symbols. Thus, though I cannot individualize my general concept of triangle, except as equilateral, isosceles, or scalene, I can judge and reason about a triangle, without making any attempt to conceive it in its specific character. But the individualization of a concept, at least

in a possible object of intuition, is the true test of its logical correctness. If its attributes cannot be thought together, the concept must be rejected as illegitimate.

6. *Logical and real concepts.* — Logically, then, any concept not embracing contradictory attributes is legitimate. Such a concept is a legitimate form of thought, whether true to nature or not. As there is nothing contradictory in the combination of attributes, we can as easily, and hence, in a logical sense, as legitimately, conceive the particles of matter repellent of each other as attracting each other. But metaphysically, or really, conceptions are true or false, according as they correspond or not with the facts of nature. Thus, a person never having seen water congealed, might conceive it as necessarily fluid, which, not embracing all the essential facts in the case, is a false conception. Hence the truth of our conceptions depends upon the extent and accuracy of our knowledge of objects.

7. *What is conceivable is possible, but not necessarily the reverse.* — Whatever is conceivable we regard as possible. As it is construable to thought, as there is no difficulty in our thinking it, we can see nothing insuperable in the way of its being realized. What we can think, we are constrained to believe that Almighty Power might render actual. And even what we cannot think, we do not necessarily consider as beyond the reach of Almighty Power to realize; so that *inconceivability* is not regarded by us as equivalent to *impossibility*. (N. p. 253, bottom.)

8. *Limit to the application of the term conception.* — Conception being the contemplation of the internal character of a class of related objects, and thus, in a general sense, the construing to thought, or the viewing

in connection with each other and as consistent with each other, of various attributes and relations, we may be said to conceive a judgment, a process of reasoning, a system composed of various co-ordinated or subordinated parts, a machine, or other structure embodying abstract ideas and relations. But conception should not be used in so wide a sense, as is often done by Dr. Reid, as to include *understanding*, *comprehending*, *supposing*, *assuming*, etc. We may *understand* the statement that *a part is greater than the whole*, but we cannot *conceive* the relation assumed in the judgment. We may *suppose* or *assume* that *two straight lines enclose space*, but we cannot *conceive* the relation implied in the sentence.

SECTION II.

FORMATION OF CONCEPTS.

1. *We first distinguish individual things.* — In our first perceptions, especially by sight, different objects are regarded only as variations in, or different parts of, one whole. By degrees, these variations are distinguished as different objects, and more or less of their qualities perceived, varying with the sense employed in their perception. And in time, by the use of our different senses and powers, we acquire a knowledge of all the properties of an object which we are capable of acquiring. The knowledge thus acquired of an individual object, whether at once or by repeated efforts, is called an intuition.

2. *We then combine them in classes.* — In the mean time, we have perceived a large number of objects,

which, from a natural tendency of the human mind to disregard differences, are distributed into classes according to their substantial resemblances, the individuals of each class being recognized as virtually the same and being designated by the same name. Thus objects are rudely classified almost unconsciously. But reflection follows the unconscious process, and confirms or corrects its results, as the case may require. We thus come, at length, even in ordinary perception, almost wholly to disregard the individual features of classified objects, and in conceiving or thinking of the class by its type, to fix exclusively on certain attributes common to all the individuals, while all others are neglected as non-essential.

3. *And then combine classes into one.*— Our concepts, in the course of observation and reflection, are continually becoming more and more accurate, and more and more extended, exhibiting a constant tendency to higher and higher generalizations. The primary concepts which we form from limited observation are gradually enlarged with our growing experience, by admitting to the class other and still other kindred classes of objects, till the general class embraces various subordinate classes, each having its separate type, but all coinciding in certain interior common attributes. Thus the notions which we form from observation of the *rose*, *lily*, *violet*, etc., are afterwards united in the more general concept of *flower;* while the notion of *flower*, *tree*, *fern*, etc., are embraced again under the still wider concept of *plant.* And thus our concepts embrace wider and still wider circles of objects, tending ever towards the absorption of all things into one grand unity, the *summum genus*, Substance or Being.

4. *Breadth and depth of concepts.* — In this gradation of concepts, it is obvious that the higher or wider the concept, the greater the number of objects and the less the number of attributes which it embraces; as the concept of *plant*, while it embraces more objects than that of *tree*, embraces them only by assuming fewer attributes to express the common nature of the class. In the language of logic, higher concepts have greater *breadth*, or a wider *extension* or. *sphere*, while lower concepts have greater *depth*, or more *intention*, *comprehension*, or *matter* (qualities).

5. *Hence conception grows out of perception.* — It thus appears that conception grows out of perception. The percept lies at the root of the concept. Concepts are secondary notions generalized from perceptions. This is accomplished through comparison, as far as it is a conscious process. The common attributes of different objects are discovered by placing them side by side in our mental view, and considering them in comparison with each other. But the withdrawing of the attention from all except the common attributes of the different objects, by which the generalization is effected, is called *abstraction*. However, even this is possible only through comparison.

SECTION III.

KINDS OF CONCEPTS.

It will tend further to elucidate the nature of conception, to enumerate and describe some of the principal classes of concepts or notions. Our concepts are either *distinct* or *confused*, *adequate* or *inadequate*, *sym-*

bolical or *notative*, *primary* or *secondary*, *positive* or *negative*, *irrespective* or *relative*, *abstract* or *concrete*, *necessary* or *contingent*. Each of these classes of concepts may receive a few words of explanation.

1. *Distinct and Confused Concepts or Notions.* — A notion is said to be distinct, when we can distinguish its marks or attributes and enumerate them. Thus, the notion of a *bridge* is a distinct notion, for we can readily discern and declare its attributes, as is done in the definition, "a bridge is a structure over any collection of water, resting on supports, and designed for the passage of men or beasts." Not that such notions are necessarily distinct in all minds, but they are capable of becoming so. A confused notion, on the contrary, is one whose attributes cannot be distinguished, such as our notions of *space*, *time*, *red*, *love*, or of any other simple intuition or feeling. Such notions are clear enough, but being without distinguishing marks, they are said to be confused or indistinct. They are often called simple notions.

2. *Adequate and Inadequate Notions.* — Notions are said to be adequate, when not only their attributes, but the attributes of these attributes, can be distinguished and enumerated, — and the attributes of these again, as far as our purpose requires. Thus, if perception be defined, "a mental energy by which we acquire a knowledge of an external world," we enumerate its attributes; and the notion becomes *adequate*, when we explain, in turn, what is meant by "a mental energy," by "acquiring a knowledge," and by "an external world." When such explanation cannot be given, the notion is inadequate.

3. *Symbolical and Notative Concepts.* — Symbolical

concepts are notions so complex, and embracing so many attributes, that the full extent of their meaning is not usually realized in employing the terms by which they are designated, the words being really used as substitutes or symbols in place of the ideas. Such words as *state*, *virtue*, *universe*, etc., are of this sort. These and many other general terms are constantly used without either speaker or hearer realizing any thing like the full conception which they designate. Indeed, all familiar concepts are practically, in a great measure, symbolical. After we have once formed a concept, we think but little of its elements, but take the general term by which it is designated as a substitute for the thought. But where the attributes of a concept are quite simple and obtrusive, so that they are readily realized, as in the concepts of *book*, *box*, *tree*, etc., it is said to be notative.

4. *First and Second Notions.* — First notions, as the term implies, are the simple, unmodified concepts which we form of things, or classes of things, as they stand in nature; such concepts as have thus far been described in this chapter. But when these primary concepts come to be thought of out of relation to the objects which they represent, and only in relation to each other, i.e., when they come to be handled purely as materials of thought, they are viewed by the mind under a new aspect. Under this new form they become second notions. Thus, the first notions of *Thomas*, *man*, *animal*, etc., can be thought of in relation to each other only as *individual*, *species*, *genus*, etc. Hence first notions are such as those of *tree*, *plant*, *stone*, *horse*, etc., while second notions are such as those of *individual*, *genus*, *species*, *premise*, *conclusion*, *syllogism*, and

other concepts of concepts, or "names of names," as Hobbes calls them. As second notions are the forms which first notions assume when they are thought of in relation to each other, Logic is said to have to do wholly with second notions.

5. *Positive and Negative (or Privative) Notions.* — A positive notion is any notion which possesses positive attributes or marks. Such are all the classes of notions thus far spoken of, and indeed, all notions except negative notions. Negative notions, then, are characterized by a want of attributes or marks. They are but the implied counterpart or reflection of positive notions. Every positive notion suggests a counter negative notion, and these together make up an entire sphere; as *kindness* and *unkindness*, *good* and *not-good*, *animal* and *not-animal*, *material* and *immaterial*. All such negative notions are merely conceived as destitute of the attributes of the positive notions to which they correspond. Such notions, however, are not without their value. They supply a negative for every positive, and give us a glimpse of what is unknowable even, by shadowing it forth as the counterpart of what is known. Of this nature are all our conceptions of the infinite and absolute.

6. *Irrespective and Relative Notions.* — Irrespective notions are such as do not imply or suggest any other notion, as, for instance, the notions of *horse*, *tree*, *flower*, and indeed, the great body of our notions. Relative notions, on the contrary, are those which usually or always occur to our minds in pairs, the one seeming necessarily to imply the other. Such are the notions expressed by the words *debtor* and *creditor*, *parent* and

child, *male* and *female*, *young* and *old*, *true* and *false* etc. Positive and negative concepts are also relative notions.

7. *Abstract and Concrete Notions.*—All concepts are abstractions, but certain concepts are technically known as abstract, in comparison with others which are called concrete. Abstract notions are qualities viewed under a substantive form, or apart from the subjects to which they belong. These qualities may either be of a general nature, such as belong to various classes of things, as *whiteness*, *roughness*, *justice*, etc; or such as belong to only a single class of beings, as *humanity*, *royalty*, etc. But when these qualities are directly attributed to existing beings or things, our notion of them is said to be concrete, as when we speak of the *white* snow, the *just* man, *human nature*, *man*, *king*, etc.

8. *Necessary and Contingent notions.*—What are commonly called necessary notions are more properly, perhaps, either necessary intuitions, or necessary judgments. Our ideas of space, time, causality, etc., can be considered *concepts*, only as they extend the qualities presented to us in their respective intuitions to all possible time, space, etc., and hence, in a certain sense, are generalizations. On the contrary, the various logical and mathematical axioms are rather judgments than concepts. Strictly, therefore, all concepts are contingent, except such as are necessary in that very limited sense implied in the fact, that our perceptions having been such and such in regard to any class of objects, our conceptions are necessarily in accordance with our experience.

SECTION IV.

THEORIES OF CONCEPTION.

The controversy about general notions is one famous in the history of philosophy, and has been marked by three distinct theories on the subject; denominated, respectively, *realism*, *nominalism*, *conceptualism*.

I. REALISM.

1. *What this theory holds to.*— According to this theory, concepts have a *real* objective existence, independent of the mind conceiving them, and even of the objects in which alone they appear to us. They are neither mere modifications of the mind, nor combinations of qualities in objects, apprehended by the mind and abstracted from them. They are to be regarded, rather, as proper representative objects, mediating between the mind and the phenomenal world. They are thus only a peculiar form of the *representative ideas*, which figure so largely in the history of philosophy.

2. *The Platonic view.*— According to Plato, the phenomenal world (i.e., all external objects) addresses itself only to the *sensitive soul* (as he calls it), and gives rise merely to sensations, not perceptions. All that is really perceived is *ideas*, and hence objects are perceived only as they *participate* in these ideas. These ideas he regards as existing *actually* in the mind of God and as having determined him in creation,— they being the types or models after which all things were made; but only *potentially* in the mind of man, as he is only conscious of them as elicited by experience; i.e., by the recurrence to sense of various phenomenal objects which are the embodiments of these ideas. Thus

the ideal world was the only real world; all the rest was only changing, fleeting, phenomenal. These views of Plato were adopted by his followers among the Schoolmen of the Middle Ages, and employed by them, especially, as a theory of conception, or an account of general notions,—though conception and perception are all the same, on this theory.

3. *Criticism of the theory.*—This theory of conception (like the corresponding theory of perception) errs, in assuming the existence of actual, representative entities in thought, which are not mere modifications of the thinking mind itself,—i.e., real mental apprehensions reached through experience. It substitutes representative ideas for thoughts proper. Conceptions, thoughts, are indeed real, both in the mind of God and in the mind of man, though not distinct, real entities,—certainly not in the mind of man. God has stamped certain types upon things, and man reads them there.

II. NOMINALISM.

1. *What the theory is.*—This theory does not deny that we apprehend certain common qualities in different objects, and classify them accordingly. It only contends that these common qualities are none the more general, for being perceived in several objects,—that they always stand in the mind, as perceived in some particular object of the class, but accompanied by the consciousness that they belong equally to every individual of the class. All the generality, therefore, which there is in such notions, consists in the idea of *relation* to various individual objects, which is involved in them.

2. *Further developed and illustrated.* — The nominalist, therefore, holds, that strictly, there are only general terms, notions being always singular. In other words, that in employing general terms, or words which designate classes of things, the object before the mind is always individual, only accompanied by the consciousness that this individual object is like various other individual things in certain qualities or respects. There can be, therefore, no such general notion, as was formerly contended for by some philosophers, which embraces the distinctive characteristics of every individual of a class, yet so generalized as to apply to no one in particular; as, for instance, of a triangle, which is at the same time rectangular and oblique, equilateral and scalene, and yet neither the one nor the other. This is now generally admitted, and the only difference between nominalists and conceptualists seems to be, as to whether the mind in using general terms always and necessarily calls up individuals, or is concentrated, as far as it realizes any thing beyond the word, upon the bundle of qualities common to the class, abstracted from any and all particular objects. The latter is the view of the conceptualist, and as it seems to me, the true view. (N. II. 2, p. 254.)

III. CONCEPTUALISM.

1. *What the theory is.* — This is the theory of conception described in the previous sections of this chapter, and that now more commonly held by philosophers. According to this theory, general notions exist, indeed, but only as thoughts, or products of the mind. They are mere formal representations of classes of objects, constructed by the mind from its observation of their

common marks. They are thus but mental modifications, or thoughts of certain attributes common to classes of objects.

2. *The use of general terms according to this theory.* — Doubtless language is of great use — nay, indispensable, even — in conception, as in other mental operations. When we have formed a concept, we give it a name, which fixes and records it, and thus preserves it for future use. This name, ever afterwards, stands as the sign of the concept, and recalls it whenever it occurs. Some of these general terms are mere arbitrary signs of the things signified, and some of them contain in their etymology some allusion to the qualities represented by them; as, *animal* (something having *life*), *vegetable* (something that *grows*), *happiness* (something which we owe to *hap* or fortune); so also, *inertia*, *gravitation*, *isomorphism*, *homœopathy*, etc. Thus, as Aristotle remarks, general names are often only abbreviated definitions.

SECTION V.

IMPORTANCE OF CONCEPTION

1. *Conception compared with perception.* — Conception, as we have seen, is apprehending, or grasping together, the marks or characters which constitute the common nature of classes of related objects. By perception we become acquainted with the qualities of individual objects, by conception we form notions of classes of objects. In perception the qualities are all directly given in a single individual object, in conception the common qualities of many different yet related

objects have to be abstracted by a reflex mental effort. Conception, therefore, requires a much higher mental energy, and hence is a much more difficult process. If, then, men often use their senses so poorly that their perceptions are inadequate and indistinct, how much more danger is there of their conceptions being so?

2. *All our higher knowledge depends upon the adequacy of our conceptions.*— At the same time, all our higher knowledge depends upon the adequacy and distinctness of our conceptions. As accurate perceptions are necessary, in order that we may have the materials for forming accurate conceptions, so accurate conceptions are necessary, in order to an adequate knowledge of all above individual things. All the knowledge expressed by general terms, as indicating more than a single object, all that is reached by judgment or the longest process of reasoning,* depends upon the accuracy and adequacy of our conceptions. If our conceptions are inadequate, not only is our knowledge of classes of objects, and of all general and abstract ideas, defective, but our inferences and deductions from them are unreliable. And how large and important a portion of knowledge is thus affected, may be seen by considering how few of the ideas which form the staple of our thoughts are expressed by proper names or singular terms.

3. *Fruitful knowledge is not the knowledge of words, but of things.*— When knowledge becomes a mere knowledge of words, and philosophy only a series of logomachies, they must necessarily be devoid of fruit. It was so in Bacon's time, who, with his usual felicity,

---

* Thinking is defined by Mansel (*Prolegomena Logica*, p. 22) as "the act of knowing or judging of things by means of concepts."

pointed out the cause in a single word, by saying that science had become so unfruitful, because it had *lost its root in nature.* The leading Schoolmen, who brought on this state of things, were either nominalists or realists, both of which views tend to carry off the mind from nature, and entangle it in barren subtleties. Knowledge becomes fruitful only as our words are merely the signs of distinctly formed concepts, filled with a living content, direct from nature. The mind is enriched only as it grasps the reality of things. To show the importance of conception, let us take a few illustrative cases from the sciences.

4. *Illustrations from astronomy.* — Astronomy furnishes many forcible illustrations of the importance of conception in the study of nature. Nothing is more familiar to us than the phases of the moon, and yet how inadequate the conception, in most persons, of the actual relative positions of the sun, earth, and moon, from which those successive phases result; and how impossible it would be for them to represent and explain these relations to another, and deduce the phenomena from them! One may even have solved all the mathematical questions pertaining to the subject, and obtained the formulæ which express all the facts, as thousands have done, and yet have no adequate notion of the thing itself — no mental picture of the actual relations of the three bodies from which the phases arise. So one may be able to calculate an eclipse, without really conceiving the relation of the bodies from which it arises; nay, may have mastered, perhaps, the formulæ of the Mechanique Celeste, without having any thing more than the vaguest conception of the real mechanism of the heavens. The solution of such

questions by the algebraic method does not necessitate the actual formation of the implied concepts, nor is a true and vivid conception of all the facts and relations involved in the case always reached, though they are much more likely to be, even by the geometrical method of solution.

5. *Illustrations from other sciences.* — Other sciences furnish scarcely less forcible illustrations of the importance of conception. What knowledge is conveyed to us by the term "stereographic projection," or by the mere process of finding the formulæ which apply to it, if we do not actually form a conception of the thing itself? How are we profited by the terminology of Chemistry, Geology, Natural History, Physiology, or Psychology, unless we actually form the conceptions indicated by the different terms? Merely to learn the words and repeat them from memory is of no avail. They must be apprehended in their meaning in order to enrich the mind at all. And so in all cases. There is nothing in which men fail more than in forming distinct and accurate conceptions, and no more defective education than that which encourages a mere knowledge of words, rules, and formulæ, to the neglect of ideas.

CHAPTER VI.

JUDGMENT.

SECTION I.

NATURE OF JUDGMENT.

1. *What judgment is.* — Judgment is the power of viewing one concept as being (or not being) equivalent to or a part of another concept. Without this power our concepts would remain isolated, each being viewed by itself, without any connection between them. It is by the judgment that their relations are perceived, and that they come to be regarded as equivalents or parts of each other. Thus, having a concept of *man* and of *changeableness*, I perceive that changeableness forms a part of my concept of man, and therefore say, " man is changeable," or " changeable man." So we say, " man is a rational animal," " man is not immortal," " a tree is a plant," etc.

2. *Meaning of the word "part" in the above definition.* — In the above definition, the term *part* is used in its most general sense, as denoting *any thing belonging to.* According to Aristotle, every judgment declares either the *genus*, or the *definition*, or the *property*, or the *accident* of its subject. In the first case, the idea expressed by the predicate contains the subject as a *part*, in the second, the two ideas are *equivalent*, and in the others, the predicate expresses a *quality* (property or accident) of the subject; as, " man is an animal," " man is a ra-

tional animal," "man is a warm-blooded animal," "life is sweet."

3. *Possible judgments.* — Whatever concepts are united in a judgment must be regarded as holding one or the other of the above-named relations to each other. When, therefore, any two concepts which do not admit of such a relation are brought together in the form of a judgment, the judgment is inconceivable. We often have occasion to use such judgments, but only as *suppositions.* Though inconceivable in themselves as positive judgments, they are possible forms of thought, and quite conceivable as *assumptions.* Thus, for the purposes of demonstration, we may suppose a square to be a triangle, the three angles of a triangle to be greater or less than two right-angles, two straight lines to enclose a space, etc. These and the like, are intelligible as suppositions, though not as positive judgments.

4. *Conceivable judgments.* — A judgment is conceivable only when the relation asserted to exist between the two concepts is conceivable. It is not sufficient, as seen above, that the form of expression be intelligible, so that we comprehend the relation assumed; to make a judgment conceivable, it must be capable of being construed to the mind, of being thought as possible, of being brought into a consistency of representation. No such consistency of representation is possible in such a judgment as "a square is a triangle;" but that "man is mortal," "sugar is sweet," or that "space may exist either occupied or unoccupied by material objects," may be easily construed to the mind.

5. *True judgments.* — A true judgment is one which is according to the facts of nature. It expresses what is known as true. It is not enough, in this case, that

the relation asserted between the two concepts should be conceivable, it must be real. "Men are infallible," is a judgment entirely conceivable in itself, though far from being true. But the propositions, "men are fallible," "two straight lines cannot enclose a space," are true judgments, being in accordance with what we know, either from experience or intuitively. In all forms of judgment both concepts are known, but in true judgments, the assumed relation of the concepts, also, is in accordance with what we know.

6. *Judgment implies comparison.*—Judgment, of course, implies comparison. The relation which is asserted or denied to exist between two concepts, can have been perceived only by comparing them together. When one asserts, "snow is white," he implies, that, in comparing his notion of snow and whiteness, he perceives that the quality belongs to that subject. But in that affirmation by the mind, in all its operations, of the existence of some object before it, either real or ideal, which Sir W. Hamilton calls an "assertory judgment," and Mr. Mansel, a "psychological judgment," there is no proper comparison; it is only the assertion of an immediate state of consciousness. Thus, when I assert that there is a real object before my mind in perception, and an ideal object before it in imagination, I only assert what I am immediately conscious of,—there can be no comparison in such a case, except it be that of something with nothing.

7. *Depth and breadth of judgments.*— When the relation between the two concepts in a judgment is viewed as existing between the *marks* or *attributes* which they embrace, the judgment is regarded in its *intension*, *comprehension*, or *depth;* but when between

the *things* embraced under them, it is regarded in its *extension* or *breadth.* Thus the judgment, "all men are mortal," means, according to its intension, "the attribute of mortality belongs to, or is one of the attributes of man;" according to its extension, "man belongs to the class of mortal beings." The first *defines*, the second *divides*.

SECTION II.

KINDS OF JUDGMENTS.

Judgments may be divided: according to the coincidence or non-coincidence of the concepts which they contain, into *substitutive* and *attributive* judgments; according to the form of the language in which they are expressed, into *categorical*, *hypothetical*, and *disjunctive* judgments; according to the agreement or repugnance of the ideas compared, into *affirmative* and *negative* judgments; according to the matter which they relate to, into *certain* and *doubtful* judgments; and according as the predicate merely explains or adds something new to the idea contained in the subject, into *explicative* (*analytic*) and *ampliative* (*synthetic*) judgments.

1. *Substitutive and Attributive Judgments.* — This is a general division of all judgments. As we have seen in the preceding section, all judgments assert, either that two concepts are equivalent to each other, or that one is a part of, or belongs to, the other. In the first case, the judgment is substitutive, in the second it is attributive. Thus, in the judgment, "man is a rational animal," the two concepts being equivalent, the subject and predicate may change places (i.e., one may be

substituted for the other) without affecting the truth or propriety of the judgment. It is just as true that "a rational animal is a man," as that "man is a rational animal." But in such judgments as "life is sweet," "the rose is a flower," the subject and predicate cannot with propriety be made to change places, since the one concept, in each case, is but a part, or an *attribute*, of the other.

2. *Categorical Judgments.* — In modern usage, categorical judgments embrace all judgments direct in form, whether positive or negative. They thus embrace all judgments, except hypothetical and disjunctive judgments. This is the common classification of judgments from Aristotle down. But in Aristotle himself, as shown by Sir W. Hamilton, * *categorical* is not opposed to *hypothetical*, but always means *affirmative*, whether applied to propositions or syllogisms.

3. *Hypothetical Judgments.* — These are apparently pairs of judgments, related to each other as cause and effect, condition and consequence; as, for example, "if it rains copiously, the rivers rise;" "if you neglect to sow, you cannot expect to reap." But in all such cases, there is in reality only a single judgment, a single assertion, which is, that *if* one thing happens, *then* another will. Giving it, therefore, its true logical form, the hypothetical judgment becomes "*the case* (*fact, notion*) of its raining copiously IS *a case* (*fact, notion*) of the rivers rising."

4. *Disjunctive Jndgments.* — Here, too, there are apparently two judgments, but really only one. Such judgments bring together, as alternatives, two judgments, *both* of which cannot be true, but *one* of which must

* Philosophical Discussions, p. 151.

be; as, "either the miracles of Christ were real, or he was a gross impostor." The real judgment here, reduced to its logical form, is, "the possible cases in regard to the miracles of Christ are, that they were real, and that he was an impostor."

5. *Affirmative and Negative Judgments.* — Judgments which express an agreement of two concepts, as wholes, or as whole and part, are called affirmative judgments, while those which express a want of such agreement are called negative judgments; as, "life is short," "man is not immortal." But when the negative does not affect the copula, but the subject or predicate, the judgment is affirmative; as, "*not* to submit would be madness," "all human virtue is *im*perfect." A judgment like this last, with a negative or privative expression in the predicate, is sometimes called an *indefinite* judgment.

6. *Certain and Doubtful Judgments.* — Judgments pertaining to what is called necessary matter, as the relations of time, space, number, and degree, as developed in the various mathematical sciences, are made with the utmost confidence and certainty; such as, that "two and two make four," "two straight lines cannot enclose space." But judgments relating to contingent matter are made with less certainty, varying in different cases, and are received with more caution. The judgments, "truth is great and will prevail," are probable, though not certain. So of judgments based upon testimony; as, "Cato killed himself at Utica," and in the other departments of probable truth.

7. *Explicative or Analytic Judgments.* — Such judgments merely *unfold* or *analyze* the subject in the predicate, — the predicate merely draws out and repeats in

another form the idea contained in the subject. Such are the judgments expressed in the common logical and mathematical axioms and definitions; as "a whole is equal to the sum of its parts," "a circle is a curved line, every point in which is equally distant from a a point included by it, called the centre." Such, too, are judgments in contingent matter, when the predicate is thought as *necessarily* involved in the subject; as, "all bodies are extended." Analytical judgments are not strictly identical, although the concepts in the subject and predicate are equivalent to each other. The concepts are the same in substance, to be sure, but being different in form, the one is drawn from the other only by an act of mental analysis.

8. *Ampliative or Synthetic Judgments.* — These are judgments in which something is added in the predicate to the idea contained in the subject. They express an *enlargement* of our knowledge, a *putting together* of two notions not actually involved in each other and thought as necessarily belonging to each other. Such judgments relate chiefly to contingent matter and probable truth; they indicate the enlargement of our knowledge through experience. Thus, when we say, "iron is ductile," we indicate by the predicate a quality not thought as necessarily involved in the very notion of iron, but one which has been discovered to belong to it by experience.

9. *Judgments not to be classified as Propositions.* — The classification of judgments as *propositions*, and their significance as such, belong to logic. There are commonly reckoned six distinct forms of propositions, to which Sir W. Hamilton, carrying out a thorough quantification of the predicate, in negative as well as

affirmative judgments, has added two more, making eight in all. We may embrace, in both affirmative and negative judgments, the whole of the subject and predicate, a part of the subject and predicate, the whole of the subject and a part of the predicate, a part of the subject and the whole of the predicate.

CHAPTER VII.

REASONING.

SECTION I.

NATURE OF REASONING.

1. *What reasoning is.* — Reasoning, when drawn out in full, consists of a series of judgments, in which every third judgment is deduced from the two preceding. The smallest movement in reasoning consists in deducing a third judgment from two others. This constitutes a single step, and is called, in logical language, a *syllogism.* As the mind advances from individuals to classes in conception, and from classes to combinations of classes in judgment, so it advances from judgments to combinations of judgments in reasoning. In reasoning, the object always is, from judgments already formed to reach other judgments which are legitimately deducible from them. This is done by the introduction of intermediate judgments. Thus, from the given judgment "all animals are mortal," I conclude at once that "man is mortal," as soon as I learn that "man is an animal." But from the judgment, "a triangle is a figure with three sides and three angles," we reach the conclusion that "the three angles of a triangle are equal to two right angles" only through several intermediate deductions.

2. *Argument, syllogism.* — A reasoning expressed in words is called an *argumentation* or *argument;* though

properly, *argument* is only the discovery and application of the means of proof, of *middle terms.* But as already stated, a reasoning, or rather, a single step or process of reasoning, drawn out in full, so as to express the complete form and exact order of thought in deducing a conclusion legitimately, is called a *syllogism.* Thus while one would say, in common argumentative discourse, "this liquid is poisonous, for it contains arsenic," if he were required to show more clearly the order of the thought, and the legitimacy of the conclusion, he would draw it out in full syllogistic form:—

Every thing which contains arsenic is poisonous.
This liquid contains arsenic,
Therefore this liquid is poisonous.

3. *Designations of the different judgments in a syllogism.*— In a syllogism, the judgment which we wish to establish is called the *question* or *problem,* at the outset, and the *conclusion,* after it has been established; while the judgments from which it is deduced are called *premises,*— the general judgment with which we start, the *major premise,* and the mediating judgment, the *minor premise.* Thus, in the preceding syllogism, the question at the outset is, "is this liquid poisonous?" and the conclusion deduced from the other two judgments as premises is, that "it is poisonous."

4. *Reasoning is generally abridged in common discourse.*— In the language of common discourse, the process of reasoning is generally abridged, by omitting one of the premises, or even the conclusion; and often the order of the premises and the conclusion is inverted. The speaker or writer comprehending the reasoning dis-

tinctly himself does not feel the necessity of drawing it out fully, and in exact form, in expressing it to others. But such an argument being defective in form may be disputed by the caviller, or illegitimate reasoning may be passed off as legitimate under such forms. But a syllogism, drawing out the reasoning in full, cannot be disputed, and will always exhibit any latent fallacy which may lurk in the reasoning.

5. *The syllogism a test of reasoning.* — The syllogism, therefore, is only common reasoning drawn out in full, and in the best order to exhibit the legitimacy of the conclusion. It is common reasoning, though not in the precise form, nor in the exact language of common discourse. It is a universal test of reasoning, and a sure protection against all fallacies. Thus, should it be said, "trade is depressed, therefore the country must be misgoverned," this might be passed off in a political harangue as very good reasoning; but let it be drawn out into a syllogism and the fallacy is apparent at once. Thus:—

> Trade is depressed,
> Therefore the country is misgoverned,
> *For every country is misgoverned where trade is depressed.* *

Putting in, thus, the general judgment implied but not expressed in the first form, the inconclusiveness of the reasoning immediately becomes obvious.

6. *Ground of the conclusion in a syllogism.* — The object of all reasoning is to establish as true certain

---

* This form of the syllogism is called *analytic,* since the premises follow the conclusion as its reasons. The *synthetic* form, which places the premises first, is more common, but no more legitimate, or convincing The two judgments, without the general one, constitute an *enthymeme.*

conjectural judgments which occur to us in the experience of life. And as all judgments consist of two concepts, which are legitimately united in thought only as they are seen to agree as wholes or as whole and part, the object of the syllogism is to exhibit conspicuously their agreement, *through the introduction of a third notion*, which agrees with both of the notions of the judgment to be established, either in whole or in part, and hence warrants the conclusion, since two concepts which agree with a third must agree with each other. Thus, should we conjecture of a certain disease that "it is fatal" in its character, if on further investigation we discover it to be *consumption*, we have hit upon a notion which agrees with both "disease" and "fatal" (i.e., combines in itself both these ideas), and hence may say (introducing this as a middle term), "this disease (which is consumption) is fatal;" or drawing out all that is implied in this statement in the form of a syllogism:—

All consumptions are fatal.
This disease is consumption,
Therefore it is fatal.

7. *All reasoning may be resolved into syllogisms.*—All reasoning is of this nature. It is always capable of being drawn out into syllogisms; the longest train of reasoning, when fully and formally expressed, is only a series of syllogisms. It is the same in probable and in demonstrative reasoning. Logic takes no account of the matter to which the reasoning relates; its forms are the same whether applied to necessary or contingent matter. Indeed, it does not even vouch for the *objective truth* of either its premises or conclusion, but

only for the *sequence* of the one from the other. Thus, the following syllogism is a legitimate form of thought, though obviously false in fact: —

> All men are perfect.
> John is a man,
> Therefore he is perfect.

8. *The discovery of the media of proof.* — Reasoning being such as here described, it will readily be seen that the chief difficulty in the process must lie in the discovery of middle terms, or what is called in common language, the *media of proof.* As these media are always notions pertaining to the general subject of inquiry, and lying between the premises and the conclusion, they are generally best reached by an attentive study of the subject in itself and in its connections. In mathematical reasoning, where the conclusion is developed directly out of the premises, we have little more to do, in order to discover the media of proof, than carefully and patiently to consider what is given, in all its elements and contents. But in inductive reasoning, and probable reasoning generally, where truth as realized in nature and in life is to be established, the media of proof are to be sought from a wider field; though even here they are always related to both premises and conclusion, else, indeed, they could not serve as media of proof at all.

9. *Discovery of the media of proof in inductive reasoning.* — In inductive reasoning, the guide to the connecting conception is analogy or likeness, and the success of the inductive reasoner depends partly upon the closeness with which he scrutinizes every thing pertaining to the subject which he is investigating, and partly

upon the readiness with which he seizes upon analogies among the objects which pass under his scrutiny. It was thus that Newton saw the law of gravitation in a falling apple, Oken the vertebral column in the skull of a deer, and Goethe the flower of a plant in its leaf. Newton, as he has informed us, owed his discoveries chiefly to the patience with which he studied his subjects, while the other discoverers here named, seem to have owed their success more to a lively imagination, which enabled them to see analogies that escaped duller though more patient students.

10. *The object of reasoning.* — From what has been said, it will be seen that the object of reasoning is, to extend our knowledge from what we know to what we do not know — to enable us to form wider and wider judgments with regard to things. The human mind tends irresistibly to a unity of knowledge. It seeks so to arrange, and classify, and subordinate its knowledge, that in its highest synthesis, it may all stand under a single relation, and be embraced in a single affirmation. In this generalizing process, reasoning follows upon conception and judgment, and completes the work which they begin.

SECTION II.

KINDS OF REASONING.

1. *All kinds of reasoning are the same in form.* — As already stated, reasoning in all cases is the same in form, being always capable of reduction to the form of a syllogism. But there are certain recognized distinctions in the process, depending either upon the

order of the thoughts or the matter to which they pertain, which deserve a passing notice.

2. *Inductive and Deductive Reasoning.* — This is a general distinction of reasoning into two counter wholes, depending upon the reversed order of the thoughts in the two cases. In inductive reasoning, we proceed from the particular to the general, from the parts to the whole; while in deductive reasoning, we proceed from the general to the particular, from the whole to its parts.

3. *Principle of the two processes as stated by Hamilton.* — Of the two processes, Sir W. Hamilton * remarks, "The former is governed by the rule: *What belongs (or does not belong) to all the constituent parts, belongs (or does not belong) to the constituted whole.* The latter by the rule: *What belongs (or does not belong) to the containing whole, belongs (or does not belong) to each and all of the contained parts.*"

4. *Induction usually precedes deduction.* — As general notions, with a few exceptions, are formed from experience, induction must usually precede deduction. In the investigation of nature both are necessary, and they usually alternate with each other, — induction establishing a general truth, and deduction, again, inferring some particular from it, and thus testing it. Thus, induction having rendered it probable that the diamond and charcoal were the same general substance, deduction inferred, that if so, then the diamond would burn, which was found to be the fact, and hence their identity was established beyond all doubt or cavil.

5. *Imperfect inductions.* — Induction is often used loosely for observation, or the investigation of facts

* Philosophical Discussions, p. 159.

preparatory to induction, and generally, among physical inquirers, for those imperfect inferences which proceed from *some* to *all*. In such cases, the inference is not based upon any necessity of thought, but upon the material probabilities of the case; and though all-important as a guide in the investigations of nature, is logically defective. Hence most of our general principles, established by the induction of experience, are but probable truths. We say "all men are mortal," and have no shadow of doubt of the fact, though it is far from being a complete induction. Men are mortal as far as our experience goes, and, from the uniformity of the laws of nature, we are confident that they will always prove to be so. But from the nature of the case, the mortality of man can never be universally established till the end of time.

6. *A-priori and A-posteriori Reasoning.* — This famous distinction of reasoning, at least according to present usage, depends chiefly upon the different character of the premises from which the reasoning proceeds. The reasoning in both cases is deductive; but in the one case the premises are derived from experience, in the other they are not. Of the use of the two terms, as designating elements of knowledge from which inferences may be made, Sir W. Hamilton * remarks, "The term *a priori*, by the influence of Kant and his school, is now very generally employed to characterize those elements of knowledge which are not obtained *a posteriori* — are not evolved out of experience as factitious generalizations; but which, as native to, are potentially in the mind antecedent to the act of experience, on occasion of which (as constituting its

* See Wight's Hamilton, p. 66.

subjective conditions) they are first elicited into consciousness."

7. *Distinction between the two kinds of reasoning according to Hamilton.* — As applied to reasoning, the same author * says of the terms: "Previously to Kant, the terms *a priori* and *a posteriori* were, in a sense which descended from Aristotle, properly and usually employed,—the former to denote a reasoning from cause to effect, the latter, a reasoning from effect to cause. The term *a priori* came, however, in modern times, to be extended to any abstract reasoning from a given notion to the conditions which such a notion involved; hence, for example, the title *a priori* bestowed on the ontological and cosmological arguments for the existence of the Deity. The latter of these, in fact, starts from experience — from the observed contingency of the world, in order to construct the supposed notion on which it founds. Clarke's cosmological demonstration, called *a priori*, is therefore, so far, properly an argument *a posteriori*." (N. 7, p. 254.)

8. *Probable and Demonstrative Reasoning.* — This is a distinction of reasoning depending upon the effect which it produces upon the mind in different cases. The one kind of reasoning carries with it evidence which is irresistible, the other, only such as renders the conclusion probable. Yet, the process of reasoning is precisely the same in the two cases. The whole difference lies in the matter to which the reasoning, in the two cases, is applied. Reasoning on necessary matter is demonstrative or apodictic, on contingent matter, only probable.

9. *Necessary and contingent matter.* — Necessary

* See Wight's Hamilton, p. 66.

matter includes all objects of thought on which we always and *necessarily*, in any given case, think the same; and contingent matter, all other objects of thought. Hence, space, time, number, and degree — i.e., in brief, *quantity* — in their various relations, constitute the only absolutely necessary matter. All other matter is more or less contingent. Our knowledge of facts may be definite and certain, and various first principles of knowledge, as well as modes of conception, may be necessarily received as such by all men, but nothing except quantity presents an object of thought on which, in its various parts and relations, all men not only do, but *must*, think alike, if they think at all.

10. *Mathematical reasoning.* — In mathematical reasoning, — which alone, in the strict sense of the word, is demonstrative reasoning, — both the question and every step in the solution are not only perfectly definite, but incapable of being apprehended differently,— if really apprehended, they must be apprehended alike by all and at all times. Thus, the definition of a circle, of a square, a triangle, etc., is one and the same to all, and any relation between their parts must always be apprehended alike by all. Space is apprehended by all as admitting of perfect figures of all sorts, and of fixed relations between their parts, whether any such figures are ever actually constructed or not. There is the like ideal exactness and perfection in our conceptions pertaining to the other forms of quantity.

11. *How the case stands in probable reasoning.* — But in probable reasoning the case is different. Here the object to be reasoned about is not fixed and deter-

mined by our conceptions, but is variable and contingent, conforming rather to the laws of nature and the realities of things. Suppose we wish to prove the existence of the soul after death, the obligations of morality, or any of the ten thousand questions pertaining to life and reality, we find no definite notion to start with, as in mathematics, which really contains the conclusion in itself, and which can be developed to the end through a series of necessary judgments; but are obliged to start from this or that admitted fact or truth (and these, perhaps, not *universally* admitted), and proceed by merely probable inferences drawn from various, diverse, and often uncertain, relations, till we reach the conclusion. Such reasons may be sufficient to incline the mind to a particular conclusion, as against those which tend to any other conclusion; but they are never quite sufficient to necessitate the conclusion, and render any other impossible. Still, if sufficient to control the reason, they are sufficient to control the conduct (*mores*) also; and hence it is that probable reasoning is sometimes called *moral* reasoning.

12. *Demonstrative reasoning not the most important because the most convincing.* — But we are not to infer that demonstrative reasoning is the most important, because it is the most convincing. A conclusion which is probably certain ought to control our conduct as readily as one which is demonstrably certain. That the proof preponderates on one side is sufficient to determine the reason, and should be to determine the conduct. If it does not, it is evidence of something wrong in our character; and thus the fact that every question cannot be made demonstrably evident, becomes an important test and trial of character. Be-

sides, as life has to do chiefly with things contingent, probable reasoning is much more used by us, and hence is much the most important to us. As remarked by Bishop Butler,* "to us [beings of limited capacities, as we are] probability is the very guide of life."

13. *Abstract Reasoning.* — This is reasoning from a general notion to its conditions or consequences. In terms it embraces mathematical reasoning, and indeed, all reasoning where there is no appeal to experience. But it is chiefly applied to that species of probable reasoning, which deduces conditions or consequences from general notions; as, for instance, the existence of God, from our conception of space; or future rewards and punishments, from the fitness and unfitness of actions.

SECTION III.

FIRST PRINCIPLES OF REASONING.

1. *The whole structure of knowledge depends on reasoning.* — As we have seen, it is by reasoning that our thoughts are combined and the whole structure of our knowledge reared. Nay, even the very foundations of knowledge depend upon reasoning. All thoughts are compared with each other by the reason, and are either accepted or rejected according as they are found to be consistent or inconsistent with other things. All knowledge being thus at the mercy of reason, it becomes important to know within what limits its authority is legitimate, and what are the bounds to its action fixed in the nature of things. Even the reason must be reason-

* Introduction to the Analogy.

able. It may not cavil, nor expect to prove every thing by demonstrative reasons. Being limited in its nature, it must not attempt to pass certain bounds; but, on the contrary, should accept as final certain well established judgments of fact, certain necessary conceptions, and certain laws of thought.

2. *Primary judgments of fact.* — Primary judgments of fact relate to things contingent, and are such as these: *thought implies the existence of a thinking being to whom the thought belongs; quality implies a substantive existence in which it inheres; whatever is perceived by the several senses exists, and substantially as perceived; whatever is recalled by the memory did exist as remembered;* and in general, *consciousness makes a true and reliable report of our experience.* And not only so, but, that in the natural and unperverted state of things, men not only experience the truth, but speak the truth, and hence, that *facts may be established by evidence.*

3. *All probable reasoning is impossible unless these facts be accepted as final.* — Without the admission of these, and perhaps other kindred judgments of fact, as primary and indisputable, all moral, or probable reasoning is impossible. All reasoning of this sort rests ultimately upon experience, and hence requires that the primary elements of experience be received as indisputable facts. If they be not thus received, there is no end of controversy, nothing in life can be settled, and the whole fabric of practical and empirical knowledge at once falls to the ground. It was thus that Hume subverted the fabric of knowledge in his time, and it was only by building upon these primary truths of fact, in a more sure and cautious manner, that it was again restored by Reid and his followers.

4. *Necessary first truths.* — Much of reasoning, also, rests upon certain *necessary* truths or judgments. Such judgments are: *every effect must have a cause; all objects exist in space and time; space admits of various definite and perfect relations both among objects and the different parts and positions of the same, as time does among events and the different periods of the same existence.* We think every effect as necessarily having a cause, and can neither annihilate space and time in thought, nor conceive them otherwise than as media which admit of all possible forms, poportions, motions, successions, and relations of quantity.

5. *Consequences of denying these truths.* — Our conceptions of space, time, and number, lie at the foundation of mathematical reasoning. If denied, therefore, the mathematical sciences are undermined. But they cannot be denied; they are necessary truths, forcing themselves upon us with a power which defies disbelief. Hence, the mathematical sciences, as being at least formally true beyond all possibility of doubt, have never been seriously assailed by scepticism. This is not true, however, of the doctrine of causation. Our idea of causation being regarded by Locke as wholly empirical, it fell, with other empirical knowledge, before the scepticism of Hume, and with it the proof of a First Cause, until restored on a surer foundation by subsequent philosophers.

6. *Axioms and laws of thought.* — Reasoning, also, rests upon certain axioms and laws of thought. Some of these *axioms* are employed exclusively in mathematical reasoning; as, "a straight line is the shortest distance between two points," "two straight lines cannot enclose a space," etc. Others may be employed, also,

in probable reasoning; such as, "the whole is greater than its part," "things that are equal to the same thing are equal to each other," and the like. And besides these axioms, there are three well-known *laws of thought*, which apply to concepts and judgments, as well as to reasoning. These laws are denominated the Principle of Identity, the Principle of Contradiction, and the Principle of Excluded Middle.

7. *What these laws teach as applied to thought.*— These laws are usually expressed by symbols as follows: A is A (Identity); A is not *not* —A (Contradiction); B is either A or *not* —A (Excluded Middle). As laws of thought, they are designed as a guide to the right use in reasoning of the *three forms of thought*,—the concept, the judgment, and the reason. They teach that in reasoning, having assumed a concept or judgment with a certain content and extent,—i.e., one embracing certain attributes and things,—we are bound to keep it, under every form of expression, always the same, recollecting that A is always A, and cannot be made any thing else, or *not* —A: while every particular thing, as B, must be either A or *not* —A; since A, and *not* —A, cover the whole sphere, and do not admit any thing between them. There is no middle course. In other words, these laws teach that a concept, or proposition, maintains its sameness or consistency under different forms of expression, only so long as the *meaning* of the words remains the same; that they become inconsistent, or contradictory of themselves, when confounded in any degree with that which they are not; and that every concept, or proposition, must be either consistent with or contradictory of itself: the assertion of the one involves the denial of the other. There is no middle course.

8. ***What they teach as applied to things.*** — Applied to things, these laws teach such truths as these: That the same attribute cannot be affirmed and denied of the same thing; that the attribute cannot be contradictory of the subject; that a thing cannot *both* be, and not be; that a thing cannot be both *white* and *not white;* that no proposition can be both *true* and *false.* And, on the contrary, they teach that every thing must *either* be, or not be, and every proposition must *either* be true or false; and this even when we comprehend neither the affirmative nor the negative of the proposition. Thus we say of time, that it *must have either* an absolute beginning or an infinite non-beginning, though we can conceive of neither. Also, that there is something in every object which constitutes it such, and makes us conceive it the *same;* and, hence, that the recurrence of the same complement of qualities is always to be taken as evidence of the presence of the same object. We are not at liberty to question its sameness every time it recurs, but are required to receive it in the character in which it presents itself.

9. ***How these first principles are to be regarded.*** — These and the like primary truths and principles form the starting-points, and warrant the procedure, in all reasoning. They are to be regarded as primary and indisputable, because they are all well established, and capable of being proved, either demonstratively or with the highest probability.

SECTION IV.

IMPROVEMENT OF THE REASONING POWERS.

1. *They are improved by use.*—The reasoning powers, of course, are improved by reasoning, as the other powers are improved by their appropriate exercise. Action is the grand condition of improvement for all our powers. As we can improve our senses only by a careful and persevering use of them in the perception of external objects, and our memory only by tasking it in the association and recollection of events; so we can improve our reasoning powers only by their frequent and earnest employment in reasoning, or what in some way pertains to it.

2. *We should arrange our knowledge in logical order.*—In order then, to improve our reasoning powers, it is necessary, in the first place, that we should be in the habit of arranging and frequently retracing our knowledge in its logical order. By the "logical order" of things I mean, the order of their dependence in thought, as part and whole, means and end, premise and conclusion, reason and consequent, etc. It is not enough that we arbitrarily connect our thoughts by the thread of association, and recall them in that order—this is merely an exercise of memory, not of the reasoning powers. We reason, only as we proceed from thought to thought as logically dependent upon each other, and compelling our assent at every step. Reasoning is proving, and hence we reason when we seek to establish the truth on any subject. The investigation of truth, therefore, is the great field for the improvement of the reasoning powers.

3. *Mathematical reasoning as a source of improve-*

ment. — Mathematical reasoning, as we have seen, is virtually coincident with demonstrative reasoning. Of the effect of this kind of reasoning in improving the reasoning powers, different and even quite opposite opinions are held. Sir W. Hamilton, in an article truly marvellous for its compass and ability, comes to the conclusion, that mathematical studies exercise the reasoning powers but feebly, being chiefly "conducive to the *one sole intellectual virtue of continuous attention.*" * Others, again, consider mathematics as absolutely the most efficient means of cultivating the reasoning powers.

4. *What the truth in the case seems to be.* — These are the extreme views, and the truth, undoubtedly, as usually happens in such cases, lies between them. It is true that the object-matter of mathematics — *quantity* — is simple and uniform, and the various conceptions pertaining to its different parts and relations, clear and even necessary, while conclusions, however remote, are always implicitly contained in the premises, and are simply evolved out of them. Hence the course of deduction in mathematics seems to be of the simplest kind. The path being so plain, direct, and even hedged in on both sides, it scarcely seems possible for one to wander from it. Still, in mathematical, as in other reasoning, the object is, not simply to make *a* deduction, but the right deduction — a deduction not only true, but important; to come to a conclusion, not only correctly drawn from the premises, but establishing a particular point, and admitting of particular applications. Though the conclusion is always involved in

---

* Discussions on Philosophy, etc., p. 310.

the premises, it takes a good deal of reflection to perceive it, and something more than mere patience to trace it through a long line of deduction, which at the same time is but one line among many that might be followed. Though mathematical reasoning has no very wide application in the ordinary affairs of life, there can be no doubt that it is an important instrument for sharpening and strengthening the reasoning powers.

5. *Probable reasoning as a means of improvement.*— Probable reasoning embraces all reasoning which is not demonstrative in its character, and hence, in general, all except mathematical reasoning. It occupies a wide sphere, therefore, and from the diverse, variable, contingent, and uncertain elements with which it has to do, must require the most careful and intense exercise of our powers in order to conduct it safely. Its processes may be shorter than in mathematical reasoning, but the variableness and contingency of its matter make it more difficult to manage. The effect of this kind of reasoning in improving the reasoning powers will be seen by considering its procedure in those departments of study and mental exertion where it has the greatest scope.

6. *Influence of metaphysical and ethical studies in improving the reasoning powers.* — There is a large demand for the use of probable reasoning in metaphysical and ethical studies. Here the object is to establish the truth with regard to knowledge and duty, — to solve the questions, *What can we know?* and, *What should we do?* These and the collateral questions are among the most abstruse and subtle which the human mind has to deal with, and can be settled only by weighing

a thousand probabilities — often in themselves apparently as light as air — and observing the slightest preponderance of one over the other. The arguments by which the truth on these subjects is to be established, are so abstruse and subtle, as to task the human powers to the utmost to discover and appreciate them. I know of no better gymnastic for the reasoning powers, than Butler's discussions on Morals, and Hamilton's on Philosophy.

7. *Effect of forensic discussions in improving the reasoning powers.* — But the field where probable reasoning has its widest scope, is in the proof of facts. The proof of facts by "circumstantial evidence," as it is called, is but the proof of facts by probable arguments, and has always been considered as presenting the finest field for the exercise and display of the strength and ingenuity of the reasoning powers. When the fact to be established deeply affects human interests, and arouses the popular mind by its public importance, as the fact of a murder, or some great public outrage or fraud, it has always been a favorite theme for the orators, and, in different ages, themes of this sort have called forth such prodigies of argumentative eloquence, as the speeches of Cicero against Verres, of Burke in the impeachment of Warren Hastings, and of Webster in the trial of the Knapps. The construction of such arguments is among the highest efforts of the human reason, and even the careful reading and analysis of these great efforts of the master minds of our race are among the most profitable studies in which we can engage.

8. *Logic as a means of improving the reasoning powers.* — I might name, as another means of improving

our reasoning powers, the study of logic. Not that logic teaches the art of reasoning; logic is rather a *critique* of reasoning, than a system of rules for conducting it in practice. In the nature of the case, there can be no art of reasoning, except what is the result of the practice of reasoning. Reasoning proceeds by internal perceptions, not by external rules. We improve our reasoning powers, therefore, only as we improve our perception of the logical relations of ideas, — only as we sharpen our mental acumen. And it is in this way that the study of logic improves the reasoning powers. It treats of the logical relations of thought, and hence trains the mind to their perception. It analyzes the canons of thought, and thus lets us into its mechanism and familiarizes us with its processes. The study of logic, therefore, tends to improve the reasoning powers, but only as other studies and mental exercises do, by promoting the perceptions and habits which are essential to reasoning.

9. *Conclusion.* — It is by these, and the like means, that our reasoning powers — the last and noblest in that gradation of powers which it has been attempted in the preceding chapters to describe — are trained to that wondrous clearness of perception and facility of movement, which conduct us, step by step, with unerring precision, to the most remote and hidden truths. Reasoning is a search for causes, or first principles. It proceeds from things as they present themselves to us to things as they are, from thoughts to the conditions which they involve, from facts to principles, from effects to causes, and from nature to God. It is ever moving towards

unity, towards wider and still wider conclusions, as if instinctively tending towards that highest and sublimest affirmation of the Christian faith—"GOD ALL AND IN ALL."

CHAPTER VIII.

SPECULATIVE KNOWLEDGE, OR METAPHYSICS.

SECTION I.

INTRODUCTORY.

1. *Speculative knowledge defined.* — Speculative knowledge is not that common, obvious knowledge which we acquire by the ordinary exercise of our faculties, but those more subtle, more fundamental principles of knowledge which arise to our view in *speculating;* i.e., contemplating or scrutinizing the objects and products of knowledge as they exist in the mind. On a close scrutiny, these products are found to be all cast after given forms, and seem to embrace more than can be gained by the regular action of our different powers. All our knowledge is linked together in our minds under the forms or relations of substance and attribute, cause and effect, means and end ; and nothing is known out of relation to space and time. These are called the "categories," or necessary relations of knowledge ; and, since these ideas are supposed to be furnished directly by the mind itself, — they really being there *prior* to experience, and merely elicited by it, — they are also called "*à-priori* principles." And, as being fundamental and primary to all our knowledge, they are often called

"first principles," "primary notions," "intuitive truths," and the like.

2. *Metaphysics defined.* — Metaphysics also has to do with the fundamental principles of knowledge, and means substantially the same as speculative philosophy. Etymologically considered, the term has no particular significance, and is said to have been accidentally applied to this particular part of philosophy by being added by the compiler of Aristotle's works to the treatise on these fundamental principles which happened to come *after* his treatise on Physics (*Τὰ μετὰ τὰ φυσικά, the treatise after that on physics*). Metaphysics means the same as ontology, or the science of being; i.e., of being *per se*, real being, as opposed to the phenomenal or to apparent being. In short, metaphysics treats of the fundamental forms of being, or knowledge, not only of the above-named categories, but of what Kant calls the "ideas of the pure reason;" viz., of the conception of God as the highest condition of the possibility of all things, of the conception of the world as a single designed effect, and of the human soul as a simple, immaterial, unchanging substance and self-conscious personality. That these ideas and categories exist is universally admitted; the only difference in regard to them among philosophers being as to whether they are principles original and native to the mind, or derived from experience. The intuitional school holds to the former view; the empirical school, to the latter.

3. *'Tis immaterial whether speculative knowledge is considered intuitive or acquired.* — Whichever of these views shall prevail seems to me of but little consequence as far as they affect the dignity and importance of the mind. The facts remain the same in either case. A

theory is designed to account for the facts, not to change them; and that theory is the best which accounts for them the most simply and completely. And it is to be noticed, that both theories admit the necessity of experience in order to the realization of these truths in our consciousness, — the one as the *cause* of their realization, the other as the *occasion* of it. The one view regards the truths in question as actually generated in the mind by the experience of life; while the other regards them as simply called out or elicited into consciousness on occasion of this experience. In the one case the mind gathers them up from experience: in the other it becomes conscious of them through experience. In the one case the mind acquires them: in the other they are native to it. And why should they not be of equal authority in either case? Indeed, acquisition implies more that is active in the mind than original possession does. And, after all, what can really be meant by a capacity for knowing certain truths which are antecedent to and above all experience, and which yet are never known except in connection with experience? Are not the facts in the case calculated to suggest that the whole is the result of experience? And, indeed, what need is there of any other hypothesis, unless this fails to account for the facts? Whether it will account for the facts or not will appear from the following examination of some of the principal ideas in question.

SECTION II.

OF OUR IDEAS OF SUBSTANCE AND ATTRIBUTE.

1. *An attribute defined.* — An attribute is any limitation or relation which we attribute or ascribe to an object; as when we think or speak of an object as *long* or *short*, or *round* or *square*, or *red* or *white*, or *hard* or *soft*, and the like. We sometimes use the terms *quality*, *property*, or *accident*, instead of attribute: indicating by the first of these terms that the attribute gives a certain *character* to the object, or makes it *such and such;* and by the other two terms, in the first case, that the attribute is *peculiar* or essential to the object; and in the second, that it is *accidental*, or non-essential. But, whatever term is used to denote the modifying circumstance or peculiarity, we never think of it as any thing independent, or as having a separate existence apart from the object to which it is ascribed. We may, indeed, think of a quality as an abstract or ideal existence, and, as such, ascribe to it certain qualities; as when we speak of *redness*, the *light* red, the *dark* red, &c.: but, the moment we attempt to exemplify the quality by ascribing to it a concrete existence, we think of it as belonging to some object.

2. *Of material substance and its attributes.* — Substance is the *substratum*, or the ground, of the qualities or manifestations which in our various experience address themselves to our senses or our consciousness. It is of two kinds, — material and spiritual. We will first consider material substance. Material substance is known to us directly only through its qualities; but these qualities are all regarded by us as *relative* to some

object, and it is impossible for us to conceive them otherwise. We do not conceive the qualities as constituting the object, but simply as belonging to it. We may suppose all the qualities with the exception of extension withdrawn, and yet the substance remains; and even extension, though essential to our idea of material substance, does not seem to constitute it. Yet, whatever may be the nature or essence of the ultimate particles of matter, we know that they must be of some size and shape, and occupy some portion of space; otherwise they would cease to be matter. Extension, then, being essential to the constitution of matter, in knowing material objects as extended, we may be said to know them in themselves. Extension is something more than a quality; it is a nature: as Hamilton says, "The primary qualities (i.e., extension and its subordinate forms) deserve the name of qualities only as we conceive them to distinguish body from not-body, — corporeal from incorporeal substance. They are thus merely the attributes of *body as body*." It is clear, then, that, in knowing an object as extended, we know the object itself. Hence we may know not only qualities, but the objects in which they inhere; and, always knowing them in conjunction with each other, we naturally associate them inseparably with each other, so that, when we think of the one, the other always comes into the mind as its relative.

3. *Of spiritual substance and its manifestations.* — As to spiritual substance, the account of this is more difficult. Accustomed as we are to consider matter alone as a substance, it sounds quite incongruous to hear spirit spoken of as substance. The term here, however, is used in its most extended, and indeed in

its etymological sense; as the *substratum*, or that which underlies or supports our spiritual manifestations, as realized in consciousness. As we cannot conceive qualities as existing alone, but only as relative to some material object in which they inhere; so consciousness and the various forms of thought seem to imply a thinking substance, or being, of which these forms of thought are manifestations. And as in material substance, so here, we have no direct knowledge of this spiritual substance or mind or soul except through these manifestations. But while in the former case both the qualities and the substance are material, in this both the thought and the substance are spiritual. Our thoughts become known to us in and through consciousness; and, being so entirely different from the phenomena of matter, we ascribe them to a different nature, and view them as wholly relative to that nature. Thus the knowledge which we have of our spiritual nature is indirect, or inferential, but entirely satisfactory; so that we always think of it as the ground of our various thoughts, and hence associate them together. But I do not think we can be said to be directly *conscious* of a separate spiritual nature in us: if this were the case, no one could ever doubt it, and consequently there could be no such thing as a materialist, of which there are great numbers in existence.

4. *Both material and spiritual substances have a real existence.* — Both material and spiritual substances, then, exist. The view here taken is entirely different from that advocated by Hume and Mill and his associates, though attaching something of the same importance to the principle of association. It is not held, with Hume, that what we call material substance is merely the idea generated in the mind by our various sensations of the

so-called material qualities ; nor with Mill, that it is only a "permanent possibility of impressions," but that it has a real, positive existence, and is cognizable to us through our senses. So, too, the soul is regarded as having a distinct, independent existence, and not merely as an idea generated by many rapidly-succeeding states of consciousness, nor as only "a series of feelings aware of itself as past and future." While it is held that the attribute and its object, and the thought and the thinking principle, by being perpetually known together, are inseparably associated with each other, so as to seem entirely relative to each other, it is far from being held that the whole idea and reality of substance is a mere congeries or series of associated experiences. Such an assumption of the efficacy of the principle of association is not at all necessary to my view : but it is only demanded that it should be thought sufficient to account for the coherence of thoughts and things, which, in the above-named cases, always come into the mind together ; and this, it seems to me, it is fully competent to do.

5. *All existences are either substance or attribute.* — All existences are either substance or attribute. Thoughts, feelings, and volitions are attributes of spiritual substance, as primary and secondary qualities are attributes of material substance. Even appearances, or phenomenal as well as ideal existences, — as the pictures in the air in *mirage*, and the pictures before the mind in imagination, — are but modifications of matter and mind. So our idea of force, momentum, or power, is a conception of the mind, derived, I have no doubt, from the external reality of the effect of our own action on other objects, and of the perceived action of these objects upon each other and upon our own organism. And even

space and time must be considered as ideas of the mind, corresponding to the external possibility of free motion and succession in the sphere in which we live. Nothing (i.e. *no*-thing) is not an existence, unless it be a negative existence, if any one can tell what that is. Existence, or being, is contradictory of non-being; and hence we cannot believe a thing both to be and to not be at the same time, because the two states are impossible, one necessarily excluding the other.

SECTION III.

OF OUR IDEAS OF CAUSE AND EFFECT.

1. *The question stated.* — Cause and effect are relative ideas, like attribute and object; the one always implying and suggesting the other. And that the one should suggest the other may be accounted for, as in that case, on the principle of association. The ideas, however, are not merely relative to each other, but relative in the order of time, as antecedent and consequent; and not only so, but one as being the ground of the existence of the other, and that *necessarily* and *universally*. The causal judgment, as expressed by every one, is, not that this, that, and the other event must have had a cause, but that *every change or event must have a cause.* We can conceive no change as taking place without a cause. Events are not isolated, but are linked together as causes and effects. The problem, then, here is, not to account for the mere relativity of the ideas, but for the peculiar way in which they are related, or rather in which the things represented by the ideas are related. In short,

we are to inquire why it is that every one decides at once that every event *must have* a cause.

2. *Intuitive and empirical theories of causality.*—This has been accounted for variously. Many have held that it is an intuitive perception; that we are impelled to the decision by the very constitution of our nature, and, for this reason, cannot believe otherwise. This theory is sufficient to account for the facts, provided the existence of such an intuitive perception be admitted. Another theory, started by Hume, and followed up by Brown, Mill, and others, is, that our idea of causality is wholly derived from the perceived antecedency of objects or events to others which follow them in the continued succession of things. This doubtless is sufficient to account for the simple association of the ideas of cause and effect together, but not for the fact that one is viewed as representing something which is the *ground* of that represented by the other, or of their being associated together *as* cause and effect. Others, as Maine de Biran, derive our notion of causation from our own experience in producing effects through the operation of our wills in controlling and directing our organs in action. As it requires effort in us to produce an effect, we might certainly infer from this experience that *power*—an essential element in the causal idea—is necessary in producing change, but could not legitimately conclude that *every change must be produced by some cause.*

3. *Rational theories of causality.*—It thus appears that the various empirical theories fail to account for the most important element in the causal judgment; viz., its necessity and universality. For this reason, Hamilton resorts to what may be called a *rational* theory of the matter. As change in matter, and also in force, is

merely change in form, not in amount, every effect must be considered as only its cause or causes under a different form, and hence there is an actual continuity in things; and events must be indissolubly connected with each other in our minds, as things are in fact. But, not to name other objections to this theory, it merely accounts for the universal linking-together of events in our minds, not for their universal connection *as* cause and effect; unless because we must think the effect the same as the cause, only under another form, implies causation.

Let us try another rational theory, then. It seems to me that the causal judgment is best accounted for by the doctrine of *sufficient reason:* indeed, it is little more than another form of that doctrine. We soon learn from experience, if we do not conclude from a rational view of the case, that no change can take place where there is no change in the conditions. The billiard-ball not in use remains at rest on the table, which is perfectly horizontal; the water in a pool, unaffected by any extraneous influence, remains quiet; vegetation, while the earth is bound with frost and covered with snow, undergoes no change: and so in other cases. But let the table become inclined, or the ball be struck by the billiard-stick, or the wind blow upon the water, or the sun melt off the snow and shine warmly upon the earth, and a change immediately takes place. And, in all such cases, we say there is a good reason for it: there has been a change of conditions, and these new conditions we regard as the *cause,* — as having exerted an influence which resulted in the change. And since, without such influence, no change takes place, and we can conceive no possibility of any change without it, we decide with confidence that every change takes place by a change of conditions in the antecedents, and hence that every effect must have a cause.

4. *The final cause.*—The final cause is the end or aim had in view in doing or making any thing. It is called a cause, from its being conceived of as a reason or incitement to the agent to do the thing in question; and is said to be the *final* cause, inasmuch as it lies at the end of the work, and is supposed to operate till its completion. Thus we often hear it said that the final cause, or end, which God proposed to himself in creation, was to set forth his character to his intelligent creatures, or to work out their greatest good. At all events, the world is full of correspondences and adaptations, which imply design; as of the eye for the light, the horse for the rider, and the ox for the yoke. And as it is the distinctive act of human intelligence to conceive of ends, and contrive means to attain those ends, when we discover in our own bodies and other objects around us such striking evidences of design, and adaptation of means to ends, we can but regard them as evidences of the existence of a wise and beneficent Creator.

5. *First and second causes.*—This doctrine of causation leads directly back to a First Cause. The causes hitherto spoken of are but secondary causes. The lowest hypothesis which will satisfy the Christian, or even the theistic, idea of God, is, that he *concurs* in all

---

3. The *powers* of nature are its active principle; such as gravity, light, heat, electricity, chemical action, mechanical action, and the like. "Conditions," on the contrary, are the passive qualities of objects, or other attendant circumstances, which control and regulate the action of powers; as, in the above cases, the inclination of the table allowing the action of gravity, and the presence of snow preventing the action of the heat of the sun.

changes. Or in other words, if God has endowed matter with certain powers, these powers are not independent of himself: they must be sustained and seconded by him in order to be operative. But even if all the changes and transformations which we witness and which take place in the world, including growths of men, animals, and plants, are wholly effected by powers inherent in the things themselves, yet, being uniformly dependent one upon the other, — equally effects and causes, — however numerous, they must still be a dependent series, and plainly demand for a beginning a Cause which is not also an effect: otherwise existences, however far traced up, would be found to be dependent upon what is itself an effect, and the principle of causation would be made void. Our idea of causation finds its complete exemplification, and attains its absolute universality, only in God.

SECTION IV.

OF OUR IDEAS OF SPACE AND TIME.

1. *Origin of our notion of extension.* — Extension is limited space; and it has already been stated that we get our first idea of it through the mutual externality

---

5. This is what is called the cosmological argument for the existence of God; and, with the one from design referred to in the preceding paragraph, is the most striking and conclusive. There are other proofs of his existence, and especially the ontological proof, which argues from the idea of God to the truth of his existence. We find ourselves with an idea of God as an infinite and perfect being; and, as such an idea cannot be gained from the finite and imperfect things which surround us, it implies for its cause, it is contended, the Being himself.

of our sensations. Our nervous system, in which the susceptibility of sensations resides, is spread out through and over the whole body, so that the affections which produce sensations are actually separated from each other, and reveal themselves to us thus in our consciousness. Although apprehended by the mind at the centre of the organism, yet they are always recognized as being in that part of the body where they actually are, and hence more commonly at the surface; but, in whatever part of the system they reveal themselves, they must be more or less removed from each other. But what do we mean by saying that one is removed from the other? Why, that they are so related to each other, that we have to put forth a certain amount of exertion in moving the eye or the hand from one to the other. We thus reach the notions of *here* and *there*, which imply space, and are indeed fundamental elements from which the whole idea of extension follows. So when we speak of material objects as having the three dimensions of length, breadth, and thickness, what can we mean except it be that their external character can be described by certain motions in three directions? At all events, it is certain, that, were we explaining this character in things to one who did not understand the meaning of the words, we should illustrate it by such motions. All agree that we become *conscious* of extension in some such way as this; and the empirical philosopher holds that our idea of it is wholly *generated* by this experience, while the intuitionist regards the experience as merely the *occasion* of eliciting into consciousness a pre-existing but hitherto dormant idea of space.

2. *Origin of our notion of duration.* — As extension is limited space, so duration is a limited portion of time.

How, now, do we acquire our idea of duration? Duration is continuance in succession, as extension is continuance in direction. Duration, therefore, is relative to conscious existence: it supposes some being who is conscious of succession in his own experience. It implies a *now* and a *then* in one's experience. And what do we mean by now and then, unless it be two points in our experience separated by more or less intervening incidents of experience? We recognize an interval between the two, not, however, as a blank, but as filled up with and measured by the intervening experience of life. We first get the idea of duration, perhaps, by our heart-beats, following each other in such rapid succession; or by the recurrence of other feelings or acts, as of cold, heat, hunger, exertion of the mind or muscles, and the like. And, having got the idea of duration, we soon learn to measure it, — at first loosely by such experience as that referred to above, say, by the interval between our heart-beats, or that required to move from a given point to another, and then more accurately by the recurrence of day and night; the varying positions of the sun and the other heavenly bodies; the changing shadows of natural objects, and then of artificial objects (as in the sun-dial); and, finally, by the swing of the pendulum, each vibration of which occupies a definite portion of the time required for the revolution of the sun. Few, if any, will doubt that it is by some such experience as this that we become conscious of our notion of duration; though, as in the case of extension, many hold that the idea is merely elicited by this experience, not generated by it.

3. *The intuitional and empirical theories discussed.* — As is implied in what has already been said, the intu-

itionist holds that the ideas of space and time are antecedent to those of extension and duration, and alone give significance to the experience described above. Kant regarded space and time as the *forms* furnished by the mind in perception by the senses, as the "categories of the understanding" and the "ideas of the pure reason" are the forms furnished by the mind in its higher processes of thought. According to this view, the *here* and the *there*, the *now* and the *then*, are furnished directly by the mind itself, and not derived from our experience: we rather *posit* things in space and time, in the gross, than ascertain by our experience that they are there. This is the view, which, with some variations, is held by intuitionists in general. The question, then, is, whether we really have or need, in order to account for all the facts, any other idea of points separated from each other in space and time, so-called, than different sensations in our organism, from one of which, in the one case, the hand or the eye may start, and, after a certain amount of exertion, reach the other; and, in the other case, of like sensations in our internal experience, or life, connected by a given amount of actual or possible experience intervening. And, if we need nothing more than this to make up our notion of extension and duration, — as it seems to me we do not, — why assume the latent existence of intuitive ideas of space and time which are first elicited into consciousness by this experience? Or if it be said that it is not claimed that we have ready-formed ideas on these subjects which are thus brought out, but merely the ready-furnished *power* of forming them on the occurrence of the appropriate experience, we reply, that this is precisely what is here contended for, and proved, too, by the actual form ing of them ; not, however, merely in consequence of the experience, but in and by it.

4. *Infinite space and time.* — But space and time, it is said, are conceived of by us as infinite, while our experience in extension and duration must necessarily be very limited. And if, now, our ideas of space and time are wholly derived from experience, how does it happen that these ideas are without limit? It is true that we cannot fix a limit to space, nor assign a beginning or end to time, even in imagination. But we cannot, of course, have a positive idea of infinity in any form. We merely conceive of the extension and duration of which we have continued experience as existing everywhere. They seem to us ubiquitous in their nature. As we find that space is necessary to the existence of all material objects, and time to all continued existences, we must assume the presence of space and time wherever we suppose it possible that there may be such existences: the possibility of the existences determines the necessity and universality of the conceptions. Wherever such existences may be, there must be room for them. And can we place any limit to the possibility of such existences? Wherever the universe extends, there these may be. All admit the extension and duration which we experience to be of precisely the same nature as space and time in general; to be, indeed, parts of them: and as in these we always find an overplus beyond our actual experience, always room beyond, we naturally and necessarily extend the same to all the possibilities of existence. This, as it seems to me, is all that there is in the so-called necessary conceptions of infinite space and time.

5. *Relation between space and time.* — Space and time

are both quantities, — the one *extensive* quantity, and the other *protensive* quantity, as designated by Hamilton; the one being the measure of our external, and the other of our internal, experience. But, of these two quantities, space is evidently the primary, time being but secondary to it. Hence many of the terms which belong properly to space are applied also to time, as *before* and *after*, *long* and *short*, and the like, where time is evidently conceived under local relations. So the measure of time is made sensible to us by motions of extended bodies in space; as by the movements of the heavenly bodies, the swing of the pendulum, &c. The terms *now* and *then*, also, are applied to the beginning and the end of a motion in space, as well as *here* and *there*, which properly indicate these points; the idea being, that there always is, or may be, a certain amount of internal experience during any motion. Indeed, time is more commonly conceived under the image of space; and it is easy to see why it should be so. Space is not only primary to time in being the fundamental condition of all material existences, whether animate or inanimate, but, being the measure of these material things, its physical elements are more obtrusive, and hence more easily laid hold of.

6. *Origin of mathematical axioms.* — As the relations involved in the ideas of space and time constitute the chief subjects of mathematical science, it will be proper here to consider the origin and authority of a few of the mathematical axioms; such as, that "a whole is greater than either of its parts," "two straight lines cannot enclose a space," "a number added to itself makes double that number." As to the authority of these axioms, no one questions it. They are appealed to with perfect

confidence by all, and are most unquestionably true. But there are different views in regard to their origin; some holding that they express intuitive perceptions, and others that they are judgments or conclusions arrived at through experience, or by a rational view of each case. I do not see any need of calling in the aid of intuition here, any more than in the preceding cases. Suppose it be true that a part of an object may be removed, so small as not to be perceptible by the senses, and hence that in such a case we can't distinguish between the whole and its remaining part by our natural senses: still we may be able to do it by the microscope, and can certainly distinguish the two rationally. And it should be recollected that mathematical wholes and parts are ideal wholes and parts, and are always to be viewed and judged rationally. In like manner, though we cannot actually follow out two straight lines to infinity, we can follow them far enough to conclude from the course which they are taking that they can never meet in more than one direction, and hence cannot enclose a space. And as to the doubling of a number by adding it to itself, this may be proved by counting the fingers.

SECTION V.

OF THE INFINITE AND THE ABSOLUTE.

1. *What these are, and the apparent contradictions which they involve.* — The ideas of space, time, and God, constitute what has been called the Infinite and the Absolute; or, more briefly, the Unconditioned. It is in these ideas that Kant, and after him Hamilton, find

so many antinomies, or contradictions. The chief of these are the following: 1st, If God be infinite in his nature, he must include in himself all things, and hence cannot be *distinguished from* the universe; and yet, as infinite, he cannot be *identified with* the finite things which make up the universe. 2d, Of time we cannot conceive an *absolute beginning*, nor an *infinite non-beginning*. 3d, We cannot think of space as *absolutely limited* in any direction, nor yet as *infinitely unlimited*.

Of these apparent contradictions it is sufficient to say, that, in each case the subject of thought being assumed to be infinite in its nature, we cannot, of course, positively conceive of it as such, since we are confessedly incapable of conceiving the infinite; and, being infinite, we cannot, of course, conceive of it as finite, which it is not. As, for instance, of time: time being infinite, we are incompetent to conceive of it as such, and hence cannot conceive of it as having an *infinite non-beginning;* and, since it is infinite, we cannot conceive of it as finite; i.e., as having an *absolute beginning*.

2. *The infinite and the absolute defined.* — There has been a good deal of juggling with the abstractions called the Infinite and the Absolute. Infinite is a negative term, meaning that which has no end or limit; which to us can only mean that which has no end or limit *as far as we can trace it in thought.* Thus space (being infinite) is extension carried out in all directions, so that we can place no limits to it in thought. So infinite goodness, wisdom, &c., are simply these qualities as exhibited among men, but carried out to perfection. And here we have the idea of the Absolute, which means *completed, perfected.* Infinite goodness or wisdom becomes absolute goodness or wisdom when perfect in its

kind; but, as the point of perfection is beyond the reach of our scrutiny, they may be spoken of indifferently as infinite or absolute.

3. *The unconditioned.* — Hamilton uses the term unconditioned to include both the infinite and the absolute. Strictly speaking, the unconditioned is that which bears no relations to any thing else; of which, therefore, we can neither think nor assert any thing, since this would imply some such relation. If there be any such unconditioned, we cannot, of course, know any thing about it: it must be to us as zero. There may, indeed, be many things in the universe about which we know nothing; but this is quite a different thing from saying that there are things about which nothing *can be* thought or said consistently with their nature. The fact is, the infinite, the absolute, and the unconditioned, as they have been treated by Hamilton, Mansel, and many German and French philosophers, are mere metaphysical puzzles, misleading and bewildering by their vagueness and incomprehensibility. It is absurd to say that nothing beyond our own imaginings, or which really touches the subject, can be known or said about space, time, and God, when we are continually thinking and speaking, and that, too, with a conscious intelligence, on these subjects. We do not know God in his fulness or absolute nature, it is true; but our knowledge of him is not wholly nought, nor negative even.

APPENDIX.

ABSTRACT OF THE HISTORY OF SPECULATIVE PHILOSOPHY.

1. Philosophy has been defined to be, "the research of causes." It is the fruit of the inquisitive or speculative spirit of man. By the constitution of the human mind, all experience awakens reflection. We are not merely conscious of the successive facts and changes which transpire within and about us, as they pass, but are arrested by them, and led to reflect upon them. They awaken not only consciousness, but curiosity. The mind dwells upon them, compares them, contemplates, *speculates* them; and in so doing, draws inferences from them, generalizes them, and, by degrees, ascertains their true relations and significance. Philosophy, therefore, in its incipient state, must be as old as our race. Its rude beginnings are first seen in the mythologies and cosmogonies of nations. These are as truly a search for causes, or first principles, as the later and more rational theologies and philosophies.

2. Among the ancient nations, philosophic thought advanced but little beyond its mythological tendencies, except in Greece, and subsequently in Rome. The history of ancient philosophy is little more than the history of Grecian philosophy. Among the Greeks, philosophy passed through every stage of development, and

presents, in epitome, a complete history of speculation. Here, as elsewhere, it commenced in mythologies and theogonies. The elements and powers of nature were personified and elevated into deities, as the generating and regulative principles of nature and natural phenomena. Facts were thus rudely classified and nature traced back to first causes. These causes, however, were rather imaginative than rational, assumed more as postulates of the religious instinct, than as deductions of reason. Greek philosophy, properly so called, begins with the Ionian Philosophers, *Thales*, *Anaximander*, and *Anaximenes*, about 600 B.C.

3. Philosophy, at the outset, would naturally be one-sided and partial. Thought, at first, would not penetrate very deeply into things, nor take a very wide survey of the objects of nature. It would be likely to seize upon only the coarser and more obtrusive elements and relations, and be satisfied with the most partial results. Commencing with the mere husk and shell of things, in the progress of ideas, we should expect it to penetrate deeper and deeper, and extend its survey to a wider and still wider circle, till it embraced all objects, whether near or remote, and all elements, whether coarse or subtile, and harmonized them under one consistent, rational view. And such we shall find to have been the constant tendency of thought. Philosophy has progressed as thought in general has progressed.

4. Primitive philosophy, then, will more commonly be of a physical nature. Intelligence will be regarded as little more than one of the many phenomena of the material universe, akin to, and scarcely more striking than motion, which is observed to exist in even unorganized matter. In the real ignorance of causes, all

nature will seem in some sense animated, and man scarcely more so than the rest. The first step of the philosopher, therefore, in attempting to account for what he witnesses around him, and to reduce the multifariousness of nature to unity, will be to assume some element, which may serve as the common basis of both mental and material qualities, and from whose various transformations, all the objects of nature, with all the phenomena of intelligence, life, and change, arise. At the same time, from the imaginative character of primitive ages, this *prima materia*, or elementary principle, will naturally be endowed with an inherent, dynamic force of self development, so as to operate from within all the various changes and transformations which it undergoes. Of this nature were the *archæ*, or first principles, of the Ionian philosophers.

5. THALES, the first in order, was born at Miletus, a flourishing Greek colony on the coast of Asia Minor, about 640 B.C. He is regarded by Aristotle as the first who attempted to establish a beginning of things on rational grounds, without the aid of myths. His doctrine was, "water is the beginning of all things." In looking around upon nature, organized and unorganized, this seemed the most .universal element. He found moisture everywhere. Every thing seemed to be nourished by moisture, and indeed, to be made up of it, so as to be only moisture variously transformed. Earth was but water condensed, and air but water evaporized. He assumed water, therefore, as the universal basis of all things, as the *invariable substance* of which all special objects are but the *variable forms.* Hence, it was the single problem of his philosophy to

resolve all special existences into this, to show that this was the grand residuum in all analysis.

6. Anaximander, born also at Miletus, and contemporary with Thales, though somewhat younger, is commonly regarded as having pursued the same line of physical philosophizing. With him the first principle of all things seems to have been a sort of *chaos* (*apiron*), or, as Aristotle appears to have regarded it, a *mixture* of elements in a limitless and formless state. His *prima materia*, then, was a sort of general substratum, of an unorganized and heterogeneous nature, from which sprang, apparently by an inherent dynamic* action, the various objects, beings, and changes which constitute the phenomenal world. He seems to have felt that no single element was susceptible of all the various transformations necessary to constitute the different objects in nature. His analysis found more than one element in all objects, and so he conceived the different elements as in combination from the first, and evolving themselves into different forms to constitute the sensible world.

7. Anaximenes, the last† of the illustrious Miletian trio, known as the founders of the Ionian philosophy, was born about a century after Thales (548 B.C.), and pursued the same general line of investigation. With

---

* Ritter, however, considers his philosophy as of the mechanical sort, and Lewes, as of the mathematical. But the view expressed in the text is the more common and credible opinion. See Thompson's note to Wm. Archer Butler's History of Ancient Philosophy, vol. i, p. 32[illegible].

† *Diogenes* of Apollonia, in Crete, about a century later, took up the doctrine of Anaximenes, and further refined it. With him the "air" became *intelligent*, as well as animate, the *soul* both of man and nature,—the elementary *deity*, in short, animating and actuating all things. See p. 42, 1.

him *air* was the beginning, or first principle, of all things. This seemed to him most like the general animating and constitutive principle of nature. It seemed to unite both material and spiritual qualities. It filled space, investing and nourishing all things, and was ever in motion, as if possessing an inherent spirit of life. All life was supported by air; the earth and all solid bodies were only air condensed in various degrees, while heat and cold were produced by different degrees of density in the same primal element.

8. HERACLITUS of Ephesus (born about 503 B.C.,) continued the Ionian philosophy in substantially the same spirit as its original founders, though with more breadth and a greater tendency to the spiritual. With him *fire* was the first principle and substance of the universe. It was the common ground both of mental and material phenomena; not only the animating but the intelligent and regulative principle of nature. The phenomenal world was but a successive kindling and subsidence of this primal fire. He taught that the very existence of sensible things consists in change, in becoming and subsiding. All things are in transition, in a perpetual *flow*, or change, as reported by the senses. This is of the very nature of fire, which perpetually enkindles and extinguishes itself by an internal, self-regulating principle. Material objects exhibit this character in their ever-changing phenomena, and mind in its restless and fleeting thoughts, — for even God and the soul of man are but a more subtle flame. His system, in short, was that of *unrest* in every thing, produced by a sort of pantheistic development of the subtle, intelligent element which he called fire.*

* Heraclitus is known in history, or fable, as the *crying* philosopher;

9. Anaxagoras of Clazomenæ (born about 500 B.C.) is the last of the Ionian philosophers, and even in him the system had lost much of its original character. The tendency to spirituality, which was observed in Heraclitus, in Anaxagoras was carried so far that he substituted for the vague vital force of nature, adopted by the previous masters of the school, an infinite, independent, omnipresent principle of *intelligence* (*nous*). At the same time, he held that all space was filled with infinitely small particles of inert matter of different kinds, which the regulative intelligence formed into objects differing as the primitive elements of which they were constituted differed. Natural objects were no longer regarded as self-developments of one or many elements, but as formed from an inert primitive chaos by an independent intelligent power, operating upon it from without. If we have not here the full conception of a Divine Creator and Providence, we have something very like it. Anaxagoras, though born at Clazomenæ, spent the prime of his life at Athens, and there taught his doctrine of an All-ordering Intelligence, which was afterwards so nobly carried out by Socrates and Plato.

10. We have thus seen in this series of philosophers, a constant tendency to more and more spiritual views of nature. Starting with the grosser elements as primal principles in the constitution of nature, and mind as wholly subordinate to matter, — a mere quality of

---

probably from his wearing a gloomy aspect, or, as some think, on account of the fleeting, unsatisfactory view of things to which his philosophy led. He is also called the *obscure*, most likely from the depth and peculiarity of his views. Thompson says of him (note to Butler's History of Philosophy), "He was perhaps the greatest speculative genius among the fore-runners of Plato."

it, — they gradually adopted the finer elements as first principles, and at last wholly extricated mind from nature, and placed the organization and control of matter entirely under the superintendence of a distinct principle of intelligence. Of course, it was admitted from the beginning, that the intelligence of man was superior to that of other animals around him, and especially to that of unorganized matter; but it was regarded as differing in degree rather than in kind. Every thing was regarded as having a species of animation, and hence a kind of intelligence, which was only more developed and more perfect in man and the gods, not at all different in kind. But little attention, therefore, was paid to the theory of knowledge. The Ionian philosophers do not appear to have held to any other knowledge than that of phenomena, and this, in general, they held to be very inadequate and deceptive.

11. If now we turn from the eastern shores of the Ægean to the western shores of the Adriatic, from the outlying Greeks in the east, to the outlying Greeks in the west, we shall discover a philosophical movement of quite a different kind. The line of speculation is here quite reversed. It is not so much the material which constitutes the world that is investigated, as the thought which underlies it; not so much the phenomenal world, as the intelligible and ideal. The phenomenal world seemed to these western philosophers too changeable and relative, not only to the mind, but to the particular organization of the senses of each individual, to be regarded as the real world. At a period when the true theory of perception was not understood, and the various "fallacies of the senses" were unex-

plained, sense-knowledge would naturally be discredited, and seem scarcely worthy of being considered knowledge. Thus, the inability to handle intelligibly and satisfactorily the world as it presents itself to the senses, drove these philosophers to the speculation of the ideal world, in which no such difficulties and contradictions occur. The succession of philosophers here referred to, though differing considerably in their views, and not all of them historically very closely connected, constitute what has been called the Italic School of philosophy.

12. PYTHAGORAS, the first in the series, was born in Samos, an island of the Ægean Sea, about 600 B.C., but spent the greater part of his mature life at Crotona, in the southern part of Italy. His fundamental doctrine was, "number is the principle of things." By this he could not have meant that number was the material or constitutive principle of things, but their determining principle, since number or proportion dominates in all things. Things are and can be only copies of certain forms or proportions. Such a doctrine was easily carried out into the mystical notions of number and harmony ascribed to Pythagoras and his followers. The soul, which he regarded as fire in its substance, was a copy of unity, the perfect number, and in allusion perhaps to his doctrine of the transmigration of souls, was called a "self-moving unit." At the same time, the divine mind was the primitive unit, from which all human minds were derived, and to which they stood related as units of an inferior order. The philosophy of Pythagoras has been called mathematical, but as it assumed a rational rather than a physical ground of nature, it deserves rather to be ranked as

metaphysical, with that of the Eleatic philosophers, to which we now proceed.

13. XENOPHANES the founder of the other great branch of the Italic Philosophy, called the Eleatic (from Elea, in Italy, the seat of the school), was born at Colophon, in Asia Minor, about the same time as Pythagoras, and having wandered from place to place in the character of a philosophic rhapsodist, finally settled in the above-named place in Italy. Although he alludes to Pythagoras, he does not seem to have had any proper historical connection with him. Indeed, his system, though having the common peculiarity of assuming a rational rather than a material ground for things, was entirely different, both in the character of its initial principle, and in its details. Instead of the barely harmonizing, or at most, but logically causal principle of number, Xenophanes assumed as the ground and operating cause of the changes in outward nature, an uncaused, independent, and intelligent Divinity. All outward changes were caused by the acts of his volition, and, apparently, were operated in a real world distinct from himself.

14. PARMENIDES, commonly supposed to have been the disciple of Xenophanes, was a native of Elea, and further carried out the system of his master. With him, the Deity of Xenophanes became *The One*, or Absolute Being. The phenomenal world was but an illusion — but a contexture of mental phantasms, without any reality corresponding to it. Real thought was confined to the absolute alone; so that thought and being were one. "He distinctly recognized that the existent, as such, is unconnected with all separation or juxtaposition, as well as with all suc-

cession, all relation to space or time, all coming into existence, and all change; from which arose the problem of all subsequent metaphysics, to reconcile the mutually opposed ideas of *Existence* and *Coming into Existence*."

15. ZENO, the last of the series of philosophers known distinctly as Eleatic, and a favorite disciple of Parmenides, was born at Elea about 500 B.C., and visited Athens with his master when about forty years old. He seems to have accepted the system of Parmenides as he left it, and to have devoted himself wholly to the task of defending it. To defend the *one*, he had to disprove the possibility of the *many*. This he attempted by exhibiting dialectically the contradictions involved in the common space-and-time relations. These contradictions are: 1. that as any space is infinitely divisible, no motion can commence in it; 2. that hence, the swiftest moving object cannot overtake that which moves most slowly; 3. that a body supposed to be in motion, inasmuch as it occupies space, must actually be at rest; 4. that one and the same space of time is both long and short. These are the subjects of his famous fallacies, some of which, at least, still await a solution. Zeno invented and applied to philosophy the method of *Dialectics*, which afterwards became so famous in the hands of Socrates and Plato, and was so abused by the Megarian philosophers.

16. EMPEDOCLES, of Agrigentum, in Sicily (born about 450 B.C.), belongs in spirit, as well as in locality, to the general class of Italic philosophers, though holding many Ionic and other views. He conceived the world as composed of four distinct elements, originally combined in a sort of chaos (called by him a

sphere), with two developing forces, *love* and *hate*. This totality of elements and forces he called God. He was, therefore, what in modern phrase is called a Pantheist; since his deity combined in himself both matter and developing power, so as to produce all things out of himself. The *One* or *God* of the Eleatics was thus retained, but more in the character of the self-developing principles of the Ionics. In the assumption of a chaos of different elements, he may seem to have borrowed from Anaxagoras and with him to have prepared the way for the atomic theory of Democritus, as he certainly did for the theory of perception held by this latter philosopher. Empedocles seems to have first propounded the doctrine, which, under various forms, has had so much influence in the history of philosophy,* that "like is only perceived by like." Particles, he taught, are continually emanating from objects, which, entering the body through the pores, come in contact with like particles in the human frame, and are thus perceived; as though perception was a sort of chemical action between particles.

17. Democritus, then (born at Abdera, in Thrace, about 460 B.C.), the chief founder † and cultivator of the Atomic Philosophy, related as are his views to those of both Empedocles and Anaxagoras, naturally closes the double movement of Greek philosophy on the opposite shores of Ionia and Italy, that a new and more hopeful movement may commence from Athens,

---

* See Wight's Hamilton, p. 190, note.

† Leucippus is called the founder of the school; but as he has left no record of his views, they are known only through Democritus and other reporters. Democritus, it will be recollected, is known as the *laughing* philosopher, in contrast with Heraclitus, the *crying* philosopher.

which has come to be the true centre of Grecian influence and refinement. As already stated, Democritus adopted substantially the doctrine held by Empedocles, of perception through the emanation of material particles or films from objects, brought into contact with corresponding atoms in the human frame. At the same time, the *atoms* of Democritus may have been suggested by the distinct elementary substances of Empedocles and Anaxagoras, though they differed from these elements in the important particulars of being indivisible, homogeneous, varying only in form, and, since existing in a vacuum, susceptible of motion, and hence of generation or dissolution, which they were constantly undergoing by the power of Fate, thus constituting the phenomenal world. Besides, Democritus taught that all the senses were but modifications of touch, and seems to have made the distinction between the primary and secondary qualities of matter. His system was decidedly materialistic, and was afterwards taken up and further elaborated by the Epicureans.

18. As we have already seen, the scattered rays of philosophy were fast concentrating at Athens. First issuing from the eastern shores of the Ægean, they had rested a while upon "sunny Italy," and glanced even upon the hyperborean regions of Thrace, till now they were rapidly converging upon the art-crowned Acropolis of Athena. Nearly all the more distinguished of the recent philosophers, both of the Ionic and of the Italic schools, had visited Athens, and many of them had taught and spent a large part of their life there. Thus was philosophy fairly inaugurated at this radiating centre of culture and influence. But, with the genuine philosophers, came also the sham philoso-

phers, called Sophists, or Wise Men, as professed teachers of the wisdom of the age. They were mostly from the outlying settlements of the Greeks, and generally had studied philosophy in some of the schools already described. Their object was to popularize philosophy and make it practical; to make the materials and culture wrought out by philosophy the basis of a liberal education for the ambitious youth of the free states of Greece,— in short, to adapt philosophy to public life, and make it speak and act. Their teaching, therefore, was a sort of philosophized rhetoric. Philosophy in their hands had no longer the simple aim of discovering truth; it became a sort of art, or knack,* and hence was regarded by mere speculatists, like Plato, as but a mock-wisdom, a sham. †

19. The leading sophists were PROTAGORAS, GORGIAS, HIPPIAS, and PRODICUS. As professed teachers of practical wisdom they received pay for their instruction. They doubtless differed from each other in many of their philosophical views, but all, apparently, held, with Protagoras, to a mere sense-knowledge of things, and that "the individual is the measure of all things." Hence, there was to them no absolute standard of truth and right; these varied with each one's individual perceptions. It does not seem certain that they fully carried out this view to its legitimate results in morals, though Socrates showed them that it was as applicable to moral as to metaphysical distinctions, and as subversive of the one as of the other. Though justly chargeable with narrow and unsafe views in philosophy and morals, and of having contributed to the undermin-

---

* See the Gorgias of Plato, 465, A., and at large.

† See the chapter on the Sophists in Grote's History of Greece.

ing of morality by their rash and over-confident assertion of the sufficiency of the individual reason; yet, as active, popular teachers of wisdom, they diffused knowl edge and awakened scientific inquiry much more extensively among the people than they ever had been before, and laid the foundation for that wonderful intellectual activity and culture, which henceforth distinguished Athens above all other Grecian cities.

20. Contemporaneously with the Sophists, SOCRATES (born in one of the suburbs of Athens, 468 B.C.), the most remarkable and gifted of the Greek philosophers, makes his appearance on the stage of Atheniam history. The son of a sculptor and a midwife, he united in his character and views, the ideality of the artist with the practical skill of the artisan, and was equally expert in fashioning the conceptions of his pupils and in assisting them in being delivered of them. Springing from the middle class of society, and drawing his philosophy from his own experience and thoughts, rather than from books and professed teachers, he ever retained his sympathy and intercourse with the common people, and hence held his discussions in the shops and at the corners of the streets, exhibiting and enforcing his views by such familiar and homely illustrations as all could comprehend. As described by Plato and Xenophon, he opposed himself, in these discussions, partly to the physical philosophers — whose speculations he considered not only as unfruitful, but as little less than irreverent — and partly to the Sophists. In opposition to the mere sense-knowledge and individual opinion of the latter class of philosophers, he appealed to the intuitive perceptions and general convictions of men, as a solid foundation for the stability of truth and duty.

21. Socrates left no writings, and indeed taught no complete system of philosophy. He merely awakened, "watered," and fructified the germs of philosophic thought in the minds of others. He introduced a new *method*, rather than a new system of truth. His method was that of *induction*, leading to valid *definitions* or conceptions. Starting with some one of the general notions relating to man or society, to truth or duty, he gradually *led in* the mind of his opponent farther and farther towards the centre or essence of the conception, by showing one thing after another, commonly included in the notion, to be inconsistent with, or non-essential to, it. He thus taught men how to revise and purify their thoughts, which is the great end of metaphysical philosophy.* In these discussions he necessarily exhibited his opinions upon most of the important questions in philosophy, politics, morals, and religion, which always leaned to the side of the permanent, the absolute, the ideal, as opposed to the empirical and the changeable. His most positive teachings pertain to morals, where he held the paradoxical sentiment, that virtue was but wisdom, and hence was a science which might be taught. Vice, then, was but the fruit of ignorance. This might all be true, were it not for the influence of passion and habit, or wrong bias. But these are so important disturbing influences as to entirely discredit the theory. As wisdom and virtue were the same, of course, virtue and happiness would be the same; knowing the right would lead to right action, and right

* With Socrates, philosophy first became primarily a criticism of knowledge, a scrutiny of thought in order to determine its validity and value; and this has ever since been the chief problem of metaphysical philosophy.

action to happiness, i.e., true happiness would be found alone in virtue; which, also, we find to have been a doctrine of Socrates.

22. From the vigorous root of the Socratic life and teaching there sprang up various offshoots, externally more or less akin to the parent stock, but generally quite alien in nature, and often engrafted with germs from other stocks. The extraordinary personal interest connected with the character and teaching of Socrates drew around him disciples of different temperaments and aims, as well as those with different local prejudices and variously pre-occupied by antecedent instruction in the other schools. At the same time, the wide and free scope of his instruction, as well as the peculiarity and somewhat undeveloped state of some of his doctrines, gave opportunity for different interpretations, and a basis for the rearing of widely differing systems. We should not be surprised, therefore, to find his disciples splitting up into varying sects immediately after his death. Free thought always produces sects, whether in philosophy or religion. The chief of these sects are the following: —

23. (I.) The MEGARIC SCHOOL. The seat of this school was Megara, and the founder EUCLID (not the mathematician), who was born at Megara about 440 B.C. Euclid had been a disciple of the Eleatic Parmenides before he heard Socrates. His system, therefore, very naturally partook of that of both his teachers; — it appears to have been simply that of the *One* Eleatic, invested with the *ethical* coloring of Socrates. His *one* was *The Good*, but whether he attached any distinctly ethical meaning to *the good* seems uncertain. It is doubtful whether his ethical element was any thing

more than a coloring of Socratic language, while his real views were substantially the same as the Eleatics, not merely identifying virtue and science, as Socrates had done, but absorbing the moral into the rational, and making speculation the Chief Good. Euclid was followed by EUBULIDES, DIODORUS, ALEXINUS, and STILPO in the same general line of philosophizing. Like the Eleatics, their great instrument was logic, which they abused even more than Zeno. Stilpo more fully developed the ethical aspects of *The One*, by regarding the internal consciousness of personality as but an illusion, like the external consciousness of the phenomenal world, and making a profound impersonal *indifference* the highest attainable excellence. He was thus the author of the Stoical doctrine of *apathy*, afterwards so celebrated.

24. (II.) The CYRENAIC SCHOOL. This school was founded by ARISTIPPUS of Cyrene in Africa, a man of wealth and gayety, who, visiting Athens in the time of Socrates became his disciple, and remained with him till near the time of his death, when he quitted Athens, and after several years of travel in quest of knowledge and indulgence, finally returned to Cyrene and put forth his doctrine of "Pleasure the Chief Good." With him, the doctrine of Socrates, that virtue is happiness, was inverted, so as to become, happiness, or rather, pleasure, is virtue. The rule of pleasure was the rule of right, not the reverse. Pleasure and pain were the true *criteria* of actions; there was no higher *criterion*, no other indeed. Pleasures did not even differ in kind, they were all on a level. His doctrine was, the greatest present enjoyment is the greatest good, not holding even to a regulated happiness, as the Epicureans did later. Such a philosophy was but

little more than a license to indulgence, and of course, could not have had much credit with serious and earnest men. It is scarcely worth naming, except as the precursor of Epicureanism.

25. (III.) The Cynic School.— This was established by Antisthenes, an austere disciple of Socrates, in a quarter of Athens called Cynosarges, whence, probably, the name of the school. As a school of philosophy it is of little account; it had no philosophic system deserving the name, but only a repulsive, snarling asceticism. It cannot be denied that there was something bordering upon asceticism, both in the rigid virtue and singular if not shabby dress of Socrates. There was, also, a certain contempt and defiance of common opinions in his doctrines and manners. These were easily exaggerated by austere natures into the disgusting asceticism of the Cynics. Both the founder, and his most distinguished disciple, Diogenes, were known by the common appellation, "the dog," from their filthy, snarling habits. They possessed, undoubtedly, a certain rude wit and virtue, and have left many pointed and pithy sayings, but are of little account as speculative philosophers. They are only named here as precursors of the Stoics.

26. Plato alone (born at Athens 430 B.C.), in his system of philosophy, truly represented the spirit of his master. Joining him at the age of twenty, and remaining with him some eight years, he fully imbibed his spirit. He was the "beloved disciple," who sympathetically received the whole spirit of the life and philosophy of his master into the soil of a rich and congenial nature, where it vegetated and brought forth fruit to perfection. But his system, though thoroughly Socratic

in spirit, is a great enlargement of that of his master, and embraces many other elements. After the death of Socrates, he left Athens and spent some twelve years abroad, visiting the different schools of Greek philosophy, and extending his travels even to Sicily and Egypt. He was thus prepared by his extensive acquaintance with different systems, as well as by his comprehensive genius, to survey the whole field of antecedent philosophy from a Socratic point of view, and harmonize the various conflicting views in an enlarged and purified reproduction of the system of his master. Accordingly, on his return from his travels, at the age of forty, he established himself as teacher of philosophy, just outside of the city, upon a small estate inherited from his father, within the enclosure of the public garden or gymnasium, called the Academy, which henceforth became the name of his school. Here he was soon surrounded with a band of disciples, and, with only two considerable interruptions, on occasion of his second and third visits to Sicily, continued his instruction and the preparation of his extensive works to the end of his life, at the age of eighty-one.

27. Plato continued the distinction of the Eleatics and Pythagoreans between the permanent and the phenomenal world, but in a much more fruitful and consistent form. The great aim of the teaching of Socrates, as we have seen, was to establish clear and true conceptions of things in the minds of his pupils. In perfect accordance with this, we find the central principle of the system of Plato to have been, the doctrine of *ideas*, or conceptions objectified, and made real. These were his permanent world, being both the original archetypal forms of things, and the permanent ele-

ment in nature, which alone was perceived, all else being changeable, phenomenal, producing only deceptive sensations. Matter, with him, was a mere *potentiality*, or *condition* for the appearance of ideas under a contingent form, its whole reality and perceptibility depending upon its *participation* in the eternal archetypes. The impression made on the organism, or *sensitive soul*, as he called it, by external objects, was not a knowledge of these objects; it was only the apprehension by the reason of the ideal element in the object that was true perception, which apprehension was but a *reviving* ("*reminiscence*") of a knowledge obtained in an antecedent state of existence, when reason stood face to face with being.

28. Professor Butler * thus briefly states the grounds and consequences of the Platonic theory of perception by ideas: "1st, that a true knowledge or communion of reason with the reality of things is ensured by the kindred, or even homogeneous, nature of reason and ideas; 2ndly, that this intimate connection is testified by the impassioned aspiration † of the instructed soul for the perfection to be found only in the ideal world; 3dly, that the great business of the philosophic cultivator of his intelligence, is, by the constant exercise of accurate abstraction, to fit the qualities of sense to represent the everlasting models of the sphere of truth and being; 4thly, that we may well conclude the rational nature of man, formed as it is for ideal conception, to be *eternal* as ideas themselves; and though the sensible world itself is, by the participation of ideas, as perfect as the dull obduracy of its material subject

* Lectures on the History of Ancient Philosophy, vol. ii. p. 147

† Referring to the Platonic *Eros*, or love for the ideal.

will permit, yet to the philosophic soul it can never appear in any other light than as a restriction to the inborn energies of the spirit, suggesting, indeed, the absolutely good and fair and true, but clouding and concealing the very perfection it suggests."

29. The predominant spirit and aim of the philosophy of Plato is *eminently ethical.* It proposes as its object, the purification of the soul by the contemplation of ideal truth and excellence. The True, the Beautiful, and the Good are all one; or rather, the two former are merged in the latter, — the true and the fair both alike minister to the good. The Good or the Perfect is alike the end of both. The study of truth, therefore, is the study of goodness; and philosophy is the purification of the soul. This is only carrying out to its consequences the doctrine of Socrates, that knowledge is virtue. True happiness, too, was the fruit of philosophy, with Plato, as it had been of virtue or wisdom, with Socrates. Thus philosophy was the chief good with him, but only because it was the pursuit of the Good through the True. Indeed, the Good was the grand end of God himself, both in making the world and in all his acts. The Good determined all his actions, as it should those of men.

30. To borrow again from that admirable expounder of the doctrines of Plato, Professor Butler: * "This principle of Rationality is a direct consequence from the entire scheme of Platonism. The system supposes the orginal unity of the Beautiful, the Just, and the Good, in the *True;* the True being, as it were, the supporting or substantiating; the Good, the characterizing idea; the Beautiful and Just accompanying both:

* Lectures on the History of Ancient Philosophy, vol. ii., p. 283, *seq.*

the True being the very reality of things; the Good, the final cause of their being; and the others investing the True out of the strength of that final cause,—for wherever is the ἀγαθόν [the good], there will infallibly be the highest measure of *harmonious proportion;* and proportion is the essential idea of both the Beautiful and the Just. . . The great requisite of virtue, then, is to gain the intuition of these ideal excellencies; and the original fitness of the soul to meet them is so certain, that it cannot be conceived that it can really apprehend these eternal objects without yielding to their divine attraction. . . . You will not, then, be surprised to find that the perfection, of which virtue is the effort, is by Plato described as ὁμοίωσις θεῷ, assimilation to God. This assimilation is the enfranchisement of the divine element of the soul. To approach Him as the substance of truth, is science; as the substance of goodness in truth, is wisdom; as the substance of beauty in goodness and truth, is love."

31. Plato carried the same lofty spirit of speculation into his social, political, and even his physical system. His ideal state is but a community of philosophers, in which rank and authority are determined by wisdom, and the various relations and duties of life regulated by philosophy. Blind custom, superstition and prejudice were no longer to rule, but men, on the one hand, were to be controlled by the restraints of reason, and on the other, to have all the license supposed to be allowed by reason. We are prepared to expect that a social state established on so entirely ideal principles, without any regard to the lessons of experience, and even in contemptuous disregard of their authority, would tolerate extravagances and be marked by de-

fects, similar to those seen in systems conceived in the like spirit in modern times, and even in our own day, which we find to be the case. The Platonic State, with all its lofty ideality, is in substance, a sort of compound of the *despotism* of the Monarchy of Hobbes, and the *license* of the Socialism of Fourier, joined to that of the Mormonism of Brigham Young. His physical system,* too, was wholly ideal, and conjectural. His universe was built up from his imagination, without resort to a single experiment. It was, indeed, professedly but an attempt at ideal world-building, an attempt to draw out an imaginary scheme of things which might represent "the exquisite order and simplicity by which actual results may have been brought to pass," and thus, "deepen and vivify our notions of the harmony of the universe, and the consequent wisdom and goodness of its Author."

32. The successors of Plato in the Academy were, first, Speusippus, his nephew, then Xenocrates, Polemo, Crates, and Crantor (called thus far the Old Academy), and afterwards (to mention only a few of the leading names of the New Academy), Arcesilaus, Carneades, Philo, and Antiochus; the two latter con-

---

* Plato first conceived in order to account for the celestial changes, the system of concentric orbs or cycles, revolving within each other, and bearing on their interior surface the different heavenly bodies. His system embraced but eight such cycles (see the diagragm in Stalbaum's edition of the *Timæus*, p. 36, B.). Afterwards the number was increased by others, and eccentrics and epicycles added, till it broke down from its cumbrousness. It is to this system that Milton (P.L.B., 8, 83) alludes, as the fruit of the perverse ingenuity of man, which disfigured rather than explained nature :—

"With centric and eccentric scribbled o'er,
Cycle and epicycle, orb in orb."

temporary with Cicero, who was himself, in the main, an Academician, though with strong *eclectic* tendencies None of these were men of the lofty spirit and genius of the founder, and hence were unable to maintain the dignity and glory of his school. Incapable of soaring to his knowledge of the ideal, they abandoned it as hopeless. Thus left to the empirical element alone, to mere sense-knowledge, they soon sank into a settled *scepticism* * as to the certainty of all knowledge, which they held could never rise above belief or probability. They maintained, against the Stoics, the "representative" theory of perception, and the insufficiency of any impressions or representations, derivable by the mind through the senses from external objects, to the establishment of knowledge. "The impossibility of absolute certainty [says Professor Butler], the value of high probability, — these are the dominant maxims of the Academic philosophy."

33. On the contrary, in NEO-PLATONISM, the outlines of which were first taught in Alexandria by AMMONIAS SACCAS, about two hundred years after Christ, and which subsequently spread to Rome and Athens, the ideal element of Plato was seized upon, and carried out to ruinous excess. Like the genuine Platonism, it held to a knowledge of the absolute, not, however, through the intervention of ideas in the human mind,

* The *absolute scepticism* of *Pyrrho, Timon, Aenesidemus, Sextus Empiricus*, etc., was but an exaggeration of the moderate scepticism of the New Academy, and in part, indeed, was historically affiliated with it. Their general doctrine was, that nothing actually existed as it seemed, and that such were the contradictions and perplexities in all pretended knowledge, that the repose necessary to happiness could be found only by maintaining an entire suspension of judgment and all positive assertions about things.

but by a sort of ecstatic absorption of the individual reason into the Infinite Reason, so that it became conscious of whatever that was conscious of. New Platonism was an attempt to construct, on the general basis of Plato's system, a philosophy capable of rivalling and even superseding Christianity. Hence its claim of ecstatic vision and superhuman illumination. But these very pretensions, by which it hoped to become a religion as well as a philosophy, proved its ruin. Its mystic enthusiasm soon degenerated into magic and sorcery and all manner of extravagance.* Thus the direct continuations of Platonism, in both its branches, had failed to realize the fair promise which the system gave as it came from the hands of its author.

34. ARISTOTLE, to go back now to the time of Plato, was the truest representative of his master. He was the son of Nicomachus, an eminent physician of Stagira, in Thrace, and was born 384 B.C. Coming to Athens in his seventeenth year, he soon after became a pupil of Plato at the Academy, and remained such for about seventeen years, till the death of his master. Although pursuing different lines of inquiry from Plato, and coming to quite different results, the central idea and method of his system are plainly traceable to his master. As Plato had developed the purified conceptions and definitions of Socrates into positively existing ideas, apprehended in experience as a reminiscence

---

* The chief masters of Neo-Platonism were, — at Alexandria, *Iamblicus* and *Hierocles*, — at Rome, *Plotinus*, *Porphyry*, and *Amelius*, — and at Athens, *Plutarchus*, *Syrianus*, *Proclus*, *Marinus*, *Isidorus*, and *Zenodotus* under which last teacher, in 529, the schools of Athens were closed by an edict of Justinian.

of a previous knowledge, Aristotle reduced these ideas to mere mental *abstractions* elaborated by the reason through the recollections or *reminiscence of actual experience.* In like manner, the Socratic method of *investigation* became one of *demonstration* in his hands, and the *dialectics* of Plato re-appeared as *formal logic* in Aristotle. The "idea," therefore, was no longer an objective reality, but a subjective conception or thought. Still, as he supposed, a valid science of Being might be constructed from such empirical materials by passing them through the alembic of logic. Beginning thus soundly with experience, his philosophy ended in mistaking consistency of formal thought for material truth.

35. On the general question of the relation of the permanent to the phenomenal, Aristotle introduced the distinction of *matter* and *form.* With him, what is permanent in things is the simple, unformed matter or material of which they are composed, while particular, phenomenal objects are that general material under various determinate and appreciable forms. The permanent, therefore, was mere potential being, while the phenomenal was actual being, — existence made actual by the Great Actor and Former of all things. Hence, the permanent and the changing, the infinite and the finite, were but the same general substance, in the one case without, and in the other with, form.

36. Aristotle was an extensive and profound investigator of nearly all the great subjects of human curiosity and interest, as Logic, Physics, Metaphysics, Ethics, Politics, and Rhetoric. He treated all these subjects with a copiousness and precision unattained by any of his predecessors. Instead of the vague poetic style of preceding philosophers, he adopted the most rigidly pre-

cise and technical style, which expressed nothing but his bare ideas, and aimed to establish all his principles by solid arguments. He was unquestionably the most learned and profound of all the ancient philosophers. In him Greek philosophy reached its culminating point, and soon declined through various partial systems, as *Stoicism*, *Epicurianism*, *Scepticism*, and *New Platonism*—of which, the two last-named systems have already been characterized; so that it remains, only, briefly to describe the two former, in order to complete the survey of Greek philosophy.

37. STOICISM (so called from the *stoa*, or portico, where it was taught), as already stated, was the rival and antagonist of the New Academy. The two schools were at decided variance on the theory of knowledge, the former holding, though with some vagueness and vacillation, to an intuitive or *immediate* consciousness of external objects in perception, the latter, to only an *inferential* knowledge of them, through the medium of a representative image, somehow received or formed in sensation. The difference, in this respect, between the two schools, seems to have been substantially the same as that between the two branches of the Scotch school, represented, on the one side, by Reid and Hamilton, and on the other, by Brown.* With the one, therefore, knowledge was valid and certain, with the other, only probable. The Stoics stoutly resisted the scepticism of their age, as Reid and his followers did that of theirs.

38. But the predominant aim of stoicism was *ethical.* Their psychology was but a carefully laid foun-

* See his twenty-fifth Lecture, and Hamilton's Review of Reid's Works, *Philosophical Discussions*, p. 38—98.

dation upon which they might securely raise the superstructure of their moral system. *Zeno* (of Citium, in the island of Cyprus), who founded the school, came to Athens when a young man, and became a disciple of Crates, of the Cynic school. And though he afterwards attended the school at Megara, and the Academy, he always retained the strong ethical tendency of his first instructors, and something even of their asceticism. In his system, and that of his followers, God was little more than the laws of nature, its formative and actuating soul. To act according to nature, then, was to do the will of God, and hence was the highest virtue. Accordingly, conduct was to be controlled by reason taking a calm and comprehensive survey of the order of nature, and not by impulse or the love of pleasure. Happiness and all external advantages were regarded as mere accidental concomitants of action, not as a real good, or end of nature. The system not only placed happiness below the right, but disregarded it altogether, and endeavored to replace all emotion by a profound indifference and apathy. The great masters of the Stoic philosophy, after the founder, were *Cleanthes*, *Chrysippus*, and later, *Panætius*, and *Posidonius*.

39. Epicureanism, founded and taught at Athens by *Epicurus* (born 342 B.C.), in what was called the Garden, was an exaggeration in the opposite direction. As the Stoics rejected happiness altogether, as an end of life, the Epicureans made it the chief end of life; not, indeed, the happiness of unrestrained gratification, of whatever sort, like the Cyrenaic school, but yet mere happiness, as such. Epicureanism was not a system of mere sensualism or momentary indulgence, but rather

of self-interest. It required a subordination and systematization of the different kinds of happiness, but only as such a course is necessary in order to attain the greatest amount of happiness on the whole. Conduct was to be regulated, but by no higher standard than that of an enlightened self-interest. It recognized no immutable law of right and wrong, and hence left each one to be governed by the wholly uncertain standard of his individual conception of what was for his own good. At the same time, it made happiness consist largely in the absence of pain and care, and hence exempted the gods from all interest or concern in the affairs of men.*

40. These are all the important forms assumed by Greek philosophy during the course of its eventful history. The Socratic movement, with all its fruitfulness and wide-spread influence, had now exhausted itself. Stoicism, Epicureanism, and the Academic philosophy, continued to divide the opinions of men, till they were all, together with that new and more pretentious form of Platonism, already described, superseded and absorbed by the more positive faith of the Gospel. The Greek language and philosophy were carried into the East by the conquests of Alexander, and into the West by the conquests of Rome, but they never became thoroughly naturalized in either of these regions. Stoicism was not without its admirers and disciples in the stern patriots and military classes of Rome, as Epicureanism was not, among her luxurious and self-indulgent classes, and even the Academic philosophy, among

* The physical and psychological views of the Epicureans were merely a further elaboration of the Atomic system of Democritus, which has already been described.

her men of genius and learning, like Cicero; but neither here nor at Alexandria did they receive any new development, except in the single form of New Platonism, which was rather a corruption than a true carrying out of the original system. Neither the stern, imperial West, nor the dreamy, mystic East, was congenial to the true spirit of philosophy.

41. Grecian philosophy had now run its course, and fallen before the onward march of Christianity. But soon thought began again to assert its independence, and demand a reason for the faith of the Church. To meet this demand was the object of SCHOLASTICISM. Seeing her doctrines assailed, the sages of the Church, such as *Anselm*, *Abelard*, *Thomas Aquinas*, and *Duns Scotus* (1034–1308), set themselves at work, from various points of view, to establish the rationality of their creed. For this purpose, they made use of the materials furnished by the antecedent Greek philosophy, and especially of the system of Aristotle, whom they were wont to designate, by way of eminence, "the philosopher," and who supplied them with their phraseology and chief principles. They elaborated their system with great industry and ingenuity, forming a framework of dialectical subtleties which carried the mind off from the real nature of things, and rather confused than convinced it. After a long and earnest struggle, the attempt at reconciliation finally failed, and religion was left to its own peculiar province, that of the practical reason, which proceeds upon convictions and postulates of its own, while philosophy retained possession of the sphere of the speculative reason, which deals only in conceptions demonstratively established.

42. The downfall of Scholasticism was effected only after the most obstinate resistance, and through the influence of various co-operating causes. Among these were the Revival of Letters from the dispersion of Greek scholars over Western Europe, on the breaking up of the Eastern Empire, the Protestant Reformation, and the advancement of Physical Science under *Copernicus*, *Kepler*, *Galileo*, and *Bacon*. For, though Bacon did not, like the other philosophers here named, devote himself to physical studies and experiments, he drew out in the most imposing and attractive form, the *method* of conducting such studies, and most emphatically and authoritatively asserted the necessity of quitting the barren subtleties of Scholasticism, and returning to the direct study of nature. Other philosophers, as *Bruno* in Italy, and Boehme in Germany, promoted the same tendency, though in a more obscure and mystical way. At length, thought was again emancipated, and soon began to evince its independence in commencing the foundations of Modern Philosophy.

43. MODERN PHILOSOPHY begins with *Descartes* (born at La Haye, in Touraine, 1596). Dissatisfied with the results of the philosophy of former ages, he attempted the construction of an entirely new fabric of philosophic thought — a fabric which should be solid and impregnable against all doubt. He starts with the simple consciousness of self-existence. His famous *cogito, ergo sum*, simply asserted his existence as a *thinking* being, on the ground that he was *conscious of thinking*. That we think cannot be doubted, for to doubt is to think, and hence doubting proves thinking; as far forth as one is conscious of thinking, so far forth he necessarily exists as a thinking being. The

truth of our existence, then, is established beyond cavil. At the same time, the assurance with which we receive this truth becomes a rule for the reception of other truths — we may receive any thing else as true, when we know it with the same clearness and certainty with which we know our own existence. Yet our certainty of any thing out of ourselves wants some further voucher for its actual objective existence besides our *internal* conviction.

44. Here Descartes calls to his aid the idea of God, which he regarded as *innate*, or implanted in us by God himself. And this innate conception of God he held to be such, as to forbid the supposition of his having so made us that we should unhesitatingly receive as true what is really false. Whatever, then, in the legitimate use of our powers of perception and reasoning, we feel forced to receive as true, is so. God is no deceiver, knowledge is no deception. At the same time, Descartes proceeds to deduce from the idea of God, the nature of substance, both material and immaterial, and to build up an entire philosophy of nature. This certainly is making the idea of God a pretty fruitful one, not merely in moral but in philosophical results. Such deductions may appear highly plausible, may indeed possess a high degree of probability, but must be destitute of that demonstrative certainty demanded by philosophy, especially by a system of philosophy which professes to take nothing on trust. This working backward, therefore, to establish truth and existence from the idea of God is unsatisfactory. Indeed, it seems rather crude and credulous to assume the idea of God as innate; though perhaps in this and other cases, Descartes meant by innate, merely that the *form* of the

conception is ready furnished by the mind — that our mental constitution is such that we inevitably conceive things so and so, on experience.

45. According to Descartes, matter possesses the sole property of extension, and mind the sole property of thought. They have nothing in common, but each is the negation of the other. Their intercourse is only maintained *supernaturally* by the intervention of the Deity. The soul is conceived as seated at the centre of the brain, in the *pineal gland*, and as being determined to perception by certain motions produced in that organ by the action of external objects upon the senses. External objects themselves, therefore, are not perceived, nor even the images or motions of them; they are merely, through the *divine assistance*, the occasions * of perception. Mind and matter were thus clearly distinguished, — more so, perhaps, than in any antecedent system, — but, at the same time they were made so independent of each other as to render it difficult to conceive how the intercourse between them was to be maintained.

46. Malebranche (born at Paris, 1638), a zealous Cartesian, feeling the difficulty of mediating between mind and matter according to his master's view, sought a medium of perception in which the opposition between them should be overcome. Such a medium he found in God himself. Instead of calling in the *intervention* of God in perception, like Descartes, he transferred human perception wholly to him as a medium. God as the absolute substance, from which all other

* This was virtually Descartes' doctrine of perception, though the doctrine of *Occasional Causes* was explicitly drawn out only by his disciples *De la Forge*, *Geulinx*, etc. See Wight's Hamilton, p. 205, note.

substances are derived, was regarded as containing all things ideally in himself. Nature, thus spiritualized in God, might be perceived by spirit, and was actually brought into relation to our spirits by the all-embracing presence of God. God, in whom all nature was realized, was at the same time the place of souls. Thus we know and see all things in God.*

47. Spinoza (born at Amsterdam, 1632), commencing an earnest student of Descartes, soon abandoned as hopeless the task of mediating between mind and matter on Cartesian principles, and boldly transferred the *thought* and *extension*, by which Descartes characterized mind and matter respectively, to a single subject. Indeed, thought and extension, in his system, are but correlative qualities, the one subjective and the other objective, if not, indeed, merely the opposite sides of the same quality, as apprehended by the human understanding. All finite, phenomenal objects are but modes of this infinite substance, related to it as waves are to the ocean. In man and other finite intelligent beings, the general thought of God comes to a distinct unity of consciousness, as his extension is developed into distinct forms in different material objects. The world in all its forms, and in all its aspects of thought, life, change, and motion, is but the unfolding of God according to the necessities of his own nature. Thus

---

* Arnauld, a contemporary and fellow-countryman of Malebranche, was also a distinguished cultivator of the Cartesian philosophy. But he contributed nothing towards the mediation of mind and matter, which was the chief difficulty in the system of his master. Indeed, as he does not seem to have held to an immediate perception of external objects, his discarding all mediating ideas derived from these objects — important as the step was in itself — rather increased than relieved the difficulty.

all proper personality and moral character are destroyed in both man and God.

48. The main positions of his system are thus briefly stated by Lewes: "There is but one infinite Substance, and that is God. Whatever is, is in God; and without him nothing can be conceived. He is the universal Being, of which all things are the manifestations. He is the sole Substance; every thing else is a Mode; yet without Substance, Mode cannot exist. God, viewed under the attributes of Infinite Substance, is the *natura naturans*, — viewed as a manifestation, as the Modes under which his attributes appear, he is the *natura naturata*. He is the cause of all things, and that immanently, but not transiently. He has two infinite attributes — Extension and Thought. Extension is visible Thought, and Thought is invisible Extension: they are the Objective and Subjective of which God is the Identity. Every *thing* is a mode of God's attribute of Extension; every *thought*, wish, or feeling, a mode of his attribute of Thought. Substance is uncreated, but creates by the internal necessity of its nature. There may be many existing things, but only one existence; many forms, but only one Substance. God is the '*idea immanens*' — the One and All." These points are established by a most rigid course of demonstrative reasoning, proceeding by definitions, axioms, proposition, etc., after the manner of geometry. And here precisely is the ground of his error. Mathematical reasoning develops only the contents and relations of quantitative conceptions, not the nature of being, or the reality of things.

49. The next independent attempt at philosophizing was made by John Locke (born at Wrington, 1632),

the founder of English philosophy. His philosophy is of the empirical sort, and decidedly materialistic in its tendency. He had been preceded in the same line by his fellow-countryman, THOMAS HOBBES, * but only in a random, fragmentary way. Locke's fundamental principle is, that the mind of man starts with nothing, and ends with nothing, except what it derives either directly or indirectly from experience, — that it has merely the power of receiving, retaining, and combining what is given in experience. All its treasured knowledge, when analyzed, is resolvable into ideas of sensation and ideas of reflection; i.e., into the ideas which are given directly in the perception of external objects, and those which arise in the mind from the contemplation of these. Starting with this principle, it is the great business of his philosophy to reduce all knowledge to these two classes of ideas, which he attempts to do by an elaborate analysis of the contents of the mind.

50. The defects of such a system are obvious. If the mind imparts nothing in perception, if it be wholly dependent upon experience for its knowledge, then it is altogether a subordinate power, determined wholly from without. Besides, how can knowledge be verified if there be not some fixed principles of thought — some necessary laws of thought or modes of conception, to which we can appeal as attesting the validity of our experience? If the mind does not itself conceive some things as being *necessarily* so and so, there are no starting-points to knowledge, and every thing may be doubted. And that there are such primary principles

---

* Hobbes is chiefly known as a psychologist by his theory of the Association of Ideas

of knowledge is often unconsciously admitted by Locke himself; as where he admits that it is illegitimate to dispute whether a thing can "both be and not be," and allows that we have an idea of substance, though it clearly is not and cannot be known by experience. A system so partial could hardly fail of soon being carried out to its absurd consequences, which was actually done, and that in two different directions.

51. In its most obvious tendency towards materialism, while it was universally tolerated, and in some instances even exaggerated, by contemporaneous and succeeding English philosophers, as *Newton*, *Clarke*, *Willis*, *Hook*, *Hartley*, *Darwin*, etc., it was taken up with enthusiasm in France by *Condillac*, *Helvetius*, *La Mettrie*, *Diderot*, *Holbach*, *Lagrange* (1715–1770), and the other writers who brought on the corruption in morals and the disorganization in society which ended in the French Revolution. While Locke referred all ideas to sensation and reflection, Condillac referred them all, and even the very faculties of the mind themselves, to sensation, thus converting his Empiricism into Sensualism; and Helvetius merely drew the practical consequence of this theoretical doctrine, that sensuous pleasure and pain are the only, and consequently the highest, stimulants or motives to action. La Mettrie, and the Encyclopedists and writers of the System of Nature, further elaborated these vile principles, and carried them out with shameless audacity and particularity to their legitimate consequences, the denial not only of all morality and religion, but of the very existence of God, as well as of the spirituality and immortality of the soul.

52. But Locke's philosophy, by the most opposite

tendencies, led not only to materialism, but to idealism, as well. Its empirical character, while it made it materialistic in substance, made it subjective in principle. It contained no valid assertion of the existence of the external world. By denying to the mind authoritative principles of knowledge and necessary modes of conception, as well as a direct consciousness of external things, it virtually denied all real knowledge of outward objects, and the validity of all such general conceptions as those of Cause, Time, Space, etc. GEORGE BERKELEY, therefore (born at Kilkrin, Ireland, 1684), in order to avoid the materialistic and atheistic tendencies of his system, wholly rejected matter as an independent existence, denying all objective reality to external objects — making them merely a succession of internal ideas *produced in us by the Will of the Creator.**

53. On the other hand, DAVID HUME (born at Edinburgh, 1711), gladly accepting the empirical nature and subjective tendencies of Locke's system, carried it out to its last consequences, in the denial of a substantive existence not only to matter, but to mind also, as well as all general abstract ideas, and particularly that of causation. Holding with Locke and Berkeley, that all our knowledge comes of experience, and that in experience nothing is known beyond the ideas themselves begotten in the mind, which cannot be copies, or in any way adequate representations, of

* Berkeley stoutly asserts that his system accords with the vulgar belief; that the common mind in perception, thinks it perceives, and consequently believes in the existence of, only a combination of mental affections. But this is evidently the very reverse of the fact. The common mind, far more than that of the philosopher, adheres to an external reality as the cause of perception and the substratum of the qualities perceived. It cannot believe, whatever the philosopher may do, that pumpkins and melons are merely alternately developing and decaying *ideas.*

external things, he denies all *knowledge* of substance, whether material or immaterial, or of causation, whether physical or spiritual. He admits, to be sure, a universal and unavoidable *belief* in these, but regards it as a blind instinct, or prejudice, generated by habit. He regards our idea of material substance as wholly generated by our various sensations of the so-called material qualities; our idea of self, by many rapidly succeeding states of consciousness; and our idea of causation, by association, or the habit of seeing one event follow another.*

54. While the philosophy of Locke was being carried out to its consequences in England and France, the gifted and comprehensive genius of LEIBNITZ (born at Leipsic, 1646) was elaborating a highly original and ingenious system, opposed on the one hand, — by the assertion of native and necessary forms of thought, — to the empiricism of Locke, and on the other, to the lifeless and characterless pantheism of Spinoza. An accomplished scholar and versatile courtier, he spent a large part of his time in the varied duties of diplomacy, pursuing philosophy only at intervals, and published his views mostly in a fragmentary form, and frequently in the French language. His most considerable works are the Théodicée, the Monadology, and the Nouveaux

* These, clearly, are but the just conclusions from a philosophy which holds that perception is wholly representative, and that "there is nothing in the intellect which is not first in the senses." They can be avoided only by vindicating a direct perception of external objects, and the existence in the mind, as an original endowment from the Creator, of necessary forms of thought, according to which we mould our experience; that the mind is so made, that it cannot perceive qualities without ascribing them to a something to which they belong; nor change without ascribing it to a causative power.

Essais, the first chiefly theological, and the other two metaphysical.

55. Like Spinoza, Leibnitz holds to the existence of but one general substance; yet not to a dead, characterless, indeterminate substance, but to one full of activity and life, and distributed among an infinite number of individual beings, specifically differing from each other in quality. At the same time, this substance is wholly ideal, being deprived of all real extension, and made up of mere metaphysical points instinct with life. Each of these points is a *monad*, or distinct individual, differing from every other in quality, while they all alike, and each by a spontaneous activity, represent or mirror in themselves the universe. In inorganic matter, the representations are so numerous and confused that they do not come to a unity of consciousness; in the vegetable world, the representative activity of the monads rises to a formative vital force; while in animals, the representative activity rises to an obscure consciousness,—and in man, to a distinct consciousness.

56. All substance, then, is either distinctly or confusedly intelligent. The mind of man is distinctly intelligent, his body only confusedly so. And yet by a *pre-established harmony* they are always in perfect correspondence with each other. The monads of the body always represent exactly the same things as those of the mind, the one mechanically, the other consciously, so that they are always in exact harmony; like two time-pieces, moved by mechanism of the same pattern and from the same master-hand. But the body has no influence upon the mind, nor the mind upon the body, — they simply run together. Our knowledge, there-

fore, is not mere sense-knowledge. It does not come from without, but is produced from the mind itself. All ideas are innate, in the sense that they are always *potentially* in the mind. With much that is fanciful in this system, there is much that is substantial, and forms the basis of the most approved philosophy of the present day, especially the assertion of native forms of thought, potentially in the mind antecedent to experience.

57. It was on the general basis of the philosophy of Leibnitz that CHRISTIAN WOLF (born at Breslau, 1679) reared his elaborate system of metaphysics. He did not, however, so much develop to their completeness the fragmentary but highly fruitful germs of thought thrown out by this great philosopher, as attempt from existing materials, to construct a comprehensive system of philosophy according to his general principles. Hence, while he retained the same idealistic view of things as Leibnitz, he kept his peculiar theory of nature quite in the background. After the fashion of the times, he endeavored to embrace in his system all the great problems of existence, both real and possible. His philosophy was both theoretical and practical, including logic, metaphysics, and ethics. Under metaphysics was embraced Ontology, or the necessary conceptions under which things are known, and which were thought to apply not only to phenomena, but to things in themselves; Cosmology, or the conception of the world in its cause, beginning, composition, parts, etc.; Rational Psychology, or the conception of the soul as a simple, immaterial, unchanging substance and self-conscious personality; and Speculative Theology, or the conception of a Supreme Being as the highest con-

dition of the possibility of all things. His system, comprehensive in plan, and drawn out with mathematical precision, though mistaking formal for material truth, was highly esteemed in Germany, and remained the dominant philosophy till it was overthrown by Kant.

58. We have now arrived at a point in the history of philosophy, where the stream of speculation, already many times interrupted and divided for a season, separates into two independent and diversely flowing currents, which have continued their divergent courses to the present time. The philosophy of Locke, which had ended in materialism in France, had by a reaction ended in idealism, first in England and now in Germany. The whole movement having issued in an exaggerated and one-sided view of things, it was inevitable that the philosophical faculty would seek some new point of departure and new principles of procedure, in order to reach a more satisfactory result. Such was actually the case, and that, too, at about the same time, in the two most widely removed centres of philosophical speculation, — Scotland and Germany. And not only so, but the impulse, in both cases, came from the same source — the scepticism of Hume. *Reid* and *Kant* were contemporaries, and according to the testimony of each left on record, were independently incited by the sceptical conclusions of Hume, to attempt the reconstruction of the fabric of knowledge on a new and safer foundation. And not only so, they both appealed to the same general principles of certitude — the original instincts or conceptions of the soul, though with different degrees of distinctness and consistency, and, as we shall see, with almost opposite results. We

will first briefly trace the German and then the Scottish movement, which will complete the abstract proposed.

59. The philosophy of KANT (born in 1724, at Königsberg, Prussia, where he was teacher and professor of philosophy in the university about forty years) appeared in the form of several distinct *critiques*, and is known as the Critical Philosophy. Instead of starting, as had been the fashion, with some single principle (as the *cogito ergo sum* of Descartes, or the *monads* of Leibnitz) and deducing his system from this, he starts with a criticism of the principles of knowledge, with an analysis of its conditions, in order to ascertain its possibility and limits, and mete out its domain. His philosophy, therefore, is partly destructive and partly constructive. His criticism is designed not only to clear away the dogmatic rubbish, but to disclose the genuine foundation-principles of knowledge. The result of his criticism is, that the strictly metaphysical sciences, Ontology, Rational Psychology, Speculative Theology, etc., are based upon mere assumptions, and hence, that philosophy is restricted to the sphere of the phenomenal. The unconditioned cannot be known, but only the conditioned. Our notions of a psychical, a cosmological, and a theological unity, which he calls the *ideas of reason*, are mere regulative principles for simplifying and systematizing our knowledge, not real constitutive principles of knowledge.

60. But, at the same time, he holds, against Locke and Hume, to fundamental judgments or forms of conception, by which all our experience is connected and moulded. By an inner necessity of our thinking, we not only posit every thing in *time* and *space*, but necessarily think of things under the forms either of

unity, *plurality*, *totality; reality*, *negation*, *limitation*, *substance* and *quality*, *cause* and *effect; possibility*, *actuality*, *necessity*. These are his famous Categories of Thought, or *a priori* Conceptions of the understanding. As necessary *forms* of thought they have a universal validity, but, being in themselves wholly empty, they become valid synthetical judgments only as they are filled by the matter of experience — by actual intuitions or perceptions. While, therefore, Kant connects together the fabric of knowledge by the cement of general principles, and thus saves it from falling asunder, he so dispossesses this fabric of all objective reality, as to render it little more than a fairy castle, a mere phantom of the mind. Thus, even Kant, with all the solidity and masculine vigor of his mind, remained true to the ideal character of his nation, and made knowledge virtually subjective.

61. Not that he actually denies objective existence to things. Indeed, he verbally, at least, holds on to their objective existence, and all along supposes them the cause of sensations. He nowhere clearly draws the inevitable conclusion of his philosophy. After resolving space and time into mere subjective conditions of thought, and denying any thing more than a moulding and regulative authority, respectively, to the conceptions of the understanding and the ideas of reason, he makes a labored effort to save, at least, the existence of God, and the freedom and immortality of the soul, from the effects of his destructive criticism. This he does on the authority of the *Practical* Reason, or conscience, which, as undetermined from without, demands with authority a perfect moral law, a perfect virtue, and a perfect happiness; involving, respectively, the neces-

sity for the freedom of the soul (will), the immortality of the soul, and the being of God.

62. The appearance of Kant's *Critique of Pure Reason* (in 1781) at once created an epoch. It is unquestionably the most important event which has occurred in the history of modern philosophy. Not so much from the amount of absolute truth which it contains, as from the almost new phase of speculation which it exhibits, and the surprising depth, thoroughness, and comprehensiveness with which the discussion is conducted. It turns up a hitherto almost unknown and quite unexplored side of things. Notwithstanding the extreme abstractness and rigor of its principles, and the appalling difficulties of its terminology, it swept every thing before it in Germany, and has greatly influenced the direction and tone of philosophical speculation, in all civilized countries, ever since. It was soon adopted by all the ablest teachers in the different German universities, most of whom confined themselves to expounding its doctrines in a more popular form, and supplying its deficiencies, while only a few set themselves either decidedly to oppose, or positively to develop and carry out, the system. Of these, only *Jacobi*, *Herbart*, and *Fichte* need here be named.

63. Frederic Henry Jacobi (born at Düsseldorf in 1743, and during the latter part of his life President of the Academy of Sciences in Munich) was a man of fine genius and of rich and varied culture, with a strong dash of the poetic in his nature. It was inevitable that a mind so gifted, and sentimental withal, should be repelled by the cool destructiveness of a critical philosophy which annihilated all the most cherished objects of sentiment and faith, or at most, allowed them

only a doubtful existence, as postulates of the practical reason. Accordingly, he grounds his philosophy on immediate instead of mediate knowledge ; on faith and feeling, instead of conception and discursive thinking, which were the basis of the Kantian philosophy. As he holds to an immediate apprehension of external objects by sense, so he holds to an immediate apprehension of supersensible objects by reason; and that, in each case, these primary apprehensions manifest themselves as irresistible *beliefs* or *feelings* that things are so and so. As conceiving is but conditioning (he reasons) we can never reach the unconditioned or infinite by discursive thinking, and all metaphysical philosophy is impossible, unless rational beliefs or feelings be taken as the deepest and most veritable cognitions of which we are capable.*

64. John Frederick Herbart (born at Oldenberg, 1776) was Kant's successor at Königsberg, and is introduced here before Fichte, though chronologically subsequent to him, because he completes the development of the Kantian philosophy on one side, which was continued from Fichte, on the other, by *Schelling* and *Hegel.* His system is a somewhat peculiar and unfruitful carrying out of the realistic or empirical side of the philosophy of his predecessor. In his system knowledge is only of the given; it cannot transcend experience as a basis. Even the conceptions of the understanding and the ideas of reason are based on realities, and it is the business of philosophy, not to deny their validity on account of the contradictions which they contain, as did Kant, but to *remodel* them

* In like manner, Herbert Spencer regards *belief* as our deepest cognition. See his *Principles of Psychology,* chap. ii.

so as to free them of contradictions. He attempts such a purification of conceptions through his doctrine of "reals," in which he assumes all substances to be composed of simple, unextended monads, differing from each other in quality, and affecting each other by action and reaction. Every substance, therefore, has just as many primitive and independent *reals* as it has qualities, and hence the contradiction between oneness in substance and multiplicity in phenomena disappears. So, too, a substance changes only by a shifting *to and fro* of the reals, or by the interaction among them from a mutual effort at "self-preservation;" which interaction, on the principle of "accidental views," may, on the one side, be said really to change, and on the other, not to change, each other. In like manner, the antinomies of motion may be solved on the principle of "intellectual spaces," according to which reals may be said on the one hand to be *together*, and on the other, to be *separated.* And thus of other ontological questions. The soul, however, is a *simple real*, and its perceptions but responses or re-actions against the encroachments of other objects. Herbart's doctrine of *reals*, it will be perceived, is quite similar in its general features to the "monad" theory of Leibnitz.

65. JOHN GOTTLIEB FICHTE (born at Rammenau, 1762), a man of extraordinary independence and acuteness of mind, was appointed professor of philosophy at Jena in 1793, afterwards (in 1805) at Erlangen, and finally, dean and rector of the new university in Berlin, where he died in 1814, in the fifty-second year of his age. His starting-point was the philosophy of Kant, which he regarded as virtually a system of idealism, and stoutly contended that he was right in interpreting

it as intentionally such, until publicly contradicted by Kant himself. There can be no doubt, therefore, that he was wrong as to the intention of Kant to construct a system of idealism; but that it is virtually so, must be quite as evident to every careful reader of his Critique. At any rate, such was it understood to be by Fichte and such has it proved to be in its effects. ✓

66. Kant having made perception a synthesis of subject and object, the mind contributing one part and the external object another, towards the general result, Fitchte advanced a step further, and declared perception and thought in general to be *wholly* an act of the mind, without the concurrence or co-operation of any thing external. As all thought is necessarily subjective, he found no warrant for assuming the existence of any thing out of the mind; nor any necessity for it, indeed, since all the phases of experience and thought might be easily accounted for on ideal principles. The mind is active in its nature, and in acting, it necessarily assumes something acted upon, or co-operating with it in the act — every mental act involves at the same time a *self* and a *not self*, a subject and an object. In perception, one necessarily affirms a self and a not-self as *relatives in thought*, but nothing beyond this. Besides, the different categories of thought are only the different *relations* which the subject and object may be conceived as holding to each other. External objects, then, are only objectified thoughts, or rather, that self-imposed limitation of thought by which alone we become conscious, or have any thoughts at all. Thus we make the external world by our internal activity. Self and its representations constitute the universe. Even God is nothing more than the abstract Moral Order of things.

67. Such is a hint of the character of the subjective or egoistic idealism of Fichte, of which Sir W. Hamilton says,* that it is "developed with the most admirable rigor of demonstration," and is "the purest, simplest, and most consistent which the history of philosophy presents." And yet it ends virtually in *nihilism*. "The sum total," says Fichte (quoted by Hamilton), in summing up the result of his theoretical philosophy, "is this: There is absolutely nothing permanent either without me or within me, but only an unceasing change. I know absolutely nothing of any existence, not even of my own. I myself know nothing, and am nothing. Images there are: they constitute all that apparently exists, and what they know of themselves, is after the manner of images,—images that pass and vanish without there being aught to witness their transition; that consist in fact of the images of images, without significance and without an aim. I myself am one of these images; nay, I am not even thus much, but only a confused image of images. All reality is converted into a marvellous dream, without a life to dream of, and without a mind to dream; into a dream made up only of a dream of itself. Perception is a dream; thought — the source of all the existence and all the reality which I imagine to myself of *my* existence, of my power, of my destination — is the dream of that dream."

68. Frederick William Joseph Schelling (born at Leonberg, 1775), beginning his career as a speculative philosopher while yet at the university (at Tübingen), became, on leaving the university, a student and teacher of Philosophy at Jena, in conjunction with

* Wight's Hamilton, p. 24, note.

Fichte, and afterwards, professor of philosophy, first at Würtsburg (in 1803) and then at Munich. In his philosophizing he started with Fichte, but soon passed far beyond him in the wild pursuit of the absolute. He accepts, with Fichte, the identity of subject and object, but unlike him, makes them perfectly coördinate and equally real. The object is no longer produced from the finite subject, but both alike are produced out of the infinite subject — *the absolute.* Human souls are but separate centres of consciousness in the absolute, in universal Nature; and the experience of life, in all of which subject and object figure as the opposite poles, is but the outworking of the Infinite. Ordinary experience or consciousness is possible only through the contrast of subject and object; but in the higher, and indeed, impersonal clairvoyance of *Reason* or the *Intellectual Intuition*, the contrast disappears, as polarity does at the *indifference-point* of the magnet, and subject and object, knowledge and being, become absolutely one. Schelling, in short, was a pantheist, with a peculiar theory of knowing the absolute. Further to illustrate the views of a philosopher, so subtle and occupying so important a position in the history of recent speculations in Germany and other countries, I transfer to my pages a few luminous paragraphs, descriptive of Schelling's system, from Sir W. Hamilton's celebrated review of *Cousin.*

69. This admirable critic thus sets forth and canvasses his chief positions: "While the lower sciences are of the relative and conditioned, Philosophy, as the science of sciences, must be of the *absolute*, — *the unconditioned.* But how, it is objected, can the absolute be known? The absolute, as unconditioned, identical,

and one, cannot be cognized under conditions, by difference and plurality. It cannot, therefore, be known if the subject of knowledge be distinguished from the object of knowledge; in a knowledge of the absolute, existence and knowledge must be identical; the absolute can only be known, if adequately known, and it can only be adequately known by the absolute itself. But is this possible? We are wholly ignorant of existence in itself: the mind knows nothing, except in parts, by quality, and difference, and relation; consciousness supposes the subject contradistinguished from the object of thought; the abstraction of this contrast is the negation of consciousness; and the negation of consciousness is the annihilation of thought itself. The alternative is therefore unavoidable; either finding the absolute, we lose ourselves, or retaining self and individual consciousness, we do not reach the absolute.

70. "All this Schelling frankly admits. But he contends that there is a capacity of knowledge above consciousness, and higher than the understanding, and that this knowledge is competent to human *reason, as identical with the Absolute itself.* In this act of knowledge, which, after Fichte, he calls the *Intellectual Intuition*, there exists no distinction of subject and object, — no contrast of knowledge and existence; all difference is lost in absolute indifference, — all plurality in absolute unity. The Intuition itself — Reason — and the Absolute are identified. The absolute exists only as known by reason, and reason knows only as being itself absolute.

71. "It would be idle to enter into an articulate refutation of a theory, which founds philosophy on the

annihilation of consciousness, and the identification of the unconscious philosopher with God. The intuition of the absolute is manifestly the work of an arbitrary abstraction, and of a self-delusive imagination. To reach the point of indifference, — by abstraction we an nihilate the object, and by abstraction we annihilate the subject, of consciousness. But what remains? *Nothing*. '*Nil conscimus nobis*.' We then hypostatize the zero; we baptize it with the name of *Absolute;* and conceit ourselves that we contemplate absolute existence, when we only speculate absolute privation.

72. "To Schelling it has been impossible, without gratuitous and even contradictory assumptions, to explain the deduction of the finite from the infinite. By no *salto mortali* has he been able to clear the magic circle in which he had enclosed himself. Unable to connect the unconditioned and the conditioned by any natural correlation, he has variously attempted to account for the phenomenon of the universe, either by imposing a necessity of self-manifestation on the absolute, i.e., by conditioning the unconditioned; or by postulating a fall of the finite from the infinite; i.e., by begging the very fact which his hypothesis professed its exclusive ability to explain."

73. And still further, briefly to indicate at this point, in the words of the same author, the relation of the system of Schelling's great French disciple, Victor Cousin, to that of his master: "Cousin and Schelling agree, that as philosophy is the science of the unconditioned, the unconditioned must be within the compass of science. They agree, that the unconditioned is known and immediately known; and they agree that intelligence, as competent to the unconditioned, is im

personal, infinite, divine. But while they coincide in the fact of the absolute, as known, they are diametrically opposed as to the mode in which they attempt to realize this knowledge. Cousin declares the condition of all knowledge to be plurality and difference; and Schelling, that the condition, under which alone the knowledge of the absolute becomes possible, is indifference and unity. The one thus denies a notion of the absolute to consciousness; whilst the other affirms that consciousness is concerned in every act of intelligence."

74. George William Frederic Hegel (born at Stuttgart, 1770), an early friend and college chum of Schelling, at Tübingen, was subsequently professor of philosophy at Jena, at Heidelberg, and at Berlin, where he died in 1831. Starting from the stand-point of Schelling, he reduced his system to order, and carried it out to its last logical consequences. Schelling, while assuming the identity of subject and object *at the point of indifference*, had yet assumed the reality of both poles. Hegel, on the contrary, abolishes alike the reality of both poles, and admits only the reality of their *relation*. The equipoise of subject and object thus becomes a mere *abstract relation* of the two. The Indifference Philosophy becomes the Absolute Philosophy, and the Intellectual Intuition only Logical Conception. For, not only are subject and object absolutely one, but being and non-being, light and darkness, and all other contraries and contradictories. Indeed, the fundamental principle of his system is, the *identity of contraries*. All possibility of contradiction is thus avoided, and the way opened for the wildest revelry of thought. Philosophy becomes the possible in thought, with the principle of contradiction eliminated. Theoretically, his system

is the evolution of such a system of thought, while practically, it is the application of it to nature, life, opinion, history, etc., i.e., the explanation of the apparent world, and course of events, according to such abstract and fantastic forms of thought. In such a system, nature, man, and even God, can be only an evolution of the absolute, and in the last analysis, only a *process of thought*, a *nothing*, in short. Here we have Absolute Idealism, following upon the Objective Idealism of Schelling, as that had followed upon the Subjective Idealism of Fichte.

75. With Hegel the German movement closes. He seems to have pushed Idealism to its utmost limits, rendering any further development impossible; at all events, there has been no further development since his time. And if, now, having traced this movement to its close, till it has "vanished in thin air," we return again to Hume, to trace in few words the Scottish line of speculation, we shall find a movement of a very different order, and of a much more sober and hopeful character. The Scotch school of philosophy was founded by *Thomas Reid* (born at Strachan, 1710, and successively professor of philosophy at Aberdeen and at Glasgow), and has embraced a succession of able men but of these only two besides the founder are of sufficient importance to deserve particular mention in a mere abstract of the history of philosophy — *Dugald Stewart* and *Sir W. Hamilton* (both professors of philosophy at Edinburg). While Reid originated the system, Stewart illustrated and rendered it attractive, and Hamilton perfected it. Reid and Stewart are generally at one in doctrine, it is only in Hamilton that we find any considerable advance upon the founder.

76. The general principles of the school are thus admirably stated by Hamilton in his review of Cousin: "In Scotland, a philosophy had sprung up, which, though professing, equally with the doctrine of Condillac, to build only on experience, did not, like that doctrine, limit experience to the relations of sense and its objects. Without vindicating to man more than a relative knowledge of existence, and restricting the science of mind to an observation of the fact of consciousness, it, however, analyzed that fact into a greater number of more important elements than had been recognized in the school of Condillac. It showed that phenomena were revealed in thought which could not be resolved into any modifications of sense, external or internal. It proved that intelligence supposed principles, which, as the *conditions* of its activity, cannot be the *results* of its operations; that the mind contained knowledges, which, as primitive, universal, necessary, are not to be explained as generalizations from the contingent and individual, about which alone all experience is conversant. The phenomena of mind were thus distinguished from the phenomena of matter; and if the impossibility of materialism was not demonstrated, there was at least demonstrated the impossibility of its proof."

77. These primary principles of knowledge or forms of thought native to the human mind, Reid called "principles of common sense," and hence the Scotch school of philosophy has usually been denominated the School of Common Sense. As regards perception, or the nature of our knowledge of external objects, which is the grand distinguishing feature of all systems of philosophy, the Scotch metaphysicians are Natural

Realists. They hold to an immediate knowledge of external objects, without the intervention of any mediating mental representation or idea. This doctrine was intentionally, though not in all respects consistently, held by Reid and Stewart, and has been fully and consistently carried out by Hamilton.

78. According to Hamilton, the mind, present in all parts of the organism, or at least at its central terminations, is directly conscious of the affections of that organism, through corresponding affections of its own, and, in the mutual outness of these affections, apprehends the body as something extended. At the same time, through our power of locomotion, and the resistance to this locomotion which we meet with in our experience, we become conscious of the existence of objects exterior to our bodies, which also become known as extended objects, by the impressions which they make on our organism, already known as extended.

79. But as the principles of the Scotch philosophy are well known in this country, and form the general basis of most of our treatises, nothing further need be said on the history of this school. And having thus completed the abstract of philosophy which I intended; having traced in outline — distinct, I hope, though meagre — the wayward course of speculation from the earliest times to our own, I leave the subject, trusting that the bare sketch here presented, will prove sufficient to stimulate the curiosity of the student to pursue in detail a department of history so interesting and fruitful.

EXPLANATORY NOTES

AND

QUESTIONS ON THE TEXT.*

I.

EXPLANATORY NOTES.

INTRODUCTION.

1. IN the expressions "I think," and "I am present," the *I* or self is evidently used in different senses, including in one case only the mind, and in the other the whole person. So when I say "I raise my arm," while I distinguish self from the arm, I at the same time make the arm *mine*, or a part of self.—For the meaning of the word *affection* here, see p. 20, note.

2. The term *person*, properly includes the body; as to be "present in person" is to be present *bodily*. But when we inquire what one's personality consists in, as in the question about "personal identity," we find that it embraces the body, at most, only as a type or form; since in substance the body is continually changing, and only the interior conscious self remains absolutely the same.—In saying that "the mind first becomes conscious of itself through the

* These notes and questions are allowed to remain, although a part of them have become inapplicable by the changes in the text.

various affections which the body suffers," the mind is spoken of merely in its present state as connected with the body, without any reference to its antecedent state.

3. *Microcosm* and *macrocosm* mean respectively "little world" and "great world." As all the primitive materials of knowledge must come in through the senses, so can they be retained and used only within; hence, when we speak of roaming in thought through the universe, we simply mean that we represent to ourselves in our minds various objects throughout the universe.

4. *Extension* and *resistance* are general properties of matter, containing various subordinate properties under them. For which, see p. 57, 4 and 6.

5. *Phenomena* means "appearances," "manifestations," and is used to designate indifferently any state, change, modification, or quality, whether of mind or matter.

6. By the *participating* of the mind in an affection, is meant its sharing in it, its being itself affected, modified, or changed, together with the organ; thus making every sensation at the same time an organic and a mental change.

CHAPTER I.

SECTION I.

2. The mind, of course, can receive knowledge only according to its nature or powers, just as the mirror receives images only according to its peculiar nature, and thus modifies them as it receives them. Our knowledge of things, then, is determined partly by the forms or moulds which our minds present for its reception. These primitive determinations of thought which decide its possibility and form, *ab initio*, are variously denominated "native or first principles of knowledge," "primary facts and truths of con-

sciousness," "first principles of reasoning," etc. See Chap. II. Secs. 2 and 3, and Chap. VIII. Sec. 3.

6. A condition is always a limitation of that to which it is applied, since it always *specifies* some relation, quality, or circumstance concerning it. The conditional, therefore, is the limited, the finite, while the *unconditional* is the infinite, the absolute, i. e., that of which no condition or limitation can be named or conceived. Now, as we can know only that which can be marked off, or presented under some particular form or relation to the mind, we cannot know the unconditional; as, for instance, the absolute nature of matter, of mind, or of God,—we can know these only under certain definite relations which they bear to us. Hence, things in themselves, or the essence of things, or the *ideas* of things, as expressed by Plato, cannot be known by us. See Hamilton's article on the Unconditioned, Wight's Hamilton, p. 441.

SECTION II.

8. In such expressions as "I use *my* mind," what can the *I* indicate but the will? that which controls the mind—a self deeper than the mind as a whole? If our wills are not *free*, then are we not moral agents; and if not moral agents, what evidence have we that God is a moral governor? Indeed, if our thoughts and wills are determined, as in physical causation, why assume a spiritual nature at all for our minds? Why not regard what we call intelligence as the result of organization? And if there be no spirit in man, why any in nature? *Nullus in microcosmo spiritus, nullus in macrocosmo Deus.* See Bowen's Hamilton, pp. 17–19.

CHAPTER II.

SECTION I.

3. The automatic theory supposes a physical connection between the different parts of a process to become established by repetition;

so that, for instance, the movement of one finger, in playing a tune, awakens such a local irritability as to cause the movement of the finger which has usually followed it in performing the process, and so on. But if the mind is not really superintending and directing the process, why should it always be suspended when the attention is suddenly arrested by any thing which wholly engrosses the mind for the moment?

SECTION II.

2. We announce our consciousness of a self and a not-self in our expression of every perception; we always say, *I* perceive *this* or *that*. We have no recollection, of course, of our *first perceptions*. Hence we do not know from actual experience how they seemed to us. But, from the nature of the case, and from the experience of persons who have first acquired the use of some of their senses in mature life, it seems probable that first perceptions, in the case of most of the senses, must appear as mere affections of the organ.

3. There must be some object before the mind in all thought; and hence, in perception, if the object itself is not perceived, there must be some representative image of it before the mind; which is the view taken of perception by some philosophers.

5. By the "*figment* of the imagination" is meant, the image or imaginary object conjured up by the mind, and held before it as its object.

SECTION III.

I. 3. "Outness" is a term first used, I believe, by Berkeley, to express the fact that both our bodily sensations and external objects all appear to have different localities, or reveal themselves, as perceived by us, as out of each other. If they all appeared to us as occupying the same locality, we could never have any notion of space.

I. 5. As both mental and material qualities must have a *substratum* to which they belong, "substance" may be either material or immaterial.

I. 7. "Empirical ideas" or knowledge stands opposed to *a priori* knowledge. Ideas of the first class are simply generalizations from experience, while those of the latter class are original, native, or necessary notions, — those primitive convictions of the mind already so often referred to.

I. 9. The idea that physical antecedents are only secondary causes, and that all real causal power is in God, is objected to chiefly on the ground that it supposes such an incessant and multifarious exercise of power by God as to render it highly improbable. But if God made the world, is there any thing improbable in the idea that he operates it by his power? Is there any thing more inconceivable in the latter than in the former?

II. 3. In admitting that we are not *continuously conscious*, it is not denied that there is a sort of sub-consciousness which is continuous. Sleep is but a dormant state of the senses, sometimes shallower and sometimes deeper, but never, probably, wholly suspending an undercurrent of thought. But this does not come to the surface, and is not properly consciousness.

III. 2. (3.) A "*deliverance* of consciousness," is simply what is reported or given in consciousness, or what is revealed there, i. e. some fact or truth of consciousness.

CHAPTER III.

SECTION I.

2. "Natural dualism," called dualism because it holds to the consciousness of *two* elements in perception, which is implied in the word.

3. "Actually perceived," i.e., a real knowledge of their externality is gained through their resistance. See Sect. III. 2. The doctrine of *occasional causes*, first taught by Descartes (see p. 217), has affected, more or less, nearly all systems of philosophy since. According to this doctrine, the impressions made upon the senses by external objects are merely the *occasions* of awakening such ideas in our minds as God wills; impressions of an entirely different character would answer just as well, if God should so will. The impression or sensation, then, is of no consequence in itself, except as a sign, and does not, as in the view presented in the text, really furnish the conditions or elements of the perception itself. See note, Sec. III. 9.

5. "Phenomenal modifications," i. e., mere appearances, transitory states. In man, the two phenomena of thought and extension, or of mind and matter, confront each other. In him thought apprehends or perceives extension, or mind, matter.

7. "Or else it regards them (i. e., our ideas of external objects) as merely self-limiting forms of the consciousness itself." This is Fichte's view, for which see Appendix, No. 66.

8. Consciousness, being a direct and simple knowledge, is certainly much less liable to be at fault than logic or reasoning, which consists of many steps. We may, indeed, be mistaken as to what we are really conscious of, but genuine consciousness can never be at fault.

10. "Sceptical . . . dogmatic," i. e., negative and positive, by way of doubt and by positive teaching. Scepticism simply criticizes or doubts the truth or validity of a system, rather than teaches any of its own. This was the method of Hume.

SECTION II.

6. If we press the hand against any hard substance, we are *resisted* outwardly, or objectively, while the organ is *pressed* inwardly, or subjectively. "Considered physically," i. e., as they stand in nature. All that is here meant is, that the various qualities embraced under the general notion of resistance, are to be divided into three classes, according to the sources whence the resistance springs.

(1.) As every body must have *extension*, this distinguishes body from not-body; but bodies differ *from each other* in hardness, weight, color, odor, etc.

(2.) As extension belongs necessarily to all bodies, and does not arise from the relation of one body to another, it may be said to arise from the relations of body to itself. But as every body resists or repels (more or less) every other body which is moved against it, resistance may be said to arise from the relation of one body to another; while color, heat, flavor, savor, and the like, arise from the relation of bodies to our sentient organism.

(3.) Matter could not exist without extension; separate objects could not exist if there was no resistance among them (they would all blend into one); and we could hold no communion with nature without the qualities of color, heat, flavor, savor, etc.

(4.) As the real self is a spirit, any thing which is extended is a not-self; in resistance, we are conscious of being *ourselves* resisted by something *foreign to self*; while we recognize the sensations of heat, savor, etc., as affections of our sentient organism, and infer their cause in certain external objects.

(5.) Extension is perceived simply as a quality of bodies; but heat, odor, etc., are apprehended as affections of our sentient organism; while resistance without becomes pressure within.

(7.) That is to say, the three classes of qualities affect our organism under the three different points of view here named.

(8.) See the illustrations to No. (5.)

(9.) Mathematics has to do with extension, number, etc.; and force (the subject of mechanics) arises from the various forms of resistance; while the secondary qualities are recognized as affections of our physical system, or sentient organism.

(10.) Perception is, strictly and properly, merely the apprehension of extension in bodies; but heat, flavor, etc., are recognized as mere sensations in our organism; while resistance is objectively (outwardly) a perception, and subjectively a sensation.

(11.) The perception of extension is, in the first instance, merely the apprehension of our organism as having parts out of parts; and although this is effected only through sensations in that organism, still the sensations are entirely subordinate to the perception, and, indeed, if at all obtrusive, interfere with the perception. On the contrary, the mind merely receives or suffers the sensations of heat, flavor, etc.; while it both apprehends resistance and suffers its sensation.

(12.) See the illustrations to No. (11.)

(13.) All our senses being susceptible of sensations, and these sensations revealing themselves as out of each other, they all, of course, furnish the conditions for apprehending extension.

(14.) It is impossible for us to conceive of any body without extension; but resistance, on the contrary, though a common attribute of matter, is not conceived as necessary to it, but as only contingent; while heat, sound, flavor, etc., are not only contingent or accidental qualities, but are peculiar, as being specifically adapted for determining our nervous system to the peculiar sensations of which we are susceptible.

(15.) See the illustrations to No. (11.)

SECTION III.

2. "We can but conclude, therefore, that the resisting object is distinct from and external to us." Professor Porter, however, regards the simple sensations of touch as a sufficient ground for inferring the existence of objects external to our organism: since, in touching other objects, one simply feels; while in touching himself he not only feels, but *is felt.*

5. "An object and a medium." Formerly the light, the agitation of the air, and the effluvia, were regarded as merely the media through which objects communicated with the eye, the ear, or the nose, and not as the very things which alone are perceived. Our knowledge of the object which emits the light, sound, or effluvia, is reached only through experience.

9. If sensations are merely mental affections, then in the experience of sensations, we apprehend nothing exterior to the mind (which according to the hypothesis is alone affected); whereas if sensations are equally mental and organic affections, then we actually experience sensations out of each other in an extended organism, which is a veritable perception.

10. "Perhaps." I am aware that this is a very unphilosophical word. If we consider the sensation suffered by the mind in any particular affection of a nerve, or nervous filament, as always of a given character, then the sensation would be the same whether experienced at the centre or at the extremity. We should have a combination of sensations of a particular character, all out of each other, which very naturally, it may be, would be carried out to the extremities of the nerves, where we know the organic affection generally originates, even though really apprehended at the centre. See Wight's Hamilton, p. 385, note.

SECTION IV.

I. 3. Our sensations, in the exercise of all the senses, reveal themselves as out of each other, and hence all of them furnish the conditions of apprehending our organism as extended; but the sense of touch furnishes these conditions the most "obtrusively," since the whole body serves as the organ of touch, while the organs of the other senses are quite limited in extent.

IV. 3. "That the organ is thus affected we know from observation." Take the eye of an ox, or any other animal soon after it is killed, and peel off the integuments on the back side, and hold it up before any object, and you will see the image upon the retina.

5. (2.) By "the organism affected," is here meant, of course, the retina of the eye, which presents a considerable expanse, that is always affected or modified by the image in every act of vision.

8. "Following out the ascertained lines of vision," etc. The image being all that is recognized at first, would then be the sole object contemplated. As we gradually learn by experience that this represents an object, we learn also (as described in No. 9) that the different points in that object are seen in straight lines at right angles to the eye. Now if we suppose the image to be moved out (as it would be in our experience) on these lines (which cross each other at the pupil) to the object, every point in the object will correspond to its projected image upon the retina. One has but to draw a diagram, with the rays from an object crossing each other at the pupil and projecting themselves upon the retina, to see this.

CHAPTER IV.

SECTION IV.

7. "An irrespective object," i. e., an object having no respect or relation to any thing else. It is rather viewed as a part of the

whole where it has been once perceived, and as such tends to revive the remembrance of the other parts.

21. "Mental movement," i. e., progress, through associations among our ideas. One thought follows from, or is suggested by, another. As we have already seen, thoughts related by contiguity of time or place, by likeness, or by contrast, tend to suggest each other. And it is through these relations among our thoughts that Aristotle here represents us as excogitating the object to be remembered.

CHAPTER V.

SECTION II.

7. "More perfect than ever actually occurs in any one object in nature." This must be so if there is any distinction between the ideal and the real. No single face or form can be found with all its features or lines perfect. So there is no single flower but has defects in some of its leaves or petals. And the same is true of other things. But in the ideal face, flower, or other object, the imagination supplies these defects, and rounds out the whole.

8. What is here called "conception" is such, considered as something thought of, or construed to the mind; but as represented in a concrete image, it is an act of the imagination. See Wight's Hamilton, p. 454.

CHAPTER VI.

SECTION I.

7. "*Inconceivability* is not regarded by us as equivalent to *impossibility*." What is inconceivable seems impossible *for us*, indeed, but not necessarily so for Almighty Power or Wisdom. We cannot conceive how matter can be either created or destroyed, and yet we do not regard it as impossible to God.

SECTION IV.

II. 2. The real difference between the nominalist, the conceptualist, and the realist, is, that the nominalist wholly rejects concepts proper, as different from percepts; while the conceptualist holds to concepts as formed by the abstraction of such common qualities of related objects as actually occur to us in our experience; and the realist to concepts which embrace only the *essential* qualities of objects, such as those upon which the classification of objects turns. With the nominalist, there is nothing general but class-names, directly applicable to every individual of the class without the intervention of a mental concept; with the conceptualist, the class-word is expressly designed to designate the mental concept, but, at the same time, is applicable to individual things through the intervention of the imagination; while, by the realist, the concept, or general notion, is regarded as expressing the very essence of things, as determining their classification, and, by the extreme realist, as determining their existence.

CHAPTER VII.

SECTION II.

9. For Hamilton's scheme of propositions, see his Logic, p. 529

CHAPTER VIII.

SECTION II.

7. The "ontological argument" for the existence of God is this: That, as we have in our minds the *idea* of an infinite and perfect being, this necessarily implies the *existence* of such a being as its cause, since the finite and imperfect things around us are not adequate to produce such an idea. The "cosmological argument" infers the existence of God from the dependent and changeful

nature of things around us, which implies an independent and unchangeable being. The succession of causes and effects which we witness in nature must originate in a cause which is not at the same time an effect; otherwise the principle of causation is made void, and there is merely an infinite series of *effects*.

II.

QUESTIONS ON THE TEXT.

INTRODUCTION.

1. When does *self* include the mind only? When the body, and why? What is the body to the mind, and how animated? Of what affections are we conscious, and how do we become so?

2. In what sense is the body animated by the spirit? What is the body always to be distinguished from? How is the mind first awakened to consciousness?

3. How is the body the *microcosm* of the human spirit as the universe is the *macrocosm* of the Divine Spirit? When the mind is spoken of as roaming through Nature, what is really meant? By what are mind and matter distinguished?

4. How is the body known to us? What is it composed of? Is it possible to conceive that the body thinks? Why is the mind said to be *immaterial*? By what energies does the mind manifest itself?

5. What are some of the lower elements of life in man? Can they be explained by mechanical or chemical laws? What do the conscious phenomena of life evidently depend upon? What does the disappearance of these phenomena at death prove?

6. In what two ways may the mind become conscious of the affections of the body, and in which of them does it probably do so? What is the effect of obtaining knowledge through material organs, and what is it evidence of? How is it with pure intelligences?

7. What antithesis and what mystery do we meet with at the outset? What do the various psychological systems turn upon?

CHAPTER I.

SECTION I.

1. What is the general conscious principle in man called? What is its most important function? Is intelligence a single process? Is it designated as a whole? How do the different designations represent it?

2. What of the term *intellect* as a designation of the knowing principle? How is the intellect regarded by some philosophers? In this sense what relation does it bear to the knowing powers? What are treatises on the cognitive powers in general called?

3. What does the term *understanding* sometimes denote? How is it used by Locke? What does Hamilton say of it? How does the term represent the mind?

4. What does *reason* sometimes, and what does it properly denote? How is it opposed to the receptivity of sense? How to the blindness and excitability of feeling? Why is *proof* called reasoning?

5. What distinction does Milton make in reason? What of the reason intuitive? Can the reason give reasons for every thing? What can it do?

6. What of reason transcendental? What distinction does Kant make between the reason and the understanding? Of what does each take cognizance? Why may this meaning of reason be disregarded?

7. What might be said of consciousness? How does it not, and how does it denote knowledge?

8. Why is intelligence distributed among several faculties? What is perception? Give an account of the term, and other terms explained in the note. What self-consciousness? What memory? What imagination? What conception? What judgment? What reasoning?

SECTION II.

1. Besides knowing, what do we do? What are some of the feelings of which we are susceptible? What are some of the processes connected with willing? What relation do those phenomena bear to knowledge?

2. What feelings are called *organic?* What are some of them? What *intellectual* or *moral* feelings? What are these properly denominated? What are some of them?

3. What constitutes physical pleasure and pain? What intellectual? What *good* and what *evil?*

4. When are the feelings called *affections?* When *emotions?* When *passions?* When *propensities* or desires and aversions? What sort of affections are feelings really? What relation do they bear to knowledge? Give the illustrations.

5. What are the moral feelings consequent upon? What does Butler say of the moral faculty? What are the moral sentiments

forms of, and how awakened? What are the pleasures and disgusts of taste, and what consequent upon? Can there be any æsthetic feelings without a previous æsthetic perception?

6. What is the third phase of the mind revealed in consciousness? What is said of deliberation? What of choosing and resolving? To what does the question of the independent power of the will belong? What is said of it in passing? What is said of the question practically?

7. What is said of the question *how* the will acts through the organism? To what science do this, and the kindred question of how the external objects affect the mind through the body, belong? What hypotheses have been made on these questions by physical philosophers?

8. Which of the three great classes of mental phenomena seem to proceed from the deepest principle in our nature? If the will be free, what is the consequence? And what if not?

CHAPTER II.

SECTION I.

1. What alone can we properly be said to know? When we do thus note objects, what happens? What must all real knowledge be then? Why, then, are knowledge and consciousness equivalent? What is said of knowing, and knowing that we know?

2. What is said of the probability, from the nature of things, of there being a species of knowledge wholly fugitive and transitory? What do many of our acts seem to imply? How can we know that we ever have such thoughts? If there be such mental states, what must they be considered? What do they seem to constitute?

3. In what kind of processes are such states of sub-consciousness implied? What are such operations when first performed? What do they become in time? How does Hamilton regard them? How are they regarded by others? What is meant by automatic? What is Stewart's view of the case?

4. Do the usual antecedents of knowledge always awaken any mental apprehension? In what cases do they not? Can we be quite certain of this? What is said of the striking of a clock? How shall we account for the recalling of such an impression? Why does the rapid revolution of a lighted torch produce the appearance of an entire circle of light (note)?

5. What, then, is consciousness not, and what is it? How does the mind work as compared with a machine? How can knowing, willing, and feeling, become distinct acts, and how can they be realized? What, then, is consciousness? How is it related to perception?

6. What is embraced under the facts of consciousness? What is the meaning of *subjective* (note)? What may consciousness be considered as the subjective side of? As such, what may it embrace? What, then, does consciousness, in its most general sense include? What may the mind do with these primitive materials? What is the limit, then, of human knowledge?

SECTION II.

1. What is the most important question in philosophy? What do we want here? What should be rejected and what admitted? What is to be taken as final? What is the sole question here? In what respect is this question to be attended to here?

2. What are we conscious of in perception? Of what in the perception of a tree, for instance? Suppose that in our first per-

ceptions we are conscious of nothing beyond the affection of the organ? What does our experience of resistance lead to?

3. How then are the two elements presented in perception? Do we ever regard the two as the same? Is the object perceived ever regarded as a mere thought of the mind? How, then, does the mind always regard perceived objects? Do all men so regard them? What conviction can we never get rid of?

4. What is there not a consciousness of in memory? What is the mental action in memory? What do we reproduce and recognize in memory? Does consciousness directly reveal any thing out of the mind in memory? What have we, then, in memory?

5. What are we conscious of in imagination? How is the figment of the imagination regarded? What, then, are we conscious of, respectively, in perception, in memory, and in imagination?

6. What is the object before the mind in intuition and conception? What in judgment? What in reasoning? What in feeling? What in willing?

SECTION III.

1. What is here said of the facts of consciousness? What of the truths of consciousness? If they are not mere secondary notions, what authority do they rest upon? If original convictions, what then? How are these primary principles to be regarded?

I. What is the first class of these truths?

1. What is said of the possibility of directly perceiving space? How must it be reached, if reached at all through the action of the organs? But what is change of place, and how alone can it be understood? Can we, then, derive our idea of space from motion?

2. When we say that we see objects here and there, and move here and there, what are the real facts in the case? What does the truth seem to be? How do our sensations reveal themselves, and what does this give rise to? Would objects appear extended unless the mind so conceived them?

3. What is the most conclusive evidence that our idea of space is not a generalization from experience? In what sense may we be said to experience space? Why, then, should our notion of space, if derived from this source, be finite? But what is our notion of it in fact? Can we place any bounds to space even in imagination?

4. Can we perceive time by the senses? Can we derive our notion of it from succession, and why not? How, then, are the *now* and the *then* added? Do we conceive time as limited? What appears, then, with regard to space and time? Can we think of any thing as out of space and time?

5. Can we directly perceive substance? What alone do we directly apprehend in perception? But how are we compelled to think of these qualities and states? How are they conceived? How, then, do we come to assume a substantive existence for ourselves and other objects?

6. What idea springs up within us on observing changes? What do we mean by causation? Can we directly perceive the exertion of power in causation? What was Hume's inference in regard to causation, from this?

7. In order to save the idea of causation, then, what must be shown? What do those who regard the idea as empirical derive it from? But what may we, and what may we not, be said to experience in the exercise of our wills? What do we really infer in the case? What are we here actually conscious of? Can we doubt the causal connection in the case of our wills especially? But what kind of knowledge is this?

8. Of what character, then, must our idea of causation be? What does our mental constitution compel us to? What form does the causal notion assume in our minds? Does the extent of our experience make any difference in regard to the universality of our notion in the case?

9. Why is it not necessary to suppose that the real causal power lies in the antecedent? Can we perceive any particular adaptedness in one object over another to produce a given effect? Is it easy for us to believe that one form of matter has any real power over another?

10. To what does this doctrine of causation lead? What is true of a succession of finite beings or events? What besides Revelation attests to such a beginning in man, and other races of animals and plants? As what other cause, besides the first cause, do we regard God? Where does our idea of causation find its complete exemplification?

II. What is the second class of these truths?

1. What are we not, and what are we conscious of in memory? What do we firmly believe in? What authority does the recollection have with us?

2. How do we know that the representative thought is not delusive? What determines us to the conclusion that it is not? Do we believe any more firmly in the perceptions of our senses? What shows the firmness of our belief in the truthfulness of memory? What is effected by this law of our nature?

3. What is meant by personal identity? What is it in us which seems always the same? In what sense are we not continuously conscious (explanatory note)? How alone can past states of consciousness be known? Upon what, then, must our belief in our

personal identity **rest**? How would you state the case? What does memory predicate in the case? State the argument.

III. What is the third class of these truths?

1. What are some of the logical axioms? What the mathematical? Can these axioms be verified by experience, and what is their character?

2. Does this enumeration exhaust the primary truths of consciousness? How is this section to be closed?

(1.) When is a conviction incomprehensible? What is the case when we are unable to comprehend why or how a thing is?

(2.) How is the simplicity of a cognition a test of its originality?

(3.) How are necessity and universality coincident? What are the two kinds of necessity here spoken of? What are the cognitions characterized by the two kinds of necessity respectively called?

(4.) What is the fourth character of original beliefs? How are the third and fourth characters expressed by Aristotle? How is the latter expressed by Buffier?

SECTION IV.

1. What is the question here? Why, especially, is it necessary to consider this question? What has been thought necessary to establish the truth of any thing?

2. To what do proofs owe their validity? What do they start with and proceed by? Why cannot every thing be proved? What must the starting points in knowledge be?

3. What is said of some of these first principles? What is the probability about the truth of such convictions? What is the case with others? Suppose they are not realities, what then?

4. How alone can the presumption in favor of the truth of these primary intuitions be removed? What is it always allowable to deny? But what must the doubter show?

5. How is philosophy here defined? What should such a philosophy exclude, and what admit? What is one particular fact, then, which it must admit? What should be the simple object of inquiry here?

SECTION V.

1. What is attention? When is there no special exercise of attention? What is the state of the mind in such cases? But when does attention begin, and what is the case in its highest concentration?

2. When the consciousness is concentrated, how is it with the mind, and why? When the attention to any thing is complete, what is true of other mental operations? What is the state of the mind, then, in attention?

3. How is the attention concentrated? How far is the attention under the control of the will? How far can the will resist distracting influences? What are thus indicated?

4. To control the will, what should we cultivate? What should we form a settled purpose of doing? When we turn our attention to any thing, with what determination should we do it? With what state of mind should we always work? What will be the effect of such a course?

5. How may distracting influences be diminished? What do wandering thoughts come of? What are our minds formed for?

What is the natural order of thoughts? How is it in memory and reasoning? What have we to do, then, to exclude wandering thoughts? How else may we protect ourselves against disturbing influences? When we wish to command our attention, to what influences should we not leave ourselves exposed? What do intense or protracted mental efforts require?

6. What is another means of controlling the attention? What are instances of this? What will be the effect upon the mind?

7. What is reflection? What is a more precise definition? Of what is a mental state, as a passing phenomenon, the object, and of what, when taken up for examination?

8. Why need no extended remarks be made upon reflection? In what sort of studies is the power of reflection specially necessary? What does psychology rest upon? What, then, does the success of the student in this science depend upon? How may the power of reflection be acquired?

CHAPTER III.

SECTION I.

1. What two elements does consciousness embrace? How may we accept this fact in the first place? How else may we accept it? How else? How else? How else? How else? How many theories of perception, then, may there be?

2. What does the first theory of perception hold to, and what is it called? What does realism receive, and why? What does it not attempt to explain, and what does it hold to be conceivable?

3. How does realism hold that objects are *immediately* perceived? What does it hold the impressions made upon the senses

to be? How does it conceive the mind as connected with the organism? How does such a connection lead to a knowledge of external objects?

4. What is here said of this theory? Whose theory was it intentionally, and who has lately expounded it anew?

5. What is the second theory of perception called? According to this theory, what is true of mind and matter, God and Nature? Or, how may the case be stated more accurately? What then are mind and matter? What is consciousness on this theory? What is perception? Who are the representatives of this theory?

6. What does this theory do violence to? State the case. Why cannot the system be generally received?

7. What does the third theory make perception? How does it account for the origin of ideas in the mind? What does this theory do with the external world? Who are its representatives?

8. What can no one deny? How may the idealist logically prove that no external world can be perceived? Can the mind rest in such a conclusion, and why not? How can life become ideal, and what is the consequence?

9. What does the fourth theory make thought, and what is it called? What is said of the danger of adopting this theory? What office does the body perform in perception? How far may we trace up the mechanical part of perception? Can we conceive that matter thinks?

10. What is the fifth theory called, and why? Why cannot states of consciousness be denied? What is allowed? But what then? How does this theory err? Who are its representatives?

11. Why has the sixth theory received different designations? What is the first name which it has received, and why? What are the second and third names which it has received, and why?

12. What objection is there against this theory? Is its assumption of the existence of the external world warranted? What belief does it deny, and what assert? Is the belief denied less clear and strong than that affirmed? Suppose the mind really knows nothing of external object, what then?

SECTION II.

1. What do we not, and what do we directly perceive in mind or matter? In what sense do we know even these qualities and states? For aught we know, what may they be? What, however, is the presumption in the case?

2. What remark of Cicero is here quoted? What is consciousness, as far as revealed to us? How does consciousness always reveal itself? What does it say? What is the *I* in such expressions? What, then, do we necessarily assume for ourselves?

3. What is here said of matter? What, then, becomes important for us? What classifications have been made of the qualities of matter?

4. What are the primary qualities of matter? What is said of motion and situation?

5. What is the character, and what the names, of the secondary properties of matter? How are these properties known? How are they really apprehended?

6. How many phases do the secundo-primary qualities of matter have? How do they manifest themselves on their primary phasis? How on their secondary? To what classes are these qualities to be reduced?

7. Why are the following observations from Hamilton introduced here, and from what work of his are they taken?

(1.) Under what point of view do the primary qualities deserve the name of qualities? Why do the other two classes more properly deserve the name? Illustrate (see explanatory note).

(2.) What do the primary arise from? What the secundo-primary? What the secondary? Illustrate.

(3.) What do the primary determine? What the secundo-primary? What the secondary? Illustrate.

(4.) What do we apprehend under the primary? What under the secundo-primary? What under the secondary? Illustrate.

(5.) How are the primary apprehended? How the secondary? How the secundo-primary? Illustrate.

(6.) In which of the classes are the names of the qualities univocal, and in which equivocal? What are some instances of the equivocal names of qualities? Illustrate.

(7.) Under what relation to our organism are the primary qualities, qualities of body? Under what the secundo-primary? Under what the secondary? Illustrate.

(8.) What are the primary? What the secondary? What the secundo-primary? Illustrate.

(9.) How may the primary be characterized? How the secundo-primary? How the secondary? Illustrate.

(10.) What are the apprehensions of the primary? What of the secondary? What of the secundo-primary? Illustrate.

(11.) What is the state of the mind in the apprehension of the primary qualities? What in the apprehension of the secondary? What in that of the secundo-primary? Illustrate.

(12.) What relation does the sensation hold in the perception of primar qualities? What in the perception of the secundo-primary? What in the perception of the secondary? Illustrate.

(13.) What furnish the conditions for the perception of the primary qualities, and what the sensations of the secondary? How are the secundo-primary qualities apprehended as percepts, and how as sensations? Illustrate.

(14.) As modes of matter, how are the primary thought? How the secundo-primary? How the secondary? Illustrate.

(15.) What is the apprehension of a primary quality principally, and what secondarily? What the apprehension of a secondary quality? What of a secundo-primary quality? Illustrate.

SECTION III.

1. What is not expected here? What is the object here? Is perception wholly arbitrary? What about it is fixed?

2. What is the medium of the mind in perception? Through what are the mind and its object brought most directly face to face? How is the body, however, essential even here? What does the possession of an organism and of the power of changing place render us capable of? Of what two things are we conscious? In such a case, then, what do we know? Of what two things are we conscious here? What relation do they hold to each other? What sort of a perception is this?

3. Of what, however, are we really conscious here? What two things have already been repeatedly stated? When we become conscious of resistance, what do we immediately assume? What is true then of a quality and its subject?

4. What of the body in perception by the senses proper? What is an indispensable condition here? What is meant by this? State the case in regard to the different senses.

5. What is here said of the distinction of an object and a medium? What is the distinction here referred to (see note)? What alone can we perceive? When is an object in relation to an organ? What are all the senses modifications of?

6. What happens to the organ in all cases of perception? By what is the organ modified? How does the case stand in sight? How in the other cases?

7. Is it certain that there is in perception any modification of the organ below the surface? What has been the common supposition on this point, and what are the theories to which it has given rise? What is said of these theories? What question here still remains unsettled?

8. What is the first argument for a special sensorium at the centre? What the second? What the third? But what are the first and the last really arguments against?

9. What is the first argument against the notion that the mind is confined to the centre of the organism? What the second? What the third? What the fourth?

10. On the whole, what is the view in the case which is attended with the fewest difficulties? What follows from this view?

11. What, then, is a sensation? How, through sensations, do we apprehend extension? To what is direct perception by the senses confined? How do we become conscious of our organism as extended? How do we infer extension in external bodies? How do we infer the existence of the secondary properties in matter?

SECTION II.

I. 1. What sensation is called touch? What is the more internal sensation caused by pressure called? What that caused by violent contact, etc.? What is the muscular sense? What other peculiar and occasional feelings are there?

2. In what nerves do these sensations have their seat? Describe these nerves? Whence comes the feeling experienced in the use of the other senses? What is said of the nerves of each sense? How do we learn this in the case of sight?

3. What is said of the extent of our experience through touch? What do its sensations furnish? What other sensations do we experience through this sense?

4. What is the most important organ of this sense, and why? How is this shown in the case of the blind man? What is said of determining the form of small and large bodies respectively?

II. 1. What is the organ of this sense, and how furnished? What nerve alone is susceptible of the sensation of taste? What substances alone affect this sense, and why? What arrangement is made in consequence? What injures or destroys the taste?

2. What is a taste properly? How do we learn the cause of a taste? Do we know the nature of the property which gives rise to taste? What physical elements does a taste involve? But what are these sufficient for? What do we often do in recalling a taste?

3. What tendency is there with regard to articles which have an agreeable taste, and the opposite? What sort of a test of its wholesomeness is the taste of an article? What assistance do the other senses render in this matter?

III. 1. What is the organ of smell, and how is it constructed? How can an organ thus situated and constructed be reached? What substances, then, are odoriferous?

2. What is a smell, properly? How do we learn its cause? What do we learn on further inquiry? What do we conclude then? What may be said of the physical character of a smell?

3. In what does the importance of smell appear? What does it enlarge?

IV. 1. What is the organ of vision? What is the course of the rays of light to the chamber of the eye? What from this point? Why do they form an inverted image?

2. Where does the susceptibility of sight reside, and what is required for perfect vision? Of what adjustments is the eye capable in order to secure a distinct image, etc.? How far are these powers of adjustment competent to the end? What of glasses?

3. What is vision? What effect does the light produce upon the retina? How do we know that the organ is thus affected, and that it is this affection of which we are conscious? What is sight, then, previous to experience?

4. What is color, then? Whose statement of the case is here introduced?

5. How does Hamilton state his doctrine on this point? How many peculiarities does he state there are in the case?

(1.) What does he say of the organic affection of color? What of its apprehension, as far as it is a sensation?

(2.) Under what conditions do we become conscious of the affection of color? How is it apprehended in consequence of this?

(3.) What do the filaments of the optic nerve afford us? How alone can these sensations be realized? What do these circumstances show? What do they not warrant?

6. What becomes of the fallacies of sight according to this view of vision? What are some of these fallacies? Is there any deception here? How do we learn the actual size, etc., of things?

7. What do we soon learn to infer from the affection of vision?

What is the first step? What the next? What do we hence conclude? What do we soon verify, and why? What do we soon come to take the visual affection as the sign of? How is the rest learned?

8. What further do we learn by experience? How alone can we become conscious of the inverted position of the image on the eye? In learning this, what other corrective fact do we learn at the same time? What does the law of visible direction show?

9. How alone is an object distinctly and satisfactorily seen? Are all objects thus scrutinized by us? What do we learn by this scrutiny? What do we soon come to understand? What correspondence is there between the image and its object?

10. How do we learn the form of objects by sight? Why can we not see form except in a single dimension? How do we judge of the form of a solid body from sight? How when rays of light from it can reach us from only one side?

11. What is not, and what is, the question here? How may this question be answered in a general way? Why have we double organs? On what principle does no confusion arise from this arrangement?

12. Why must the two eyes take in different aspects of the same object? When does this become consciously so to one? Why do not all objects appear so to us? How are the two images brought together? But what shows that in practice we do actually recognize the two images and combine them into one? What is the arrangement of the stereoscope, and what the result?

13. How do we learn to judge of distance by sight? Can we see distance, and how is it shown that we cannot? How do we learn to infer it? From the distance of an object, what else do we infer? What does vision thus become the source of?

14. Why do our judgments from vision require uniform conditions in the atmosphere? If the light from an object is bent out of its course, how will the object appear? What is the effect of a hazy atmosphere upon the appearance of objects? What is the cause of the increased apparent size of the sun and moon when near the horizon, according to Berkeley? What according to Descartes?

15. How are these illusions of sight rectified? How may they be explained? What is here said of sight?

V. 1. What is the organ of hearing? What is the structure and different parts of the ear? How are the vibrations collected and conveyed to the auditory nerve?

2. What is sound? What is the immediate, and what the remote cause of the affection? What is considered as the real cause? What assists us in determining the direction of a sound, and tracing it to its source? On what is the art of ventriloquism founded? How does the ventriloquist accomplish his object?

3. What information do we derive through the sense of hearing? How does the exercise of our powers of speech depend upon hearing?

SECTION V.

1. What is said, in general, of the comparative importance of the senses? The loss of which is the most fatal? Of which the most deplorable? What, however, is true of the loss of hearing?

2. What of their individual and combined importance? What is accomplished by them? What by taste? What by smell and hearing? What by touch and sight?

3. What do the senses collect, then? What constitute all our knowledge? What, then, depend upon the materials collected by

the senses? What, then, is obvious? Without the proper use of the senses what must always be the case?

4. What sciences are founded upon observed facts? What is the principal thing in most of these sciences? What is the case in all branches of natural history? What in natural philosophy and astronomy?

5. What is language largely built upon? What is the first meaning of most words? What do a large part of the words of every language refer to? What is the case with the other words? Upon what, then, must the force and meaning of a language depend?

6. What is true in regard to these facts? What alone is necessary on our part in order to perceive them? What will an ever-wakeful attention enable even the common man to do in regard to them?

7. What, then, does great importance attach to? What is effected by this? What must one do in the exercise of this habit? What will such an exercise put him in possession of? What alone does one, with such materials, want to make him a great philosopher?

8. What inference is made from the above? What should parents and teachers do? How should observation by the senses be conducted in our schools?

CHAPTER IV.

SECTION I.

1. What does the term memory designate loosely? What wner we speak with precision? What according to its derivation? How does what we perfectly remember seem? How does recollectior ~ecognize the reproduction of the past?

2. What, then, is the difference between memory and recollection? How does the object sought present itself in the two processes? What are instances of the two kinds of reproduction? Is this distinction between the two words always maintained?

3. Who is said to have a ready, and who a tardy memory? What is this difference in memory owing to? What promotes a ready, and what a tardy memory?

4. What has tended to disparage memory as a mental endowment? What does not, and what does readiness of memory imply? What does any extraordinary capacity in one power seem to imply in regard to the others? Why is great readiness of memory likely to prove a fatal gift? But may not memory be in excess? But what must a good mind have? What form does memory assume in such minds? How is their knowledge associated and recalled? How is it with such in regard to the random power of memory?

5. Do memory and recollection often coexist in equal degrees in the same mind? What is the case with the desultory memory? What with the philosophical memory? In what rare characters are the two species of memory found united?

6. Which prevails more in youth? Which in mature age? Why should it be so? How is it in old age?

7. What is said of the above account of the distinction between memory and recollection? What does Hamilton limit the term memory to? What is all conscious reproduction of the past according to this view? Is this admitted? But with what reservation?

SECTION II.

1. What is it to remember any thing? What is it not? What is said of the thing remembered? What is the mind occupied with then? What is the thought of the object suggested by?

2. What does the mind do in remembering any thing? Why should this picture appear almost like the thing itself? What arises from this as to our knowledge of the past?

3. What is obvious at the outset? Why are objects of sight easily imaged to the mind? Give the illustrations. Can the object remembered be described?

4. What else is conceded? Why can a remembered object of touch be described? What does the blind man who reads by raised letters remember? But how are objects of touch more commonly recalled?

5. What is proof that we remember sounds? How only can a sound be described to another? But why must a sound be reproducible in memory? What are its physical elements, and to what may these be likened? What can a musician do?

6. What else must be admitted? What is said of their physical elements? What are they at all events? What is the evidence that we do recall them by their physical elements? What does the uniform recognition of them on their recurrence show?

7. What else may we remember? Give the illustrations. Under what relations may many of these be remembered?

8. Is there any sense in which a process of reasoning may be remembered? Is reasoning itself a process of memory? By what does reasoning proceed? Under what point of view, then, may it be remembered?

9. What does the public speaker do? How is the memory aided in this process? What does the mathematician do? How is he aided in this?

10. What else, in short, may we remember? How may they all be recalled? What must be true with regard to every thing which has a name?

11. But what is it admitted are the most readily remembered? Why? Through what senses, then, should as much of our knowledge as possible be introduced? What then is the advantage of models, diagrams, etc., in imparting knowledge?

SECTION III.

1. What is the object here? Is memory wholly a mystery? How far may it be traced up? What has been found in regard to perception, and what will be found in regard to memory?

2. What is the cause of perception, and what of memory? When is an object perceived, and when recalled? What is true alike in the simplest act of memory and the longest process of recollection? Do we remember at random or by a simple act of the will to do so? What may the will effect in the case? How alone can we reach the remembrance of the object sought for?

3. How do we remember a familiar friend? Why do we remember familiar objects the most readily? What do we mean by charging the memory with any thing? How are such special associations accomplished?

4. In case a verbal lesson is to be committed, what is noted, and what associations are formed? What does the call to recite recall? And what then? What is the process if only the ideas are to be committed?

5. What objection may be made to this, and what reply may be made? If there be no such recalling of words, notes, etc., what then?

6. When we charge the memory with any thing, do we really commit it to the memory for safe keeping? What, then, do we do? Give the illustration. Of what nature are all the little arts of memory? Explain the case of the string tied upon the finger?

7. What case of consciously voluntary recollection is given? How would a person proceed in endeavoring to ascertain where he had lost his purse? Why would every bridge, ferry, and tavern be specially recalled? Repeat the process as a whole.

8. What is evident, then? What is memory not, and what is it? If so, what then? Are ideas hoarded in the mind? What is the case then? What is memory? How do ideas suggest each other?

9. Is the mind wholly inactive in memory? What does it do? What does the physical view of memory refer the reproduction of ideas to? What is a fatal objection to this view? What other view, on the whole, is better?

SECTION IV.

1. What is the first law of memory? Why may this be called direct or simple memory?

2. What is this simple memory commonly called? How does it appear that it is really an act of memory? How does it differ from ordinary cases of memory? What are the illustrations?

3. What is the second law of memory? What does this law include?

4. What are instances of ideas recalling each other from a direct likeness? What is said of a single feature in a face, or a single strain in a tune? What are instances of ideas which recall each other from a fanciful likeness?

5. What is the first instance given of a prearranged association on the principle of likeness? What is the second?

6. What is the third law of memory? What does this law include?

7. What must be admitted, according to Hamilton? How is the thought of any thing which has been previously known as an integrant part of some whole, viewed, when reproduced? What does it tend to call up? What further than this? Give the illustrations.

8. Why does the name of a person or place recall the individual or locality? Why do we remember those places best which we have personally visited? Why should the names of places be printed distinctly on maps in connection with the localities?

9. Why are the feelings and tone of the mind affected by time and place? Give the illustrations.

10. What is the fourth law of memory? Why should contrasted objects recall each other? What are some of the contrasts which we meet with in our experience? What instance is given to illustrate the law?

11. How, perhaps, should this law be regarded? How does the relation here compare with that of real relatives, and what is the relation there? Give the examples. How should the law of relatives be regarded then? But what may be the case where the relation is looser?

12. What is the fourth law of memory?

13. What may this law be called? What is true of association and reminiscence in different individuals? Upon what does the course they take in different cases depend? By whom are these variations and their grounds well stated?

14. (1.) Who is named as remembering words more readily, and who things? What other variations are here named?

(2.) What is said of the natural organization and temperament? Who are named as having wonderful powers of memory?

(3.) What things settle deeply into the memory? Why do men of less genius often excel those of greater genius in the matter of memory?

(4.) What is the effect of feeling upon recollection? What things are remembered best then? What example illustrates this?

(5.) How is the memory strengthened? What are its effects upon the memory?

(6.) What effect does the unoccupied state of the mind have upon memory? How is this illustrated? What else in the state of mind in youth promotes the same thing?

15. What have these variations in memory sometimes been called? But what are they really? How are thoughts always associated and recalled? But upon what do each one's associations depend?

16. How does a certain Lutheran divine reach the recollection of Babylon, and why? How might an astronomer reach it, and why?

17. What is said of a merchant who has risks at sea? Where is this illustrated? What are the associations referred to in the passage quoted?

18. What should be fixed in our thinking in order to remember well? What is the case in mathematics? But how is it with most subjects? How can these be remembered readily?

19. What are the four rules of Aquinas for insuring the memory of any thing?

20. When may reminiscence be said to be voluntary, and when involuntary? Why are the following observations from different authors subjoined?

21. By virtue of what does reminiscence take place, according to Aristotle? What associations, or movements, does he say we pass

through, and what do we reach? According to what four laws does he say that we excogitate that which we seek?

22. When the dog has once got upon the track of his game, how does he proceed? How, then, should he proceed who would recover his past thoughts from oblivion? For what purpose should he speculate or think upon what remains to him?

23. What instance of involuntary reminiscence is mentioned by Hobbes? How does he explain the line of association?

24. What is said of mnemonics? What is said of the associations and symbols employed in such artificial systems?

25. In what case does reminiscence follow by a necessary sequence? But what in the case is under our control? How may we keep our associations pure and right? But suppose wrong thoughts are presented to us through association, what then?

SECTION V.

1. What is reminiscence? What is logical thinking? What are the points of difference between them? By what relations, respectively, do they proceed? Which is the higher kind of thought?

2. What is the logical order of thought, and to what does it stand opposed? What are the relations under which the mind admits the *sequence* of one thought from another? When ideas are so arranged, what is the process of passing from one to the other called? How does the mind trace the process?

3. But in what form may a process of reasoning be an object of memory? And what is obtained in such a case? How does the inferiority of such knowledge appear? To what, then, does so much importance attach?

4. How does all science arrange itself? When does the treatment of any subject become a science? Under what particular relations should the materials be arranged?

5. What has history been said to be? How do its materials seem at first view? How do they begin to arrange themselves when profoundly studied? When history is really understood, what is it not, and what is it?

6. How may much of geography and the daily experience of life be arranged? What have we no occasion to remember? For what must we depend upon memory? What is true of all the great subjects of study?

7. What results from the laws of association and logical thought? What is any considerable incoherence of thought evidence of? What is insanity?

SECTION VI.

1. What is true of memory absolutely? What are all the faculties necessary for? What do the different faculties do? What would be the effect of the loss of either of the faculties? Is it clear that any one faculty can act without aid from some of the others? What do we find to be the case in our mature experience? But how do the faculties differ?

2. What is memory inferior to relatively? What are the different functions of memory and perception? Which is fundamental to knowledge? Which depends upon the other?

3. What other power does memory rank below? Is reason wholly independent of memory? What is the aid rendered by memory? But why must reason be higher than either memory or perception? What is said of its movements?

4. What shows the inferiority of memory to reason? How does memory retain knowledge? How does reason arrange it? What

is said of the knowledge retained by the memory when thus put to double duty?

5. What is memory generically the same as? What is the difference between memory and the imagination? Which is the inferior power? Which of these powers creates new forms? May a good memory exist without a fine imagination? Can the reverse be the case? Considering them both as embraced under the representative faculty, how does the case stand? Do we find it so in fact? What, then, are the relations of memory to genius?

6. Where does the importance of memory appear most conspicuously? How alone, generally, can the details of every-day life be reached? What is this especially true of? How does the case stand with the professional man and the scholar?

7. What, then, is true of memory? What has tended to disparage memory? What are the effects of putting it to such a use? How is memory most honored?

CHAPTER V.

SECTION I.

1. What is the imagination, according to Hamilton? How is imagination distinguished from perception and self-consciousness? How from memory? State the difference.

2. How is the representative thought taken in memory, and how in imagination? What do they each involve? Give the illustrations.

3. To what is the imagination limited for its materials? What can it do with these materials? What is said of centaurs and sphinxes, etc.? What of the giant, etc.?

4. Of what form must the images of the imagination be? Why? What is said of Oriental images? What is the thinking of abstract ideas called?

5. How are our images sometimes obtained? Give the illustrations. How are the images obtained in other cases? Like what other images and feelings are these images suggested?

6. How are the images contained in figures of speech awakened? State the manner. Give the illustration.

7. In what two ways may these images come to us? When in one way, and when in the other? What kind of writers have commonly to search for their images? Give the illustration from Demosthenes.

8. What kind of movements of the imagination are called fancy? When is an image said to be fanciful? What sort of characters does the fancy form? What the imagination? What is said of the character, in this respect, of certain works which are named?

9. What are fancies? What conceits? What is wit? What do the ludicrous and grotesque depend upon?

SECTION II.

1. What is necessary in order to the possession of any thing deserving the name of intelligence? What powers are essential to this? What is said of the imagination? What does this prove in regard to the imagination? What effect does it have upon life? What is said of the intelligence which has barely the powers necessary for knowing? In what light is every additional power to be regarded? What, then, of the imagination?

2. In what is imagination here said to be of service? What does it add to conversation? What is said of a topic of conversa-

tion considered simply by itself? How may it be made attractive? What kind of conversation is best? What promotes this?

3. How is the imagination serviceable to the orator? What must the orator do? What effect does passion have upon the imagination? What are the figures of the orator called? What are these?

4. What is the object of the orator? What then must he do? What is the most important auxiliary to him in doing this, beyond the simple power of logical thought? Give the illustration from Demosthenes.

5. By what power, more than by any other, is the genuine poem made? What is a true poem? How does the poet proceed in constructing his poem? What is the source of the ornaments in poetry?

6. What is true of nearly all kinds of writing? What is said of the philosophical style? What happens in the treatment of most subjects?

7. What is said of painters and sculptors? What must they do when they copy direct from nature? But what is generally the case in the higher efforts of art? What is said of the ideal?

8. To whom is the imagination here said to be of service? What is true of all objects and systems of objects in nature? What is this imaging out to ourselves of objects, their relations, etc., called? What does this become when proved to be true to nature? Give the illustration. How does the physical philosopher succeed in interpreting nature?

9. To whom is the imagination of similar service? What is said of geometric figures? Upon what, then, must the success of the student of geometry depend? What must one be able to do in order to obtain a vivid idea of geography and history?

10. To whom is the imagination of but little service? How are the logical relations of ideas developed? How may the imagination be a hinderance in such a case? But to what kind of reasoners is it of service? What service does it render such? In what does the discursive power of the mind reside? What, then, depends upon the imagination and the reason?

SECTION III.

1. What renders the proper training of the imagination of great importance? What does it need? How may it be strengthened, and how chastened? What are the three ways in which the imagination may be improved?

2. What is true of every object which we perceive? What are we filling the mind with, then, wherever we go? How may we use the images thus obtained?

3. Is it sufficient merely to ramble among the works of nature? What images alone are of any value? What is said of the variety of nature? What will be the consequence, then, when our images are exact copies from nature? How alone can such images be obtained? What, then, do we see the importance of?

4. How else may the imagination be improved? What do books and works of art contain? What is said of the images presented more especially in books? What is true of a large part of these images? What is said of this source of improvement, compared with the study of nature?

5. How else may we improve the imagination? How is it employed in this case in comparison with the previous cases? Give the illustrations. How is the work of the imagination in this case related to its work in the others? What is the effect of these creative efforts?

6. What does the imagination need besides strengthening? What is said of improper images? What of a strong imagination without a just taste? What should be cultivated along with the imagination? What is the special province of taste? What does the imagination become without this?

7. What other faculty should the imagination be kept in subordination to? What does Bishop Butler say of the imagination? When the reason is not cultivated, what does the imagination do? With whom does it do this?

8. What has already been remarked? In what respect may the imagination be of aid to the deductive reasoner, and in what respect a hinderance?

9. What other powers, then, should always be cultivated in connection with the imagination? If these be not cultivated, what is the consequence?

CHAPTER VI.

SECTION I.

1. What does conception mean, and what allusion is contained in the term? What three things does the term embrace? What is the last of these more properly called? What, then, does conception correspond to? What does concept correspond to?

2. What is conceiving, then? Does the concept represent any particular object? But what must its attributes not be, and why? How, then, can the concept be fixed, so as to be reproducible in thought? In what alone, then, are concepts embodied? How are they recalled and applied?

3. Can a concept be presented in a concrete image? Why not?

In what, however, may it always be individualized? How is it individualized, and through what power?

4. What is the general notion of a triangle? What is obviou in regard to such a notion? Why is such a general notion inconceivable? Who rejected it on this ground? Would such a notion be a general notion? Why not? What is required that there should be such a general notion? What is such a concept of a triangle?

5. Is it usually necessary to individualize our concepts? Do we generally attempt it? What do we substitute for general notions? Give the illustration. But what is a test of the correctness of a concept?

6. When may a concept be said to be logically correct? Give the illustration. When is a concept true or false really? Give the illustration.

7. Why is the conceivable regarded as possible? What are we constrained to believe in regard to what we can think? What in regard to what we cannot think? Is inconceivability, then, equivalent to impossibility?

8. What is conception as an act? What, then, may we properly be said to conceive? What illegitimate use of the term is here pointed out? Give the illustrations.

SECTION II.

1. How do different objects appear in our first perceptions by sight? What is done by degrees? What do we acquire in time? What is the knowledge thus acquired of individual objects called?

2. What has taken place in the mean time? What does reflec-

tion do? What, at length, do we come to do in perception? What in thinking of a class by its type?

3. What are our concepts becoming by experience? How are our primary concepts enlarged? Give the illustrations. To what do our concepts continually tend?

4. In this gradation of concepts what is obvious? Give the illustration. How is this expressed in the language of logic?

5. What, then, does conception grow out of? What are concepts? How is the generalization accomplished? What is abstraction?

SECTION III.

What will tend further to illustrate the nature of conception? What are the different classes of concepts?

1. When is a notion said to be distinct? Give the illustration. Are such notions necessarily distinct in every mind? What are confused notions? Such notions being clear, why are they said to be indistinct? By what other name do they sometimes go?

2. When are notions said to be adequate? Give the illustration. When is a notion said to be inadequate?

3. What are symbolical notions? How are the terms designating such notions generally used? What is said of all familiar concepts? What are notative concepts?

4. What are first notions? What are second notions? Give the illustrations, and the list of first and second notions. What alone is logic said to have to do with, and why?

5. What are positive notions? What are negative? What is said of the relation of positive and negative notions? What are

negative notions considered as destitute of? What, then, is the value of such notions? Of what nature are our ideas of the infinite and the absolute?

6. What are irrespective notions? What are relative notions? Give instances of such notions.

7. What concepts are technically known as abstract notions? Of what two classes are they? When are these qualities said to be concrete?

8. What are the so-called necessary notions more properly? Under what point of view alone can our ideas of space, time, etc., be called concepts or general notions? What is the case with regard to the mathematical and logical axioms? What is true, then, of all concepts?

SECTION IV.

What is said of the controversy about general notions, and what are the three theories to which it has given rise?

I. 1. According to this theory, what sort of an existence are concepts regarded as having? What are they not? How are they to be regarded? What are they thus only a peculiar form of?

2. To what, according to Plato, do external objects address themselves, and to what do they give rise? What, then, is really perceived, and how far are objects perceived? How are these ideas in the mind of God, and how in the mind of man? When does man become conscious of them? What, then, was his real world? By whom were these views adopted, and how employed?

3. How does this theory of conception err? In what sense are concepts real?

II. 1. What does not this theory deny? What does it contend for? How does it represent concepts as standing in the mind? In what, therefore, does it contend that all the generality in general notions lies?

2. What, then, does the nominalist hold to? How may his view be expressed in other words? Can there, then, be any such general notion of a triangle, for instance, as was formerly contended for? What, then, is the only remaining difference between the nominalist and the conceptualist? To which view is the preference here given? (See note.)

III. 1. What is said of this view of conception? How do general notions exist according to this theory? What are they?

2. What is said of the importance of language here? What does the name given to a concept effect? Into what two classes are these general terms distributed? Give specimens of the latter class.

SECTION V.

1. What have we seen conception to be? With what do we become acquainted through perception, and with what through conception? How are the qualities given in perception, and how reached in conception? Which is the higher process then? What question is here asked?

2. What depends upon our conceptions? What are accurate perceptions and conceptions necessary for respectively? What kinds of knowledge depend upon our conceptions? If our conceptions are inadequate, what then? What shows how large a part of our knowledge is thus affected?

3. What happens when knowledge becomes a mere knowledge of words? How did Bacon point out the cause of this defect in the knowledge of his time? What was the influence of the doc-

trines of the schoolmen in this matter? When alone is knowledge fruitful? When alone is the mind enriched?

4. What science furnishes forcible illustrations of the importance of conception? What is the case with regard to the phases of the moon? What other illustrations? What is said of the solution of astronomical questions by algebra and by geometry respectively?

5. What is said of other sciences? What cases are here put? Is it of any avail merely to learn such terms? In what do men fail especially? What kind of education is specially defective?

CHAPTER VII.

SECTION I.

1. What is judgment? What would be the case without this power? What is done by the judgment? Give the illustrations.

2. How is the word "part" used here? What does every judgment declare according to Aristotle? What is the relation of the subject and predicate in the different kinds of judgment?

3. One of what relations must all concepts in a judgment be regarded as holding? When, therefore, two concepts not holding one of these relations to each other are brought together in the form of a judgment, what is the judgment called? For what purpose do we often have occasion to use such judgment? As what are they conceivable? Give the illustrations.

4. When alone is a judgment conceivable? Besides being intelligible, what must a judgment be in order to be conceivable? Give the illustrations.

5. What is a true judgment? What must the relation between the two concepts be in this case? Give the illustrations. In this

kind of judgment what must be the case in regard to the relation of the concepts?

6. What does judgment imply? How alone can the relation between the concepts be perceived? Give the illustration. What is an assertory judgment, and is there any proper comparison in this case? What alone is asserted in such a judgment? Give the illustration.

7. Between what in two concepts is the relation considered as existing, when the judgment is regarded in its depth, and between what when it is regarded in its breadth? Give the illustrations.

SECTION II.

How may judgments be divided according to the coincidence or non-coincidence of their concepts? How according to the form of the language in which they are expressed? How according to the agreement or repugnance of their ideas? How according to the matter to which they relate? How according as the predicate is merely explanatory, or adds something new?

1. What is said of this division? One of what two things do all judgments assert? In which of these cases is the judgment substitutive, and in which attributive? Give the illustrations.

2. What do categorical judgments embrace in modern usage? What judgments do they not embrace? But what does categorical always mean in Aristotle?

3. What are hypothetical judgments apparently? Give the examples. But what, in all such cases, is there in reality? What, then, is the true logical form of the hypothetical judgment?

4. What apparently is there here also? What relation do the

two apparent judgments hold to each other? What is the real judgment in the case?

5. What kind of judgments are called affirmative, and what negative judgments? Give the examples. But suppose the negative does not affect the copula? Give the example. What is this last kind of judgment sometimes called?

6. What is said of judgments pertaining to necessary matter? What of those relating to contingent matter? Give the illustrations.

7. What relation does the predicate bear to the subject in this class of judgments? What are judgments of this kind? Are analytical judgments identical? Show that they are not.

8. What is the relation of the predicate to the subject here? What do such judgments express? What do they relate to? What do they indicate? Give the illustration.

9. To what does the classification of judgments as propositions belong? How many forms of propositions have commonly been reckoned? How many more has Hamilton added? What may we embrace in both affirmative and negative judgments?

CHAPTER VIII.

SECTION I.

1. What is reasoning, when drawn out in full form? What does the smallest movement in reasoning consist in? What is this called in logical language? How does the mind advance in different operations? What is always the object in reasoning? How is this object gained? Give the examples.

2. What is called an argument? What is argument strictly?

What is a syllogism? Give an argument, and turn it into a syllogism.

3. In a syllogism, what is the judgment which we wish to establish called? What the general judgment with which we start? What the mediating judgment? Give the illustration.

4. How is reasoning generally abridged in common discourse? How does this arise? What may happen in regard to such reasoning? But how is it with the syllogism?

5. What, then, is the syllogism? What is it a test of, and a protection against? Give the illustration. What is the form of syllogism here used called (note)? How is the inconclusiveness of the reasoning here exhibited?

6. What is the object of all reasoning? What is the object of the syllogism? Give the illustrations.

7. How may all reasoning be expressed? What is the longest train of reasoning when fully expressed? Does it make any difference to what kind of matter the reasoning pertains? What is said of logic? What alone does it vouch for? Give the illustration.

8. Where does the chief difficulty lie in reasoning? How are the media of proof generally best reached, and why? What is the case in mathematical reasoning? What is the case in inductive and probable reasoning generally?

9. In inductive reasoning, what is the guide to the connecting conception, and upon what does the success of the inductive reasoner depend? What discoveries were made thus? To what did Newton owe his discoveries? To what the other discoverers here named?

10. What is the object of reasoning, then? What does the human mind tend towards? What does it seek? What does reason follow upon?

SECTION II.

1. What is the case as to the form of reasoning? But what distinctions are made in the process, and on what grounds?

2. What is all reasoning here distinguished into? What is the process in inductive reasoning? What in deductive?

3. What rule applies to inductive reasoning? What to deductive?

4. Why must induction generally precede deduction? How are the two processes used in the investigation of nature? Give the illustration.

5. How is induction often used loosely? What may be said of such imperfect inferences? What, then, are most general principles established from experience? Give the illustration.

6. What does this distinction of reasoning depend upon? While the reasoning is the same in kind, how do the premises differ in the two cases? What does Hamilton say of the term *a priori* in contrast with *a posteriori*, as denoting elements of knowledge?

7. What does Hamilton say was the usual meaning of *a priori* and *a posteriori* as denoting processes of reasoning previous to Kant? To what kind of reasoning, however, had the term *a priori* been extended? What does he say of the cosmological argument called *a priori*?

8 What does this distinction of reasoning depend upon? What is said of the degree of evidence in the two cases? What of the process of reasoning? Where does the whole difference lie?

9. What does necessary matter include, and what contingent matter? What, then, is necessary, and what contingent matter? What is said of our knowledge of facts, and of certain principles

of knowledge? But what alone presents an object of thought upon which all men not only do but *must* think alike?

10. What is said of both the question and every step of the solution in mathematical reasoning? Give the illustrations. How is space apprehended by us? What is said of the other forms of quantity?

11. But how is it in regard to the object to be reasoned about in probable reasoning? In such questions what do we not find to start with? And what do we have to start with, and how proceed? What may such reasons be sufficient for? But what are they not sufficient for? Why is probable reasoning called *moral* reasoning?

12. Is demonstrative reasoning the most important because it is the most convincing? What should be the effect of a proof upon the conduct, which is sufficient to determine the reason? If it does not determine the conduct, what is it evidence of? What, then, does the necessity of depending so largely upon probable evidence become an important test of? Which is the most used by us, probable or demonstrative evidence? What does Bishop Butler say of probability?

13. What is abstract reasoning? What does it embrace in terms? To what is it chiefly applied? Give the illustration.

SECTION III.

1. What have we seen in regard to reasoning? How do the foundations of knowledge depend upon reason? What, then, becomes important? Can the reason give reasons for every thing? What must it accept as final?

2. What do primary judgments of fact relate to? What are some of these judgments?

3. What reasoning becomes impossible if these primary judg-

ments of fact are denied? What does all probable reasoning rest upon? If, then, the primary elements of experience be not admitted, what follows? How was it that Hume subverted the fabric of knowledge in his day, and how was it restored by Reid and his followers?

4. Upon what else does much of reasoning depend? What are some of these necessary judgments? What is said of our notions of cause and effect, and of space and time?

5. What conceptions lie at the foundation of mathematical reasoning? Suppose their validity is denied, what then? Can they be denied? Have the mathematical sciences ever been assailed by scepticism? How has it been with the idea of causation?

6. Upon what else does reasoning depend? What axioms are employed wholly in mathematical reasoning? What others may be employed in probable reasoning also? To what laws of thought is there a constant appeal in reasoning?

7. What does the principle of identity teach? Are we at liberty to question the sameness of a thing every time it recurs? How does this principle lie at the foundation of all legitimate judgments? And how, especially, does it apply to analytical judgments?

8. What are the different forms under which this principle has been stated? What is the meaning in all cases? Give the illustrations.

9. What does this principle teach? What are our decisions on this principle, and on the preceding, respectively? Do we decide thus when we comprehend neither of the alternative propositions? Give the example.

10. What do these and the like truths and principles form? How are they to be regarded?

SECTION IV.

1. How are the reasoning powers improved? What is the condition for the improvement of all our powers? State the case.

2. To improve the reasoning powers, in what order should we be in the habit of arranging and retracing our knowledge? What is the logical order of thoughts? When do we merely remember, and when do we reason? What then is the great field for the improvement of our reasoning powers?

3. What is mathematical reasoning coincident with? What is Hamilton's conclusion in regard to the effect of this kind of reasoning upon the reasoning powers? What is said of the views of others?

4. Where does the truth probably lie in this case? What is true in regard to mathematical reasoning? What is said of the nature of mathematical deduction? But what kind of a deduction is required in every mathematical question? What does it require a good deal of reflection to perceive, and something more than patience to trace? What, on the whole, can there be no doubt of?

5. What does probable reasoning embrace? What must it require, and why? How does it compare with mathematical reasoning? Where will the effect of this kind of reasoning in improving the reasoning powers be best seen?

6. Where is there a large demand for the use of probable reasoning? What is the object of metaphysical inquiries? What is said of these questions? What of the arguments by which they are established? What books are referred to as fine gymnastics for the reasoning powers?

7. What is the field where probable reasoning has the widest scope? What is said of the proof of facts by circumstantial evidence? What is said of the case where the fact to be established

deeply affects human interests? What is said of the construction of such arguments? What of their analysis?

8 What is logic? Can any art of reasoning be taught? What does reasoning proceed by? How alone, then, can we improve our reasoning powers? How does logic promote this end? How, then, does the study of logic tend to improve our reasoning powers?

9. What is here said of the reasoning powers? What is reasoning? How does it proceed? What is it ever tending towards?

APPENDIX.

1. How has philosophy been defined? What is it the fruit of? What is the effect of experience? What is said of the age of philosophy? In what are its beginnings seen?

2. Where alone, among the ancients, did philosophy advance beyond mythology? What is the history of ancient philosophy then? What is said of philosophy among the Greeks? How did it commence there? What is said of the elements and powers of nature? What is said of the causes to which things were traced? With what school of philosophers does Greek philosophy begin, and at what period?

3. What, at first, would naturally be the character of philosophy? What would it do in the progress of ideas? With what has philosophy progressed?

4. What will primitive philosophy, then, generally be found to be? How will intelligence be regarded? How nature? What will be the first step of the philosopher then? At the same time,

what else will happen? What were the *archæ* of the Ionian philosophers?

5. What was the birthplace and age of Thales? How is he regarded by Aristotle? What was his doctrine? Why did he assume water as the basis of all things? What, then, was the single problem of his philosophy?

6. What is said of the birthplace, etc., of Anaximander? What was the first principle of things with him? What is said of his *prima materia?* What does he seem to have felt? What did his analysis find, and hence what did he conceive?

7. What is said of Anaximenes? What was his first principle of things? Why did he assume this?

8. What is said of the birthplace, age, etc., of Heraclitus? What was his first principle of things? What was this the common ground of? What was the phenomenal world? What, according to his view, does the very existence of sensible things consist in? What does this perpetual flow arise from? How is this exhibited in matter and mind? What, in short, was his system?

9. What is said of the birthplace, age, etc., of Anaxagoras? To what extent was the tendency to spirituality observed in Heraclitus carried by Anaxagoras? How were material objects formed? How were natural objects regarded then? To what do we here have something very like? Where did Anaxagoras live and teach during the prime of his life, and who took up and continued his doctrine afterwards?

10. What have we seen in this series of philosophers? What has been their course? What must have been admitted at the beginning? How was every thing regarded? To what kind of knowledge alone do the Ionian philosophers seem to have held?

11. From what, and to what, shall we turn to discover a philosophical movement of a very different kind? What is that which is investigated by this school of philosophy? How did the phenomenal world appear to these philosophers? Why should it seem thus to them? What, then, determined them to their course of speculation? What has the school been called?

12. What is said of the birthplace, age, etc., of Pythagoras? What was his fundamental doctrine? What must he have meant by this? What alone can things be? What was such a doctrine easily carried out into? How did he regard the soul? How the divine mind? How should his philosophy be classified?

13. What is said of the birthplace, philosophy, age, and wanderings of Xenophanes? Does he seem to have had any actual connection with Pythagoras? In what respect was his system like that of Pythagoras, and in what respects different? State the differences.

14. What is said of the birthplace and relation of Parmenides to Xenophanes? What did the deity of Xenophanes become with him? What was the phenomenal world with him? What were thought and being? How did he recognize the existent? What problem arose hence?

15. What is said of the birthplace, age, and relation of Zeno to Parmenides? To what task does he seem to have devoted himself? To defend the *one*, what did he have to disprove? How did he attempt this? What are the four contradictions which he set forth? What did he invent?

16. What is said of the birthplace, age, and relation to the preceding philosophers of Empedocles? How did he conceive of the world? What did he call this totality of elements and forces? What was he then? How was the *one* or God of the Eleatics retained then? What is said of his relation to Anaxagoras and Democritus? What doctrine does he seem to have been the first to propound? What was his doctrine of perception?

17. Where and when was Democritus born? Of what philosophy was he the founder? What does he naturally close? What has already been stated in regard to him? What is said of the relation of his *atoms* to the elementary substances of Empedocles and Anaxagoras? What did he teach that all the senses are? What distinction did he make? What is said of his philosophy?

18. What is here said about the course of the light of philosophy? What place had most of the recent philosophers visited? What sham philosophers came with the genuine? Where were they mostly from? What did they aim at? What might their teaching be called? What did philosophy become in their hands?

19. Who were the leading Sophists? What did they receive for their instruction? What was their general doctrine in regard to knowledge? Does it seem certain that they carried out this doctrine in morals? What did Socrates show them? What is said of their influence both for evil and for good?

20. At what period does Socrates make his appearance? What is said of his origin and character? With what class did he retain his sympathy, and where did he hold his discussions? To what classes of philosophers did he chiefly oppose himself? To what did he appeal against the sophists?

21. Did Socrates teach or leave any complete system of philosophy? What influence did he have upon the minds of others? What new method did he introduce? What was his course in his discussions? What, then, did he teach men to do? What did he exhibit in these discussions? To what did his principles incline? What were his views on morals? What is said of these views? Why should virtue lead to happiness according to his views?

22. What sprang from the Socratic life and teaching? What was the effect of the personal interest connected with his character? What was the effect of the free scope of his instruction? What should we not be surprised at then?

23. Where was the seat of the Megaric school, who was its founder, etc.? Who had been Euclid's teachers? What is said of his system? What is said of the ethical element in his system? Who was he followed by? What was their great instrument? What did Stilpo develop, and how? Of what doctrine, then, was he the author?

24. By whom was the Cyrenaic school founded, and what is said of the history of its founder? What doctrine of Socrates did he reverse? What were his *criteria* of actions? What was his doctrine, then? What is said of such a philosophy?

25. Who was the founder of the Cynic school, and whence its name? What is said of its system of philosophy? What is here said of Socrates? Who were his peculiarities exaggerated by? What was the common appellation given to both the founder and to Diogenes? What did they possess?

26. Who alone truly represented the spirit of Socrates? Why should he imbibe his spirit? What, however, is said of his system compared with his master's? What of his travels? What was he thus prepared for? Where did he establish himself as teacher of philosophy? What is said of his labors there?

27. What distinction did Plato continue in his philosophy? What was the great aim of the teaching of Socrates? What was the central principle of the system of Plato? What was his doctrine of *ideas*? What was his view of matter? What was sensation, and what perception, with him?

28. In the statement of the Platonic theory of perception by Professor Butler, what is the first item? What the second? What the third? What the fourth?

29. What is the predominant spirit and aim of the philosophy of Plato? What does it propose? What is the relation of the true, the beautiful, and the good? What is the study of truth, then? What is the effect of philosophy? What is this only

carrying out? What was happiness the fruit of according to him? What is philosophy, then, and why? What is said of the good?

30. What, according to Professor Butler, does the system of Plato suppose? State the relation between the beautiful, the just, the good, and the true? What, then, is the great requisite of virtue, and what the consequence of the fitness of the soul for this end? What is it to approach God under different forms?

31. Into what other departments did Plato carry this lofty spirit of speculation? What is said of his ideal state? What are we prepared to expect in regard to such a state? What is his ideal state in reality? What is said of his physical system? What was it but an attempt at?

32. Who were the successors of Plato at the academy? What is here said of Cicero? What is said of these successors of Plato? What did they soon sink into? What did they maintain against the Stoics? What are the dominant maxims of the academic philosophy?

33. What element was exaggerated in new Platonism? What is said of its history? What did the system hold to? What was it an attempt to do? What did its pretensions prove? What did its mystic enthusiasm degenerate into?

34. What of the history of Aristotle? What is said of the central idea of his system? How were *ideas* treated by Socrates, Plato, and Aristotle, respectively? What, respectively, did the investigation of Socrates, and the dialectics of Plato, become with Aristotle? What did the *idea* become, then? What, however, did he suppose? Beginning with experience, how did his philosophy end?

35. What distinction did he introduce? What was the permanent, and what the phenomenal, with him? What was potential, and what actual being? What the infinite, and what the finite?

36. What are the different subjects which he investigated? What is said of the style in which he treated of these subjects? What is his position among ancient philosophers? Through what systems did philosophy decline?

37. What was Stoicism the rival of? On what point were the two schools at variance? Point out their respective views on this point. What was their difference on this point like? What did the Stoics resist?

38. What was the predominant aim of Stoicism? What of its psychology? What is said of its founder? What was God in his system? What was it, then, to act according to nature? How was conduct to be controlled? How was happiness regarded? Who were the great masters of this philosophy?

39. Where, and by whom, was Epicureanism founded and taught? What did the Epicureans make the end of life? What view did they take of happiness? How was conduct to be regulated? What did it not recognize? In what did it make happiness to consist?

40. What is said of the Socratic movement? By what were the various systems of Grecian philosophy finally absorbed? What is said of the Greek language and philosophy? What classes at Rome adopted the different forms of Greek philosophy? But what new development alone did they receive out of Greece?

41. What did Grecian philosophy fall before? What did thought soon begin to do? What was the object of scholasticism? Who were the leading doctors of this system, and in what age did they live? What did they use for this purpose? What is said of their system? What is said of the sphere of philosophy and of religion respectively?

42. What is said of the downfall of scholasticism? What are among the causes which produced its downfall? What is said of Bacon? What of other philosophers? What at length happened?

43. With whom and at what period does modern philosophy begin? What did Descartes attempt? What does he start with? What is said of his *cogito ergo sum?* What does the assurance with which we receive the truth of our own existence become the rule of? But what of things out of ourselves?

44. What *idea* does Descartes here call to his aid? What did he hold that this idea of God forbid? What is true then? What else did he deduce from the idea of God? What is said of such a use of the idea of God? What is said of such deductions? What is said of his view of innate ideas?

45. What, according to Descartes, are the sole properties of mind and matter? How is their intercourse maintained? How was the soul conceived by him? What is said of external objects? What is said of his assumed relation of mind and matter?

46. What is said of Malebranche? What was his medium of perception? How was God regarded by him? How is nature brought into relation with the human spirit? Where is the place of souls?

47. Where and when was Spinoza born? What important change did he make in the Cartesian philosophy? What are thought and extension in his system? What finite objects? Where is thought, and where is extension developed? What is said of the world in all its forms, etc.? What, then, becomes of personality and moral character?

48. According to the system of Spinoza, what alone exists? What are the relations of phenomenal objects to God? What is *natura naturans*, and what *natura naturata?* In what sense is God the cause of all things? What are his two attributes? What is every *thought?* What every *thing?* What is said of his method?

49. Who was the next independent philosopher, and where born? Of what sort is his philosophy? Who had preceded him in the

same line? What is Locke's fundamental principle? What, then, is the sum of our knowledge? What is the great business of his philosophy?

50. What is the first defect of Locke's system? What the second? How does Locke unconsciously admit primary principles of knowledge?

51. By whom was Locke's philosophy, in its materialistic tendency, tolerated? By whom taken up with enthusiasm? To what consequences did Condillac and Helvetius develop his system? To what excesses did La Mettrie, etc., carry it out?

52. To what else did the philosophy of Locke lead? What was the double effect of its empirical character? How did it virtually deny all knowledge of external objects, etc.? What, in consequence, did Berkeley do?

53. To what last consequence did Hume carry out Locke's system? On what ground did he deny all knowledge of substance and causation? How does he regard the universal belief in these? How does he regard our notion of them as generated?

54. To what was the system of Leibnitz opposed? What is said of his pursuit of philosophy, and his method of publishing his views? What are his most considerable works?

55. How does the general substance to which he holds differ from that of Spinoza? What is this substance composed of? What is his *monad?* How does the representative power of his monads differ in different objects?

56. Through what, according to Leibnitz, is the correspondence between the mind and the body secured? State the manner of the correspondence. What, then, is true of our knowledge? What is said of his system?

57 What philosopher reared his system upon the general basis

of that of Leibnitz? What, however, did he not, and what did he attempt? What peculiar theory of Leibnitz did he keep in the background? What did he endeavor to embrace in his system? What is ontology? What cosmology? What rational psychology? What speculative theology? What is said of his system?

58. At what point in the history of philosophy have we now arrived? What had been the issue of Locke's philosophy? What, then, was inevitable? Did this result actually follow, and at what two centres? What, alike, stimulated Reid and Kant to attempt to reconstruct the fabric of knowledge? To what principle of certitude do they alike appeal?

59. In what form did the philosophy of Kant appear? What does he start with? What is his philosophy, then? What is the result of his criticism? What does he call the *ideas of reason?*

60. To what does Kant hold against Locke? What does he hold are the forms under which we necessarily think of things? What does he denominate these forms of thought, and how does he regard them? What is said of his fabric of knowledge? What did he remain true to?

61. Does he, however, expressly deny the objective existence of things? What does he make a labored attempt to save? How does he attempt it?

62. What is said of Kant's *critique of pure reason?* In what does its importance consist? What has been its influence? What course did German professors take in regard to it?

63. What is said of the position and character of Jacobi? What was inevitable in his case? What does he ground his philosophy on, in distinction from Kant? What does he hold to? How does he reason in regard to this matter?

64. Who was Herbert, and why is he introduced here? What is his system a peculiar carrying out of? What is his view of

knowledge? What is his doctrine of *reals*? What contradiction disappears through this doctrine? How, on his principles, may an object be said to change, and yet remain the same? How does he solve the antinomies of motion? What is the soul in his system? To what is his doctrine of *reals* similar?

65. What is said of the position and character of Fichte? How did he regard the philosophy of Kant? Was he virtually right in his view?

66. What advance did Fichte make in Kant's doctrine of perception? What did he find no warrant nor necessity for? What does the mind necessarily assume? In perception, what does one necessarily affirm? What are the different categories of thought? What are external objects, then? What is God?

67. What sort of idealism is Fichte's? What does Hamilton say of it? And yet, in the language of Fichte himself, what is its sum?

68. Where did Schelling begin his career as a philosopher? On leaving Tübingen, what did he first become, and what afterwards? What relation is there between his philosophy and that of Fichte? What are human souls and the experience of life on his system? Where does the contrast between subject and object disappear? What was Schelling, then?

69. What, according to Schelling, was the subject of philosophy? Can the absolute be known except as we ourselves become the absolute? Can we become the absolute without losing our consciousness? What is the alternative, then?

70. How, then, can we know the absolute? What does Schelling call such an act of knowledge? In such an act what disappears?

71. What does Schelling found philosophy on? What is the intuition of the absolute evidently the work of? What is the process?

72. What has been impossible to Schelling? What has he variously attempted?

73. In what do Cousin and Schelling agree? In what are they diametrically opposed?

74. What is the history of Hegel? What did he do for the system of Schelling? What was Schelling's view of subject and object, and what Hegel's? What did the indifference philosophy become? And what the intellectual intuition? What other contrasts disappear, and what, indeed, is the fundamental principle of his philosophy? What does philosophy become? What, then, is his system theoretically and practically? In such a system, what is nature, man, and even God? What kind of idealism is this as compared with that of Schelling and Fichte?

75. With whom does the German movement close? What do we find in the Scotch line of speculation? Who was the founder of the Scotch school? What two other eminent men are named as belonging to the school? What relation do they sustain to the founder?

76. By whom are the principles of the school admirably stated? What did the school profess? To what did it not limit experience? While restricting the science of mind to an observation of the fact of consciousness, what did it analyze that fact into? What did it show? What did it prove? What was thus distinguished? What was not, and what was, demonstrated?

77. What did Reid call these primary principles of knowledge? To what theory of perception do the Scotch metaphysicians hold?

78. How, according to Hamilton, do we apprehend our own organism as extended? How do we apprehend objects exterior to our organism? And how do we know these to be extended?

79. Why need no extended account of the Scotch philosophy be given? What is it trusted that this abstract may do?

SUBJECTS FOR COMPOSITION, CONNECTED WITH THE TEXT.

1. Draw out the antithesis between mind and matter (p. 14).

2. Give some account of the Platonic sense of the term *idea*, and of its use by subsequent philosophers (p. 17). See Ritter's History of Ancient Philosophy, Vol. II. pp. 261–300. Also, Wight's Hamilton, pp. 200 and 211.

3. Set forth the distinction between the three great mental processes of *knowing*, *willing*, and *feeling* (p. 22). See Bowen's Hamilton, Chap. VIII.

4. Explain the effects of habit, according to either of the theories suggested in No. 3, p. 25. For the *automatic* theory, consult Holland's Chapters on Mental Physiology; and for the other theories, Bowen's Hamilton, Chap. XIV., and Stewart's Elements, Chap. II.

5. What is the state of the mind in sleep (p. 26). See Bowen's Hamilton, Chap. XIII.

6. Are our ideas of space and time original, native notions? (pp. 32–35.) See Kant's Critique of Pure Reason, Part I. Also, Spencer's Principles of Psychology, pp. 230–264.

7. In what does our *personal identity* consist? (p. 39.) See Butler's Dissertation at the end of the Analogy.

8. Give some account of Spinoza's system (p. 51). See Lewes' History of Philosophy.

9. Give some account of *idealism* according to Berkeley (p. 52) See his Principles of Human Knowledge.

10. Give some account of *nihilism* according to Hume (p. 54). See his Principles of Human Nature, and Inquiry concerning the Human Understanding.

11. Give some account of the different theories which have been suggested for conveying in impressions to the mind (p. 64). See Reid's Essays on the Intellectual Powers, Essay II.

12. Show the advantage which we derive from double organs of perception (p. 78).

13. Compare the perceptions of *touch* and *sight*, as to their certainty, their extent, their utility, agreeableness, etc. (p. 84.)

14. Show the importance of the physical element in language (p. 85). See Trench on Words, and Swinton's Rambles among Words.

15. Show the importance of an ever wakeful use of the senses (p. 86).

16. Give an account of Hamilton's view of memory (p. 91). See Bowen's Hamilton, Chap. XXII.

17. Give some account of the physical view of memory (p. 102). See Hobbes on Association of Ideas, and Hartley's Observations on Man.

18. Illustrate the distinction between imagination and conception (p. 114).

19. Illustrate the distinction between imagination and fancy (p. 126).

20. Show the importance of the imagination to the artist (p. 130).

21. Show the importance of *taste* in the use of figures (p. 136).

22. Give some account of Hamilton's view of proposition (p. 162). See Hamilton's Discussions, Appendix II.

NOTE.—The above are given merely as specimens. Each teacher can multiply such topics at his pleasure.

www.ingramcontent.com/pod-product-compliance
Lightning Source LLC
LaVergne TN
LVHW020239110826
845151LV00003B/979

* 9 7 8 1 4 2 5 5 2 9 4 9 9 *